How to Read a Moment

I0889335

FLASHPOINTS

The FlashPoints series is devoted to books that consider literature beyond strictly national and disciplinary frameworks and that are distinguished both by their historical grounding and by their theoretical and conceptual strength. Our books engage theory without losing touch with history and work historically without falling into uncritical positivism. FlashPoints aims for a broad audience within the humanities and the social sciences concerned with moments of cultural emergence and transformation. In a Benjaminian mode, FlashPoints is interested in how literature contributes to forming new constellations of culture and history and in how such formations function critically and politically in the present. Series titles are available online at http://escholarship.org/uc/flashpoints.

SERIES EDITORS: Ali Behdad (Comparative Literature and English, UCLA), Editor Emeritus; Judith Butler (Rhetoric and Comparative Literature, UC Berkeley), Editor Emerita; Michelle Clayton (Hispanic Studies and Comparative Literature, Brown University); Edward Dimendberg (Film and Media Studies, Visual Studies, and European Languages and Studies, UC Irvine), Founding Editor; Catherine Gallagher (English, UC Berkeley), Editor Emerita; Nouri Gana (Comparative Literature and Near Eastern Languages and Cultures, UCLA); Susan Gillman (Literature, UC Santa Cruz), Coordinator; Jody Greene (Literature, UC Santa Cruz); Richard Terdiman (Literature, UC Santa Cruz), Founding Editor

A complete list of titles begins on page 243.

How to Read a Moment

The American Novel and the Crisis of the Present

Mathias Nilges

NORTHWESTERN UNIVERSITY PRESS | EVANSTON, ILLINOIS

Northwestern University Press
www.nupress.northwestern.edu

Copyright © 2021 by Northwestern University. Published 2021 by Northwestern University Press. All rights reserved.

Printed in the United States of America

10 9 8 7 6 5 4 3 2 1

Library of Congress Cataloging-in-Publication Data

Names: Nilges, Mathias, author.
Title: How to read a moment : the American novel and the crisis of the present / Mathias Nilges.
Other titles: FlashPoints (Evanston, Ill.)
Description: Evanston, Illinois : Northwestern University Press, 2021. | Series: Flashpoints | Includes bibliographical references and index.
Identifiers: LCCN 2020044729 | ISBN 9780810143425 (paperback) | ISBN 9780810143432 (cloth) | ISBN 9780810143449 (ebook)
Subjects: LCSH: American fiction—20th century—History and criticism. | American fiction—21st century—History and criticism. | Contemporary, The, in literature.
Classification: LCC PS374.C596 N55 2021 | DDC 813.5409—dc23
LC record available at https://lccn.loc.gov/2020044729

Contents

For Maïca Erin Poirier Murphy
my love

Acknowledgments

Most importantly, I owe all the gratitude in the world to Maïca Murphy, my wife, my best friend, my most attentive and toughest reader, my partner in dreaming, hope personified. All those who have had the pleasure and fortune to meet her know why my wedding vows required footnotes. This book would not exist without Maïca nor without the encouragement, advice, and steadfast support that I have received from Madhu Dubey, Nicholas Brown, and Emilio Sauri over the years. Madhu read every chapter and offered incisive commentary while also keeping me sane throughout the writing process. I have said this before, but it cannot be said too frequently: together, Madhu, Nick, and Emilio have taught me how academics ought to treat their work, their students, and each other, and their intellectual rigor and generosity continue to serve as my model for the kind of writer, teacher, and colleague I aim to be.

I would like to thank the following people for their collegiality, their intellectual and professional guidance, and their continued friendship: Eugenio DiStefano, Dan Stout, Sarah Brouillette, Imre Szeman, Walter Benn Michaels, Jennifer Ashton, Helen Jun, Phil Wegner, Susan Hegeman, Carolyn Lesjak, Cristie Ellis, Maureen Moynagh, Rod Bantjes, Jason Potts, Mitchum Huehls, Rachel Greenwald Smith, Anna Kornbluh, Lisa Siraganian, Mark Canuel, Bev Best, Ericka Beckman, Paul Stasi, Bret Benjamin, Mitch Murray, Jeff Diamanti, Kristin Bergen, Peter Hitchcock, Stephen Shapiro, Sharae Deckard, Lee Medovoi, Andrew Hoberek, Sheri-Marie Harrison, Samuel Cohen, Gordon Hutner, Tim

Lanzendörfer, Clemens Spahr, Merve Emre, Caren Irr, Tim Bewes, Ellen Rooney, Matthew Hart, Günter Leypoldt, Matt Mullins, Madhu Krishnan, Josh Toth, Alice Haisman, Neil Larsen, Rich Daniels, Jeff Williams, Jen Hedler-Phillis, Davis Smith-Brecheisen, Vincent Adiutori, Joe Ramsey, Barbara Foley, Leigh Claire La Berge, Rei Terada, Eyal Amiran, Lauren Berlant, Kristy Ullibari, Pete Franks, Brent Bellamy, Cory Rushton, Michael D'Arcy, Michele Janette, Don Hedrick, Jamie Daniel, Tim Dayton, Karin Westman, Greg Eiselein, Ken Warren, Justin A. Joyce, Ryan Brooks, Maryanne Lyons, Lisa Freeman, Jordan Cook, Matt Prins, Katie Olthuis, Matt Scott-Moncrieff, Kevin Wamsley, and Marie Gillis.

I consider myself immensely fortunate to be able to rely on the love, encouragement, and support of my family. Thank you to my parents, Susanne and Jörg Bill and Sylvie Poirier and Ron Murphy; my grandmother, Gisela Märker; my brother Christoph Nilges; my sister-in-law Elisabeth Nilges; and my lovely niece Tilda Nilges. Thank you, too, to Angelika and Jürgen Märker; Ute, Roland, and Catrin Ploss; Melissa, Tomas, and Caitlin Murphy; Nathalie Poirier; and Bruce Campbell.

Thank you to my students at St. Francis Xavier University, and in particular my superb assistants, Laura Blinn and Brennah Agnew. I would also like to thank the wonderful editors at Northwestern University Press and FlashPoints, especially Trevor Perri, Susan Gillman, Michelle Clayton, Maia Rigas, and Elizabeth Berg. I am deeply honored to have been able to work with you.

This book is also dedicated to the memory of my dear friend and colleague Kevin Floyd.

Early versions of some sections of chapter 4 are reprinted with permission of Oxford University Press and Johns Hopkins University Press and appeared in my articles "The Presence of Postmodernism in Contemporary American Literature" (*American Literary History* 27, no. 1 [2015]: 186–97, doi:10.1093/alh/aju065); and "Fictions of Neoliberalism: Contemporary Realism and the Temporality of Postmodernism's Ends" (in *Neoliberalism and Contemporary Literary Culture*, edited by Mitchum Huehls and Rachel Greenwald Smith, 105–21, © 2017 Johns Hopkins University).

INTRODUCTION

The Time Is Now

Amazing how time flies while it stands still.
—Art Spiegelman, *In the Shadow of No Towers*

"Time is a thing that grows scarcer every day," observes Vija Kinski, one of the central characters of Don DeLillo's 2003 novel *Cosmopolis*.[1] Other characters in the novel find life today "too contemporary" (27), which, Vija suggests, is a result of the future's absorption into the present, a problem for which we must find a solution: "We used to know the past and not the future. This is changing. We need a new theory of time" (86). DeLillo begins to address this problem of temporality, which has come to structure his recent novels, in particular *Cosmopolis*, *Point Omega* (2010), and *Zero K* (2016), in the early aughts. "Time is the only narrative that matters," notes the narrator of *The Body Artist* (2001), but the only narrative that matters, DeLillo tells us, is experiencing a moment of severe crisis.[2] In his 2001 article "In the Ruins of the Future," DeLillo writes, "We seem pressed for time, all of us. Time is scarcer now. There is a sense of compression, plans made hurriedly, time forced and distorted. But language is inseparable from the world that provokes it." "We like to think America invented the future," DeLillo continues. "We are comfortable with the future, intimate with it. But there are disturbances now, in large and small ways, a chain of reconsiderations. Where we live, how we travel, what we think about when we look at our children."[3] Similarly, Hubertus Bigend, one of the central characters of William Gibson's *Pattern Recognition*, published the same year as DeLillo's *Cosmopolis*, proposes the following:

> We have no idea, now, of who or what the inhabitants of our future might be. In that sense, we have no future. Not in the sense that our grandparents had a future, or thought

> they did. Fully imagined cultural futures were the luxury of another day, one in which 'now' was of greater duration. For us, of course, things can change so abruptly, so violently, so profoundly, that futures like our grandparents' have insufficient 'now' to stand on. We have no future because our present is too volatile.[4]

In *A Singular Modernity*, Fredric Jameson forwards an account of just this problem. According to Jameson, our historical moment is characterized by the standardization of fragmentation and volatility, which leads to "the persistence of sameness through absolute difference." The experience of "perpetual change," Jameson argues, introduces at its climax the impression of ultimate homogenization and standardization: "Absolute change equals stasis." "What we begin to feel," he concludes, is that, as a paradoxical result of the centrality of perpetual change, "nothing can change any longer."[5] Cayce Pollard, the protagonist of *Pattern Recognition*, provides us with an even more pointed and memorable description of the seemingly tautological nature of the perceived expansion of the contemporary in a memorable description of our time: "It's more the way it is now than it's ever been."[6]

The problem looms large in recent critical discourse. Lauren Berlant's *Cruel Optimism* (2011) centrally revolves around the epistemological, literary, and political challenges that our "broad, stretched-out present" brings with it, and Hans Ulrich Gumbrecht argues that

> it is clear that, during the final decades of the twentieth century and within Western culture at least, the future progressively lost its quality of being an "open horizon of expectations," and turned into a zone that now appears both inaccessible for our predictions and tendentiously unappealing for our desires. Between a future that seems to be closed and a past open to inundate our present, the present has begun to expand from that "imperceptibly short moment of transition" into a broad dimension of simultaneities.[7]

We find similar propositions in works such as Mark Fisher's *Capitalist Realism: Is There No Alternative?* (2009), in which Fisher examines forms of subjectivity and psychological conditions that are associated with what he terms our "endless Eternal Now." Today, Terry Smith argues, the relation between the present and the notion of contemporaneity seems profoundly troubled. "The world as it is now," Smith suggests, "no longer . . . feel[s] like our time." Consequently, our experience of contemporaneity is one of simultaneous temporal captivity and exclusion. Our present, Smith consequently suggests, is not really "a time" at all, since "the only potentially permanent thing about this state of affairs is that it may last for an unspecifiable amount of time: the present may become, perversely, 'eternal.' Not, however, in a state of wrought transfiguration, as Baudelaire had hoped, but as a kind of incessant insipience, of the kind theorized by Jacques Derrida." In our present, contemporaneity is defined by "its immediacy, its presentness, its prioritizing of the moment over time, the instant over the epoch, of direct experience . . . over distanced reflection." The "incessant incipience" of a present that has "become, perversely, eternal," Smith argues, is contemporaneity's "volatile core."[8]

The notion that the future may have ended, however, is not just a concern for authors and theorists. It has risen to a widespread cultural narrative about our moment in time. Gurus of venture capitalism such as Peter Thiel note with some dismay that the future and its associated imagination, and with it the basis for venture capitalism, seem to have disappeared. In his 2011 essay "The End of the Future," Thiel argues that our era is defined by a profound change, one that marks in his mind the end of progress and innovation. Our historical moment is witnessing the end of the future and the rise of presentism. At best, Thiel argues, we are offered a pseudo-future, one without futurity, a "strange future where today's trends simply continue." Thiel's essay offers a sweeping indictment of our present. We live "in a world where little grows or improves with time," he writes, and we have decidedly moved beyond those eras "when people still had concrete ideas about the future." But while the core of Thiel's essay and of his frustration with the current crisis of futurity is quite clearly motivated by his concern for the operations of venture and finance capitalism and a mournful longing for those future imaginaries that propped up some of the basic operations of capitalism, he also suggests that the disruption of the future results not only in capitalist crises but also in political and cultural ones. "Voters today prefer Victorian houses," he laments, a point underscored by the recent political shift in the United States and a growing number of other countries toward right-wing nostalgia and a politics that further amplifies the crisis of futurity by promising not better futures but instead the return to a romanticized past. In literature, too, Thiel proposes, we are able to see the consequences of the crisis of futurity: "Science fiction has collapsed as a literary genre."[9] Commentators like Noah Berlatsky agree. Science fiction, he writes in a think piece published in *The Atlantic*, is increasingly abandoning the future or has stopped caring about it altogether.[10]

And yet, while a wide range of commentators, scholars, politicians, and entrepreneurs continue to rehash this by now ubiquitous narrative about our moment in history, the novel tells a strikingly different story. In particular, the multiethnic American novel has in recent years engaged with the category of time to generate new future imaginaries. Indigenous or Afro-Futurisms make significant contributions to a moment that is associated, even by popular actors like Will Ferrell, with a crisis of futurity. In a special contribution to *Wired* magazine, Ferrell asks, "Where's the future?" We were promised food in pill form and flying cars, Ferrell notes. The state of our present, however, leaves him wondering what went wrong and why the future we were promised never arrived.[11] Similarly, the thirty-year anniversary of Robert Zemeckis's 1985 movie *Back to the Future* gave rise to a widely circulated meme that reflects on the differences between the film's idea of 2015 and our own reality in 2015. The "Where's my hoverboard!?" meme expresses the tension between the exciting futures of the past and the crises and problems that define our present reality. The nonexistence of the hoverboard in 2015 became a popular symbol for the collapse of the future into our present—for the absence of the exciting, positive changes that culture once imagined and for which people continue to long. But the absence of the hoverboard does not just indicate that the past we were promised never arrived. More significantly, it expresses a general loss of faith in the idea of the future.

It is precisely this loss of faith in futurity that greatly concerns venture capitalists, for it inevitably gives rise to a crisis in capitalism. For instance, Thiel writes, "A credit crisis happens when earnings disappoint and the present does not live up to past expectations of the future." In particular since the 2008 crash, capitalism itself has been experiencing a crisis of futurity, one that Thiel sees as connected to a widespread cultural, social, and political crisis of our imagination of the future. Juxtaposing Ferrell's concern with promises of the future that were broken, the discontent that underlies the demand for the hoverboard that never arrived—and one of the most popularly successful cultural engagements with the futures of the same year, Disney's 2015 movie *Tomorrowland*—would seem to underwrite Thiel's concern. *Tomorrowland* strikingly represents the crash of the future into its own retrofuturistic aesthetic. The movie's indulgence in romanticized reproductions of past cultural futures and its idealization of the naive techno-optimism of decades past furthers the suspicion that our moment is marked by a frustrated, disillusioned longing for the future. Unable to produce our own cultural futures, we nostalgically reanimate those of a different time and long for idealized moments when easy futures were said to be readily available. The futures of our present are thus temporally intriguing. They are untimely and strikingly anachronistic—not in the sense of a present in which we imagine a time yet to come, however, but in the sense of a true anachronism, as futures that belong to a different moment in time. Accordingly, in an article in *Future Tense*, a partnership of *Slate* magazine, New America, and Arizona State University, Ed Finn concludes that science fiction suffers from an "inspiration drought." Echoing the concern voiced by Thiel, Finn suggests that science fiction is in dire need of new dreams. We do not seem to have our own images of the future, Finn argues, wondering why "all our narratives about the future [are] 50 years old."[12]

The impression that we have lost the ability to imagine the future, Nathan Silverman argues in an article published in *The Baffler*, is poignantly expressed through the posts of @Shitty_Future, a Twitter account that has been gathering evidence for the future's crash. As this Twitter feed shows, our present is defined by shitty futures, Silverman argues, by a time when "the future is most decidedly now." Instead of exciting futures, we only have futures that, Silverman argues, are ultimately "letdowns." As a result, the present is nothing more than an "extended anticlimax." Our present, Silverman reasons, is marked by a "radical future malfunction" that is laid bare by the work of "the Shitty Futurists," by those who "know that the future is shitty" and who "have realized what many have not: things didn't have to be this way, and it's too late now." Faced with the choice between shitty futures brought about by climate change and versions of the future that are reserved for oligarchs and the superrich, Silverman reasons, we all must surely conclude that "the future is irrelevant, over and retailed, entirely kaput." "The future is gone," Silverman continues, and "after years of failed salesmanship" we should finally come to terms with this new reality: "It's time to bury the concept, and don't bother with the QR scannable headstone." The present should be our sole focus, because the future, "with all of its ideological baggage, and its smoldering graveyard of unfulfilled dreams, has failed us." Faced with the failure of the future, Silverman concludes, we are left with only one option: we must abandon the future "and start figuring out how we might survive the present."[13]

All we have, it seems, is now. The future has ended, and we are witnessing the rise and absolute expansion of the present. And as it turns out, faced with this development, even futurists are deciding that it may be best to change professions. In their Editors' Note to the "Futurist Forum," a series of articles "by some of the world's leading futurists," CO.EXIST editors argue that because established conceptions of time and futurity are "no longer operable in a digital age when everything—emails, tweets, TV shows, finance—happens instantly," former futurists are now becoming self-described "presentists."[14] One of these (former) futurists, media theorist Douglas Rushkoff, suggests in his book *Present Shock* that whereas the twentieth century was characterized by futurism, the twenty-first has thus far been defined by "presentism."[15] Historians David Armitage and Jo Guldi, authors of *The History Manifesto*, likewise propose that current public debate is centrally defined by short-termism. In our moment, which is often associated with a flattened world in which we all live in a global village, they argue, "time has been compressed." "Timespans ranging from a few months to a few years determine most formal planning and decision-making—by corporations, governments, non-governmental organisations and international bodies," Armitage and Guldi write, adding that "quarterly reporting by companies," "electoral cycles," and "planning horizons of one to five years" have become the "usual temporal boundaries of our hot, crowded, and flattened little world."[16] This short-termism, they show, has a name and has been spreading since the 1980s, and as a result the future has collapsed into an ever-expanding, self-renewing present.

This broadening of the present in turn generates significant problems for art and culture, as we are able to see in critical debates that focus on the current state of contemporary art. *Contemporary art* seems like an innocuous term that refers quite simply to art produced today. And yet recent discussions of the term by art historians and critics indicate clearly that it is no longer as historically and temporally bland as it once was. While we are currently witnessing increasing interest in the category of the contemporary in literary studies, art criticism has been grappling with the term for well over a decade now. And if the by now robust discourse on the question of contemporary art and the concept of the contemporary in art criticism is any indicator of discussions to come in literary criticism, then we may be looking ahead to unhappy times. But why exactly does the term seem to enrage art critics, and should literary critics be similarly impatient with the term *contemporary literature*? Critic, art historian, and chief curator of the 2018 Shanghai

Biennale Cuauhtémoc Medina argues that we are confronted with a "pandemic of contemporariness" in contemporary art. Simply put, there is more contemporaneity in contemporary art than ever before, and that is not a good thing. Medina understands art's excessive contemporaneity, or what he calls the "frenzy of 'the contemporary' in contemporary art," as a symptom of art's immediate attachment to the logic of our moment, to the absolute presentism of a world that art is unable to critique and that it instead merely reproduces. In this sense, Medina argues, art has become truly contemporary: the signature of art's contemporaneity is "the fact that art fairs, biennales, symposia, magazines, and new blockbuster shows and museums constitute evidence of art's absorption into that which is merely *present*—not better, not worse, not hopeful, but a perverted instance of the *given*."[17] The problem with *contemporary art*, in other words, is not that the term is fairly banal and simply describes the art of today. The problem is much more substantial. The contemporaneity of contemporary art is symptomatic of a historically specific phenomenon in art, and it designates a moment when art can only register the given and has lost its ability to imagine that which may lie beyond the present. It is for this reason that Medina expresses his account of the damaging dominance of the contemporary in art via a particular variation of the term: *contemp(t)orary*. The term *contemporary art* becomes contemptible as soon as it functions as more than a mere placeholder for more rigorous critical concepts, as soon as it begins to describe a historically specific problem in the relation between art and contemporaneity.

In the late aughts, the editors of the journal *October* sent a questionnaire on "the Contemporary" to "approximately seventy critics and curators." The effort resulted in a 120-page document, "Questionnaire on 'The Contemporary,'" which was published in the fall of 2009. "The category of 'contemporary art' is not a new one," writes Hal Foster on behalf of the editors in the introduction to the document. But what the responses to the questionnaire show, and "what is new," he continues, is that "'contemporary art' has become an institutional object in its own right."[18] In her examination of the relation between contemporaneity and contemporary art, Juliane Rebentisch comes to the same conclusion and suggests that "it might sound somewhat tautological, but contemporary art is experiencing a boom." "The contemporaneity of contemporary art," however, is for Rebentisch "nothing but the nightmare of an eternal now." The contemporaneity of contemporary art mirrors a larger historical problem insofar as the "fixation on the now in art is . . .

the exact correlate of a time imprisoned by immanence." And contemporary art thus conceived, Rebentisch senses, appears to be connected to the general association of our moment with a movement beyond historicism and historical time: "This description of the current state of things corresponds to the diffuse feeling that the present is no longer defined by the directional vector of historical development; instead, it gently spreads out in a peculiar way so that it becomes 'broader,' as Hans Ulrich Gumbrecht formulates it. For Gumbrecht, the broad present marks nothing less than the end of the chronotope of 'historical time' itself."[19] Art criticism diagnoses our moment as being plagued by the collapse of the future into the long now, a development that not only can be studied in contemporary art but that indeed transforms the term *contemporary art* itself into a poignant index of art's inability to imagine anything but contemporaneity.

The London-based art collective AYR accordingly writes in *Harvard Design Magazine* that our moment in history is witnessing "a larger crisis of futurity," a crisis that "collapses modern futurity on itself." AYR, however, aiming to shift the focus away from repeatedly diagnosing the same symptoms and toward an examination of underlying conditions, suggests that the end of the future should be examined in the context of the rise of neoliberalism and the rise to dominance of finance capitalism. "Contemporary forms of 'immaterial' production, the debt economy, and the digitization of individuals and their environment," they write, all have a point in common: they require "life to be turned into data." This transformation of life into data in turn results in what they describe as a "shift in knowledge" that "obliterates the classical modern model based on the formulation of a project at the temporal scale of a human life."[20] Eric Cazdyn and Imre Szeman argue similarly that the sources of the crisis of futurity should be understood as a problem of knowledge and imagination, one that originates from the particular material conditions of our present. Specifically, they show in their book *After Globalization* that contemporary thought is characterized by what they describe as a fatal flaw: the inability to imagine an aftermath to globalization.[21] In other words, while Thiel worries about the future of capitalism and blames contemporary society for its lack of interest in the future, Cazdyn and Szeman show that the source of the current crisis of imagination and of futurity should be traced back to one of the defining contradictions of contemporary capitalism itself. This line of argumentation resonates with James Bridle's suggestion in his 2018 book *New Dark Age: Technology and the End of the Future* that digitalization and the turn to big data in contemporary capitalism ultimately lead not to greater understanding but to new forms of incomprehension. Bridle associates the end of the future with a crisis of knowledge and with our increasing inability to articulate our relation to the world. Lost in a sea of information, we are unable to chart a clear course forward, he argues, and our attempts to make sense of the world are further disrupted by the emergence of simplistic narratives and postfactual politics.[22]

The chapters that follow are dedicated to exploring the function and indeed the importance of the novel in this situation of severe crisis. Like AYR and Cazdyn and Szeman, this book strives to forward an account not only of the causes of the crisis of futurity that purportedly defines our present but also of the ways we may historicize and ultimately move beyond the limits and impasses that commentators associate with our era of full contemporaneity. In addition to mainstream, popular commentary, a wide range of scholars in fields ranging from philosophy and cultural theory to political theory and economics tend to replicate this narrative of the crisis of futurity, describing our era as limited by a "presentism" or "short-termism" that creates significant problems for our sociopolitical and cultural imagination. But time has, of course, not ended, and the crisis described by commentators is entirely fictional. And yet *How to Read a Moment* shows that crises which are more fiction than fact can nevertheless create all-too-real consequences. This book explores how exactly a fictional crisis can give rise to quite concrete, material consequences. And since we are confronted with a particularly fascinating fictional crisis—for time is itself a matter of a delicate relation between fiction and fact, between the real world and the realm of ideas—this book proposes that we can learn much about the origins and consequences of this crisis by looking at how literary fiction has engaged with the purported crisis of time over the past few decades. In particular the "contemporary" novel addresses contemporaneity as a problem that is as much historical as it is aesthetic, as much a matter of the ways in which particular forms of time shape and prop up our material world as it is about changing forms of our temporal imagination, offering counternarratives of our present that show why the ubiquity of the crisis of temporality is to be treated as one of the most pressing problems of our current political and cultural imagination. Moreover, this book suggests that we may understand the rise of real-time capitalism as one central source of this crisis of temporality and, by showing that the material consequences and contradictions of the transition into real-time capitalism are bound up with significant changes in time as a form of imagination and narrative, that the novel is able to respond to this crisis by returning to its strengths as an art form. The novel emerged as an art form under conditions similar to those we face today: in the context of a historical crisis in the fiction of time and during the emergence of a new temporal regime (a new way of conceiving of temporality, contemporaneity, and "presence"). And just as it did at the moment of its rise, the novel today provides us with new, alternative ways of understanding the temporality of a changed historical moment, thus transcending what is elsewhere simply understood as a limiting crisis.

Allow me to elaborate. The end of the future is connected to a crisis of established forms of telling time, which is in turn bound up with a crisis of knowing, of making sense of our relation to the world and to our moment in history. But far from presenting us with the actual end of futurity or of time itself, the currently prevalent belief that the future may have ended should be understood as a problem of knowledge, as a crisis of our imagination that is directly bound up with a transition in material reality. What has exhausted itself is not the future itself. Rather, we are witnessing a large-scale shift in material reality that throws into crisis those narratives and forms of knowledge that stabilized and made thinkable prior modes of existence. Such exhaustions of our temporal imaginary have often accompanied moments of significant historical transformation. Yet, although they are by no means new or unique, crises in established ways of imagining and telling time bring with them significant cultural and sociopolitical upheavals. After all, what we are losing, as we have already begun to see in the examples above, is not just a set of ideas about time, a few stories about the future, or a particular orientation toward the world that is helpful for venture capitalism. More significantly, we are losing one of the fundamental ways of understanding our relation to material reality, a complex understanding of time joining the material world to the world of ideas that firmly established itself in our cultural and sociopolitical imagination as a historically specific constellation of connected forms of telling stories about and thus making sense of our world. What is helpful in such a moment, and has helped us navigate such crises productively in the past, is a turn toward literature in general and the novel in particular, toward those art forms that are quintessentially defined by their commitment to interrogating, delimiting, and innovating our narratives of time as a historically changing form of thought.

Thiel is correct when he suggests that "it is not easy to find a path back to the future." Of course, solely confronting the problem within the self-imposed confines of the capitalist imagination from which the crisis emerged in the first place certainly does not make things easier. But Thiel's general point, that we ought to reflect more rigorously on the future and that "the first and the hardest step" of such reflection may be "to see that we now find ourselves in a desert, and not in an enchanted forest,"[23] is nevertheless well taken, and it is precisely what this book aims to do. In a 2014 interview dedicated to the problem of the seeming end of the future, Gibson suggests that we are indeed experiencing a historically significant crisis. "During the 20th century," Gibson notes, "the phrase, 'The 21st century' was uttered and printed uncounted times. When did you last hear someone say, other than this conversation, 'The 22nd century'? We've quit talking about [the future] in those terms."[24] And yet the crash of old futures and of established ways of imagining time does not mark a categorical end for Gibson. Rather, it identifies a moment when we are called upon to develop new temporal imaginaries, temporal narratives that are in keeping with our time. This is to say that we are called upon to historicize our temporal imagination and time itself, which is the starting point for an important effort to develop a temporal understanding of our world that is able to make meaning of and tell the time of the new historical moment that we inhabit. In this sense, as Gibson stresses, the end of the future, understood as the end of our attachment to previous, often strikingly simplistic or even naive narratives of the future, "may actually represent a degree of maturity on our part as a culture." As I show, the novel in general and the time novel in particular are crucial to this attempt to historicize time and formulate new temporal narratives suitable for our moment, and I suggest not only that the contemporary American time novel assumes a crucially important role in our ability to come to terms with the current crisis of temporality and futurity but that the recent return of the time novel also marks a degree of maturity in American fiction after postmodernism.

A TIME FOR THE NOVEL

Timothy Bewes argues that the attempt to "temporalize the present" is one of the most significant tasks of contemporary literary criticism. Temporalizing the present, Bewes suggests, which includes attention to important categories of our time such as the contemporary, means to struggle with the infamous problem of the vanishing present, for "to describe the present implies that it is already past."[25] But what exactly is literary studies to do when the present has stopped vanishing? In a time when the present no longer functions as a productive boundary that creates the temporality of both past and future but instead expands into an absolute limit that constrains our ability to imagine the future as difference, it would seem that art forms whose histories are directly bound up with temporality and engagements with the moving present—first and foremost the novel—should also experience profound crises. What, then, happens to the contemporary novel, and what does it mean to speak of the contemporary novel, when there is too much contemporaneity? Modern times, I show in this book, became understandable to us in part through the work of the novel. The novel emerges historically as an art form that tries to make sense of a moment when virtually every aspect of the world is subject to rapid and profound change. In contradistinction to the epic, for instance, which has been described as the narrative of a world that is imagined as completed and therefore timeless, the novel's importance lies in part in its ability to address itself to the ever-changing present of modernity, which it seeks to narrativize and thereby make accessible to thought. Given the novel's foundational connection to the very sense of time whose death it now narrates, however, does the fact that a wide range of novels grapple with the end of temporal development, as the following chapters show, mean that the novel inevitably narrates its own death? As the flow of the present stops, and the infamous problem of the vanishing present is replaced by that of a static, inescapable, and seemingly absolute Now without future, we must wonder: Does the term *contemporary novel* finally designate a specific moment in time for the novel, the moment when contemporaneity becomes the novel's defining aesthetic problem as well as its ultimate point of exhaustion?

Already in 1986, Milan Kundera suggests that "the spirit of our time" is so "firmly focused on a present that is so expansive and profuse that it . . . reduces time to the present moment only." This temporal crisis, Kundera warns, may also exhaust the novel: "Within this system the novel is no longer a *work* . . . but one current event among many, a gesture with no tomorrow." "Does this mean," he consequently wonders, that "'in a world grown alien to it,' the novel will disappear?"[26] More recently, critics like Annette Van have been asking the same question. And if Van is correct, then the outlook for the novel is bleak. When we examine the status of the novel today, Van suggests, we must inevitably ask, "Is this a form that can survive the future?"[27] Van is not confident that it can. In fact, she is not even sure that "we still need the novel": "I still read lots of novels. . . . [T]he novel remains a key source of pleasure . . . but it is just one pleasure among others provided by music, film, reality television. But survival of the novel for the novel's sake? Convince me."[28] At first blush, it might seem as though the contemporary novel itself may not be able to convince Van. In fact, it seems to confirm Van's suspicion that there is no future for the novel—quite literally in some cases. "I woke one morning to find myself excused from time," the narrator of John Wray's *The Lost Time Accidents* (2016) tells us in the novel's opening passages. And given that Wray's novel is about time travel, this is a particularly troubling issue. The sense that the future and indeed time itself have collapsed into the present gives rise to a rather strange version of the time travel novel. *The Lost Time Accidents* formally expresses the problem of futurelessness that drives its plot via an epistolary narrative in which each entry is marked with the same date and time. The narrator of Charles Yu's 2010 novel *How to Live Safely in a Science Fictional Universe*, who works in the time travel industry, faces a similar problem. At the beginning of the novel, we find him in an uncharacteristic situation for an engineer who specializes in repairing time machines: he is stuck in the "Present-Indefinite."[29] And as the narrator of Yu's novel suggests, being stuck in the present is not a good thing for art: "The Present-Indefinite isn't even a real gear. It's like cruise control. It's a gadget, a gimmick, a temporary crutch, a holding place. It is hated by purists and engineers, equally. It's bad for aesthetics, bad for design, bad for fuel efficiency" (56). Is the time of the endless, eternal present the time, then, in which the novel dies?

Far from it. *How to Read a Moment* argues that the American novel affords us striking alternatives to an understanding of our present that has become common in critical and theoretical debate as well as mainstream commentary. The contemporary novel allows us to see that we have not in fact reached the categorical end of time or the limit of our ability to imagine the future or change. We do not live in the end times, as fashionable as it may currently seem to imagine such a situation. Against the majority of established approaches to time in both art and philosophy, the contemporary novel dispenses with a focus on the experience of time and instead attempts to restore our focus on a historical reading of time. Instead of examining our perception of time and the present, in other words, the novel reminds us that time itself is a matter of specific forms of knowledge, forms that emerge and are useful under specific historical conditions but that also have shelf lives and thus expire. This book illustrates the novel's crucially important contribution to our ability to grapple with the temporal crises of our time by developing ways to examine the current problem of contemporaneity historically: as a matter of the exhaustion of a temporal regime that calls for new ways of reading the present and telling the time of our moment. It is true, our established ways of imagining time no longer make sense in a world that is aimed at immediacy and in which concepts such as "real time" describe not only instantaneity but also time's full abstraction. No traditional metaphor, analogy, or narrative corresponds to the units of time that define the speed and instantaneity of our present. And it is also true that this creates a big problem for thought and culture alike. After all, thinking and knowing time requires narrative. Time is inseparable from the stories we tell about it and through it. But precisely because "telling time" means that we know time through the stories we tell about it and that time itself is a narrative about the world and our relationship to it, the current crisis of temporality does not signal the end of time or futurity. Instead, it is bound up with the exhaustion of a particular set of temporal narratives. What is required in such a situation, as Vija suggests above, is "a new theory of time." New theories of time emerge by creating a new vocabulary and new narratives that allow us to tell the new kind of temporality that governs our lives. This new vocabulary for our time is what the American novel has been developing in recent years. Today, as during the time of its rise, the novel seeks to give us ways of knowing and speaking to the new forms of time that govern our lives. By telling the time of contemporaneity in strikingly new ways, the novel recovers a sense of possibility and hope in midst of the ruins of the future while also forwarding a dazzling argument for its own survival and importance in the present.

But how does the novel accomplish this? The suggestion that we appear to be unable to imagine an alternative or even a modest change to our capitalist present yet can easily imagine the complete destruction of the globe or that of our civilization has been popularized by and come to be associated with the recent writings of Slavoj Žižek and Mark Fisher.[30] Yet this basic argument was already introduced by Francis Fukuyama in 1992 and subsequently extended by Fredric Jameson in *The Seeds of Time* (1994), who suggested that the condition may possibly rest upon "some weakness in our imagination."[31] And here Jameson was precisely right. But what has thus far escaped critical dialogue is that the novel has been addressing itself to just this weakness in imagination for roughly three decades now—not to interrogate or confirm an end point or limit, however, but in order to historicize the crisis of temporality as a crisis of our imagination and to develop ways of moving beyond it. Wray's temporally immobile time traveler composes his narrative in order to tell us how he became stuck and also as a way to get himself unstuck. The solution to his problem, we learn, lies in the act of writing and rewriting the narrative of his captivity and of the complex, problematic temporal lines that led up to it. In Yu's novel, too, the answer to the problems of time with which the novel grapples lies not in trying to live safely in a science fictional universe but instead in reimagining what it means to live in the present. The contemporary novel addresses itself to the crisis of time today by understanding it as a crisis of narrative, treating time as a form of knowledge, as a form of narrating our relationship to the world. Time, as the narrator of Yu's novel suggests, is a problem of "chronodiegetics."

This, then, is precisely what DeLillo means when he suggests not only that time is a narrative but that it is also important to remember that "language is inseparable from the world that provokes it." In fact, Peter Boxall argues that if, as Paul Ricoeur suggests in *Time and Narrative*, "'time becomes human time to the extent that it is organized after the manner of a narrative,' then it follows that narrative itself is the privileged mode in which to test this becoming meaningful of time."[32] Time, conceived as a historically specific amalgamate of narrative, vocabulary, and knowledge, emerges under and serves the interests of specific material, philosophical, and sociopolitical conditions. As these conditions change, established ways of understanding time reach the limits of their usefulness. This creates severe crises, but it also creates moments of great possibility. For if temporal regimes stabilize particular material and sociopolitical structures—modern capitalism, for instance, requires the standardization of a very specific way of understanding time—then the crumbling of such regimes calls not only for the development of new ways of understanding time but also for the restoration of those forms of telling the time of our lives that were overwritten by the previously dominant temporal regime. Such a situation is not a moment of crisis but one of opportunity for art and particularly for the novel. "To shape time in accordance with a larger historical logic," Boxall argues, "is . . . what the novel is able to do, more consummately than any other art form."[33] I show in detail in this book why exactly this is the case, and I argue that this is the very suggestion that underwrites the ways in which various contemporary novels imagine the novel's possibility and importance in our time. *How to Read a Moment* illustrates that the work of creating new ways of imagining, reading, and telling the new forms of temporality that define contemporary American life is done most effectively by the *Zeitroman*, the time novel. This art form, which strikingly and indeed bafflingly has largely been left undiscussed in anglophone literary criticism, has always wondered how we imagine time at different moments in history. The eternal Now of our moment, *How to Read a Moment* shows, is a time for the *Zeitroman*.

THE *ZEITROMAN*: SYMBOLIC FORM OF THE CONTEMPORARY

The *Zeitroman* emerges in nineteenth-century Germany, assumes a central role in the literature of the Weimar Republic, and all but disappears from the German cultural landscape as a result of National Socialism's rise to power in 1933. The term *Zeitroman* was first employed as early as 1809 by Clemens Brentano in his critical engagement with the work of Achim von Arnim.[34] Though it emerged in connection to the bildungsroman, the historical novel, and especially the *Gesellschaftsroman* (social novel), the *Zeitroman* struggled to place itself alongside these novel forms throughout the nineteenth century. It rose to greater prominence during the first half of the twentieth century and has since been chiefly associated with modernism, specifically with works such as Thomas Mann's *The Magic Mountain*, Robert Musil's *Man without Qualities*, but also, as we see in chapter 1, with Marcel Proust's *In Search of Lost Time*, James Joyce's *Ulysses*, and the work of William Faulkner and John Dos Passos. We encounter brief discussions of or references to the *Zeitroman* in A. A. Mendilow's classic *Time and the Novel* (1952), in the second volume of Paul Ricoeur's *Time and Narrative* (1986), as well as in more recent works such as Mark Currie's *About Time* (2006) and Fredric Jameson's *Valences of the Dialectic* (2009). In each of these works, the discussion of the *Zeitroman* is routed through one primary source: a lecture by Thomas Mann on *The Magic Mountain*. During the first stage of his exile in the United States, in Princeton, New Jersey (1938–41), Thomas Mann delivered a series of lectures at Princeton University, with which he was formally associated from 1938 to 1940. One of these lectures, "Introduction to *The Magic Mountain*," would serve as the point of departure for Mendilow's and Ricoeur's discussion of the *Zeitroman*, which in turn influenced those of Currie and Jameson. In his lecture, Mann describes *The Magic Mountain* as a *Zeitroman* in a double sense: first, because the novel "attempts to compose the internal picture of an epoch," and second because "pure time itself is its very object."[35] This description of the *Zeitroman* has prompted Mendilow and Ricoeur to develop sustained examinations of the ways in which this particular novel form is "about time." Ricoeur extends this basic account of the *Zeitroman* into an important formal analysis of the different aspects of time made legible by novelistic narrative that are particular to the novel. This includes, for instance, the tension between time of narration and narrated time, which is further complicated when examined in relation to the time of reading.[36] And, like Ricoeur, I believe it is important to foreground how literature in general and the novel in particular are able to read and imagine time in ways that are distinctly different from other media and other literary forms. But as Mann's lecture indicates, there is much more to the *Zeitroman* than the suggestion that it is a kind of novel that is about time itself.

After outlining the initial double sense in which *The Magic Mountain* can be understood as a *Zeitroman*, Mann adds that the *Zeitroman* "treats" time itself, which it selects as its object, "not only as the experience of its protagonist but also in and through itself."[37] By drawing a distinction between time as experience on one hand and time that can be studied in and through itself on the other, Mann stresses that one crucial project of the *Zeitroman* is the examination of time as a historically specific form of knowledge about the world. Instead of examining our experience of time, that is, the time novel examines time in time. The problem of the subjective experience of time, which in *The Magic Mountain* revolves around Hans Castorp's withdrawal from the world and into a seemingly timeless existence of introspection and interiority, becomes a point of departure for the novel's larger project. The logic of Castorp's withdrawal from historical time and into the seclusion of Davos, where only his own relation to his surroundings registers temporality, sets up *The Magic Mountain*'s inquiry into time through the form of the novel itself. Mann writes, "The book is itself that which it narrates; by representing the hermetic enchantment of its young protagonist into timelessness the novel itself tends toward the sublation [*Aufhebung*] of time through artistic means by its attempt to lend full presence at every moment to the musical-ideal total world [*Gesamtwelt*] that it circumscribes and to create a magical 'nunc stans.'"[38] The novel's relation to time, therefore, lies in what Mann understands as its commitment to the effort to unite form and content, essence and appearance, and by doing so to move beyond the initial subjective recognition of temporality and toward a theorization of time in history. The crisis of temporality in the novel is not merely a matter of Castorp's experience of time, nor is it a crisis of time itself. Instead, what comes into crisis is the way in which Castorp imagines time. That is, the problem in the novel lies in time's removal from time itself and the progress of history. This erasure of the link between time and history is historically specific and must be examined in relation to the larger political and philosophical problems with which the novel engages. It is this commitment to tracing the relation between time and history that makes the *Zeitroman* of such great value for our current moment, and it is ultimately also in this sense that we can understand the artistic and political stakes of the contemporary *Zeitroman*.

Unfortunately, this understanding of the *Zeitroman* has largely been disregarded. An example of this is the opening passage of to my knowledge the only anglophone work of literary criticism that engages directly with the *Zeitroman*, Roger Hillman's *Zeitroman: The Novel and Society in Germany, 1830–1900*. Hillman begins by citing Mann's initial definition of the *Zeitroman* but then immediately suggests that "this second sense, with Time as a philosophical problem, is not what is generally understood by the literary term and can be disregarded."[39] Hillman subsequently routes his own project through the first option and focuses on the experience of protagonists. This is not to say that Hillman's choice invalidates his project. Rather, I suggest that understanding the *Zeitroman* solely as a form that traces the temporal logic of an epoch through the experience of characters fails to register Mann's important distinction between examining time as experience and time in and through itself. This results in an incomplete understanding of the *Zeitroman*, and it precludes developing a full account of the significance of the time novel in our moment. The one-sided understanding of the time novel and the singular emphasis on the experience of characters (which is also characteristic of the work of Ricoeur) further indicate a parallel limitation of contemporary literary criticism. The focus on experience and the missing attention to form that we find in discussions of the *Zeitroman* are mirrored in recent critical and theoretical discourse on time. In his article "Prospects for the Present," Jeffrey Insko describes the temporal turn in American studies as "by now flourishing in such fertile soil that it has developed a number of distinct, if intertwined, branches: queer studies, body/affect, print and material culture, aesthetics, transnationalism."[40] And yet, while the temporal turn includes a variety of fields and areas of study, it is dominated by phenomenological approaches to time. This is not entirely surprising, given that phenomenology largely determines modern philosophies of time. But the temporal turn lacks approaches that examine time as form. I certainly do not wish to disparage phenomenological approaches to time and temporality. On the contrary, recent critical debates on time and temporality, most notably queer and gender-critical analysis, which have been among the driving forces of the temporal turn, are highly important for our understanding of time in the present and contain much-needed interrogations of the politics and power relations that link time and futurity to identity and subjectivity. This includes the work of Laurent Berlant and José Muñoz, to which I return in chapters 2 and 3, Elizabeth Freeman's stunningly argued *Time Binds: Queer Temporalities, Queer Histories* (2010), Lee Edelman's much-discussed *No Future: Queer Theory and the Death Drive* (2004), Judith Halberstam's *In a Queer Time and Place: Transgender Bodies, Subcultural Lives* (2005), and collections of essays such as E. L. McCallum and Mikko *Tuhkanen's Queer Times, Queer Becomings* (2011). However, the contemporary American novel cannot be understood fully if we miss the fact that, as I show in the following chapters, its examination of time and the temporal crises of the present is directly bound up with the continuation of the logic of the time novel as outlined by Mann: the contemporary American *Zeitroman* understands the current crisis of futurity as a result of continued attachment to temporal experience as opposed to understanding time as narrative and as a form of knowledge. What the contemporary *Zeitroman* gives us is nothing less than a new theory of time, something that is largely absent from but may form a productive addition to the temporal turn's growing, exciting body of work.

How to Read a Moment argues that literature in general and the novel in particular are uniquely able to forge a link between time and history, an ability that is crystallized in the *Zeitroman*. If, as Tobias Boes shows so persuasively in his book *Formative Fictions*, the bildungsroman can be understood as the novel form of a world newly in flux (in particular during the rise of the bildungsroman),[41] then it is possible to suggest that the *Zeitroman* takes over the bildungsroman's temporal and epistemological project in our time and becomes the novel form of the age of the *nunc stans*, the standing now. The flow of the world that gave rise to the bildungsroman appears to have stopped. Both the bildungsroman and the *Zeitroman* centrally revolve around nonsynchronicity and discontinuity. In the case of the bildungsroman, as Boes illustrates, this is an effort to register the multiple temporalities that underwrite a world newly in flux.[42] In the case of the *Zeitroman*, however, it is a matter of bringing back those discontinuities and multiple temporalities in the present that are overwritten by an overly homogeneous, overly synchronous, singularized understanding of our present. We may understand the current instantiation of the *Zeitroman* as the symbolic form of the omnipresent contemporary, an age out of which it emerges and that it immanently critiques. Cathy Caruth stresses the importance of returning to such an understanding of literature in the context of formulating a literary criticism for the twenty-first century. Literature, Caruth argues, is always precarious and always struggles with the possibility of endings and foreclosures of the future insofar as literature is "a mode of language and an institution whose very being essentially touches on the possibility and fragility of its own future."[43] From the standpoint of such an understanding of literature, any crisis of futurity appears not as an end point to literature but instead reveals itself as a common point of departure for the work of literature. In fact, since literature itself always contains a reflection upon its own possibilities and ends, it assumes a crucial function in our ability to imagine the future, since it develops forms of futurity that lead us beyond the present. "The future," Caruth argues accordingly, "cannot be thought without literary forms of articulation that exceed the language in which we refer to what we know."[44]

The contemporary American *Zeitroman* functions precisely in such a way and is thus an example of the kind of analytical engagement with the present for which Berlant calls in *Cruel Optimism*. Like Bewes, Berlant argues that the present must be opened up to complex historicization, which first and foremost means that we must develop "a historical sense of the present."[45] This, I argue, is the *Zeitroman*'s contribution to thought and politics in our time. The time novel thus also contains a utopian core, since it contributes to contemporary critical debate those kinds of impulses that José Esteban Muñoz demands of the work of utopia in the present: to present a "challenge to theoretical insights that have been stunted by the lull of presentness."[46] Muñoz's suggestion that "the present is not enough" reveals itself as particularly important, since, as Muñoz continues, "[the present] is impoverished and toxic for queers and other people who do not feel the privilege of majoritarian belonging, normative tastes, and 'rational' expectations."[47] As we will see, we may add to this list all of those whose ways of telling time and of being in time do not find a home in the dominant logic of contemporaneity, all those who are denied presence by the temporalization of the discourse of difference that binds segregation based on race, class, or gender to an imagination of temporal exclusion and noncontemporaneity. And it is also from this standpoint that the narrative of an eternal now without alternative reveals itself as particularly problematic and damaging.

Still, the suggestion that the contemporary novel engages with time on the plane of form may strike some readers as surprising. After all, as Catherine Gallagher argues, formalist literary criticism and criticisms of time and temporality are rather unusual bedfellows. In fact, Gallagher argues that formalism and time are traditionally understood as opposed. "The formalism that has been most crucial to the development of our profession in America," Gallagher writes, "is adamant in its conviction that literature cannot stop time; indeed, it has sometimes juxtaposed itself to the structural variety of formalism on precisely the grounds that molar analyses falsify 'the representation of experience in its temporality.'" "The advocates of temporality," she concludes, "have presented literary form . . . as a *refugee* from" time.[48] But as I show in this book, the time novel enlists form in the effort to engage with time, and it does so by dispensing with the focus on experience and instead conceiving of time itself as form. Understood as form, time can be made historically legible and examined as narrative via the novel. *How to Read a Moment* is therefore not only interested in illustrating what is to be gained for our understanding of the novel and indeed of time by understanding time as the movement of thought forms through history as opposed to a way of experiencing the world. I also wish to foreground the advantages of focusing on the dialectical relation between temporal form and novelistic form for our understanding of the contemporary novel and the critical possibilities of the temporal turn. I follow here a particular critical tradition that, with Theodor W. Adorno, believes that history, and therefore also time, enters the work of art on the plane of form. As Adorno suggests, "The unsolved antagonisms of reality return in artworks as immanent problems of form."[49] I am interested, that is, in how time and the historically and materially specific struggle with it in our moment give form to the novel. In turn, this book asks how we can understand what the novel is, what it does, and why we might still need it by examining how the novel addresses itself to time as one of the most pressing material and social problems of our time.

"Time without form," J. M. Bernstein argues in his classic exploration of the philosophy of the novel, "is either empty, or . . . the time that kills. The important thing is to realise that time and meaning must function together."[50] What this suggests, Bernstein reminds us, is that "time is meaningless unless and until it has been historically mediated."[51] Bernstein's demand to understand time as always formally bound up with historically specific ways of making meaning of the world is invaluable for our understanding of the recent history of both time and the novel. And by conducting such an inquiry into the logic of our time, the contemporary novel gives us a new vocabulary for our moment and a sense of time's plurality, discontinuity, and social and material contingency—of the wide variety of ways of telling time that are and that were but also those that were not, could not be, and were not allowed to be . . . but that may yet be. "The premise . . . of any convincing analysis" of time, Bernstein stresses, "must be that human time . . . is not analyzable in terms of sheer succession, a linear series of 'nows' where the line of time moves from the past through the present into the future."[52] No other art form aside from the novel is able to give us a way of imagining time in quite this way, and it is for this reason that the novel not only survives but thrives in our moment. The contemporary novel's account of its own possibility today thus evokes Adorno's emphasis on the category of form for the political function of the artwork in the present. "Aesthetic form," Adorno writes in *Aesthetic Theory*,

> is the objective organization within each artwork of what appears as blindingly eloquent. It is the nonviolent synthesis of the diffuse that nevertheless preserves it as what it is in its divergences and contradictions, and for this reason form is actually an unfolding of truth. A posited unity, it constantly suspends itself as such; . . . form is what is anti-barbaric in art; through form art participates in the civilization that it criticizes by its very existence. Form is the law of the transfiguration of the existing, counter to which it represents freedom.

"Artworks are not being," Adorno consequently argues, "but a process of becoming. . . . Whether art is in any way still possible depends precisely on this. The concept of form marks out art's sharp antithesis to an empirical world in which art's right to exist is uncertain. Art has precisely the same chance of survival as does form, no better."[53]

Chapter 1 of *How to Read a Moment* surveys existing accounts of the current temporal crisis and shows that the contemporary novel has developed an account of the sources and consequences of the purported absorption of the future into the present. The novel allows us to trace those temporal imaginaries that have reached their historical limits, it helps us understand why certain forms of telling time have been exhausted by the transition into real-time capitalism, and it highlights the problematic consequences for thought and culture alike of the emergence of a new temporal regime that grounds material life today. The time of real-time capitalism is abstract and immediate, and it seeks to collapse all forms of temporality into a standardized, uniform now: we all are expected to live in the moment, to be fully contemporary. Novelists such as DeLillo and Gibson address themselves directly to the systemic unreadability of this "now time" of global capital. By examining the novels of DeLillo as indicative of the larger commitments of the time novel that chapter 2 explores in some detail, chapter 1 shows that we may understand DeLillo as the foremost practitioner of the contemporary time novel. Novels like *Cosmopolis* (2003), *Point Omega* (2010), and *Zero K* (2016) illustrate that the time of global capital, immediate and omnipresent, demands to be experienced rather than read and interpreted. The inability to imagine and historicize the time of the present, these novels thus show, is a problem of immediacy: the time of the present leads to an experiential "darkness of the moment" that makes critical interrogation impossible. DeLillo's novels, however, model a way of telling the time of our present by showing us what it may mean to read real time and to read the moment as opposed to experiencing or living in it. This chapter also illustrates that the contemporary time novel foregrounds the novel's particular ability to critically engage with time, an ability that played a central role in the rise of the novel. Chapter 1 revisits the novel's historical relation to time, which allows us to gain important insights into the work of the contemporary time novel, and it shows that the novel's great value for our moment lies in no small part in its ability to provide us with a critique of time and direct us toward telling the time of our present in ways that transcend the limits of a purportedly omnipresent now.

Chapter 2 illustrates that Yu's *How to Live Safely*, Benjamin Kunkel's *Indecision* (2006), Gary Shteyngart's *Super Sad True Love Story* (2010), and Ben Lerner's *10:04* (2014) examine what it means to read time historically and as form through reflections on the methodology of the interpretation of art. Lerner's *10:04* and Jennifer Egan's *A Visit from the Goon Squad* (2010) forward an accounrpretation and reading that is wedded to a sincere belief in the novel's political possibility today. Reading novelistically in these novels means refusing a subjective, experiential relationship to the world. In this sense, Lerner, Egan, and Yu echo early accounts of the *Zeitroman* formulated by Ernst Bloch and Hans Robert Jauß, and answer Jean Paul Sartre's call for a "realism of temporality." The time novel gives us ways of conceiving time as form (as opposed to immediate experience), which in turn hinges upon a return to a version of literariness that is directly committed to understanding literature as the medium of mediation able to make legible the origin of the crises associated with our moment's commitment to immediacy. The novel allows us to read the time of the present otherwise, in its contradictory plurality, uncovering the latencies and possibilities in the now that, in novels such as *10:04*, become the basis for hope and a newfound sociality, and in connection to the temporally plural "coming community" that stands opposed to the fractured individualism of the now/me-time of contemporary capitalism. The chapter concludes by illustrating that the time novel and the contemporary realist novel forward immanent critiques of the existing that trace hope and possibility amid the ruins of the temporal regime of modernity.

While chapters 1 and 2 illustrate why we need a new theory of time, what such a theory might look like, what the stakes are of such a theory for the politics and function of the contemporary novel, and why the novel in general and the *Zeitroman* in particular are suited to developing this new theory, chapter 3 asks whose time the mythical omnipresent now truly is. After all, it quickly becomes apparent that the problem of contemporaneity has a strikingly different history and significance for those whose segregation on the level of class, race, or gender has always also been bound up with temporal segregation. Contemporary African American novelists emphasize that the question of contemporaneity is also always a question of privilege, of strategies for consolidating power and distinction by denying presence. By examining novels such as Colson Whitehead's *Zone One* (2011), *The Intuitionist* (1999), *John Henry Days* (2001), and *Apex Hides the Hurt* (2006), Mat Johnson's *Pym* (2011), and Kiese Laymon's *Long Division* (2013), as well as logical antecedents of this interest in time and presence in novels such as Toni Morrison's *Beloved* (1987), this chapter shows that the contemporary African American time novel unmasks the notion of an omnipresent now as troublingly tied to structures of privilege, power, and exclusion and a central component of processes of racialization. Specific forms of temporality must be ignored or actively segregated to maintain the narrative of a singular, omnipresent now. The African American time novel reveals the concept of contemporaneity as a broker of privilege and power that, particularly in the present moment, trades in the vocabulary of race for the vocabulary of time and nonsynchronicity in order to maintain naturalized racial distinction in less visible form. One of the crucial political efforts of time novels by African American writers in such a situation is the ability to make legible the heterochronies of the present, the plural temporalities that interrupt the uniform temporal regime of the "now time" of global capital. In such heterochronies the novel finds not only its own renewed possibility but also its urgent political work in the present, as the *Zeitroman* is directly wedded to a new politics of hope and possibility based on reading the present historically and thereby uncovering those latencies and unfulfilled desires that demand different times.

Chapter 4 argues that the contemporary novel's renewed attention to time and temporality and the prevalence of contemporaneity as a defining aesthetic problem of the American novel over the past three decades allows us to forward a much-needed periodizing account of literary history after postmodernism. The novel's new temporal vocabulary provides us with the basis for a new periodizing vocabulary via which we are finally able to articulate that which succeeds postmodernism. Returning to the relation between postmodernism and postmodernity, whose temporal complexity we are able to see more clearly from our present standpoint, the chapter stresses that postmodernism's aftermath does not find adequate expression via notions of a late or a long postmodernism nor via the addition of another *post-* to our periodizing vocabulary—for it is precisely the seeming inability to imagine a *post-* that might offer an alternative to repressive contemporaneity that defines much of the work of the contemporary novel. The emergence of the "contemporary novel"—the novel that addresses itself to the problem of contemporaneity—allows us to draw a clear distinction with the postmodern novel. Not only does the category of the contemporary become one of the defining aesthetic problems of the contemporary novel, but the contemporary is transformed from a temporally neutral concept into a periodizing term. To speak of "the contemporary novel" today is to express a historical relation: the moment when the novel addresses itself directly to the problem of contemporaneity in a time in which we seem to be unable to be anything but contemporary. However, this is also the moment when the novel understands its own artistic and political presence as a critical, historicizing relationship to (the time of) the contemporary.

Chapter 4 reads a range of novels in order to suggest that the problem of contemporaneity can be understood in direct relation to the rise and exhaustion of postmodernism, a historical development marked by its own, defining temporal contradictions. It asks: What are we to make of the fact that postmodernism appears to predate those historical and material structures that, according to most macrotheoretical models, gave it shape? Given that the still dominant macrotheoretical models of postmodernism (formulated by critics like Fredric Jameson, David Harvey, Jean-François Lyotard, Linda Hutcheon, Andreas Huyssen, and Ihab Hassan) tend to describe literary and cultural artifacts from the 1960s and 1970s, how can we continue to maintain the assumption that postmodernism is the cultural mediation of postmodernity when the structures we generally associate with postmodernity—globalization, digitalization, the media age, free-market economics, and full financialization brought about by the creation of floating currencies—did not rise to dominance until the 1990s? The chapter distinguishes between the postmodern and the contemporary novel by proposing a temporally more modest account of postmodernism. We are able to better understand both postmodernism and the contemporary novel by conceiving of postmodernism as a rather brief moment in cultural history that was bound up with incipient postmodernity, that is with the beginning transition into what has come to be understood as our neoliberal present: dominant postmodernity. The relation between postmodernism and postmodernity is therefore more accurately understood as one defined by nonsynchronicity and uneven temporal development. Once the transition into postmodernity reaches the status of an actual, new structural dominant in the mid-1980s and early 1990s, literary production changes, and we see the emergence of new novel forms, including centrally the *Zeitroman*. That is, once the temporal gap between postmodernism and postmodernity closes, once the postmodern new becomes the new structural now, we witness the exhaustion of postmodernism and the emergence of a new range of literary forms that attempt to make sense of the absorption of the new into the now, of the future into the present—we see the rise of the contemporary novel that probes the sources of tomorrow's crash.

Already at this point, it is important to stress that I do not seek to name a new period or establish the next big periodizing marker. Throughout the book, in particular in chapter 4, I show that we must understand periodization in far more complicated terms. *How to Read a Moment* follows the example of the novel and attempts to add to the vocabulary we need to name and describe some of the formal characteristics that make up the contemporary. Ultimately, *How to Read a Moment* is also an expression of my firm belief in the importance of art and literature in a time in which we witness everywhere the propagation of the cynical, defeatist notion that our present is a time without future or alternatives, a time defined not by possibility but by the limits of our imagination. Art gives us new forms of thought where dominant discourse and mass culture only give us formulaic repetitions of that which works, sells, and is fully part of our now. However, this does not mean that art is only a matter of the avant-garde. Instead, the contemporary American novel conceives of its aesthetic and political possibility as a matter of fully inhabiting the present. An important characteristic of the American novel that defines its recent history is its ability to show us that we have not reached the end of time, or art, and of literature but find ourselves in a moment in history in which it is vitally important to develop ways of imagining and inhabiting an always temporally heterogeneous present that neoliberalism elsewhere contracts into structural, political, cultural, and ultimately temporal homogeneity. The contemporary novel allows us to understand the crises of the present not as impasses and apocalyptic end points but as the flow of history. Art is essential to our ability to move beyond the existing by making legible in the present that which is missing and that which has been excluded or suppressed—and by doing so, it allows us to trace in the present the contours of a world and time that are, as Ernst Bloch would have it, not yet. The contemporary American novel gives us ways of thinking past an end point that seems to have left us stranded in a present without time and expresses a utopian commitment to thinking futurity as emerging from an understanding of contemporaneity as a complex, plural, and often contradictory way of being together in time. This vibrant present, alive with multiple times and potentialities, abstract and concrete alike, and not the homogenized and instrumentalized time of the endless Eternal Now, is the time of true contemporaneity and the contemporary American novel.

CHAPTER I

The Novel after Tomorrow's Crash

Have you fear'd the future would be nothing to you?
—Walt Whitman, "To Think of Time"

"When we ask what has changed in our world since the turbulent sixties," Jacques Rancière writes in "In What Time Do We Live?," "we are offered a ready-made response encapsulated in the word 'end.'" We are supposed to have witnessed the "end of specific revolutionary hopes or illusions," of "utopias and ideologies in general," or "in its most comprehensive formulation, of the 'grand narratives' and beliefs regarding the destiny of humankind." Our era is marked not only by the end of a particular historical period but by the end "of 'history' itself understood as the time of a promise to be fulfilled." "The time in which we live," Rancière concludes, "can thus be described as the time that comes after the end, a 'post' time." This post-time, Rancière suggests, is "a time of disorientation," since our "belief in a historical promise is said to have been lost along with faith in any promise of the future."[1] Contemporary novels like Cormac McCarthy's *No Country for Old Men* (2005), it would seem at first glance, confirm Rancière's analysis of our time. *No Country* is centrally arranged around lengthy meditations on the loss of old futures and associates the time in which we live with the inability to imagine the future as a time of promise. In the closing passages of *No Country*, the novel's narrator contemplates the temporality signaled by a stone water trough, the kind of temporality and promise for the future that he cannot find in his own life:

> You could see the chisel marks in the stone. It was hewed out of solid rock and it was about six foot long and maybe a half wide and about that deep. Just chiseled out of the rock. And I got to thinking about the man that done that. . . . [T]his

> man had set down with a hammer and a chisel and carved out a stone water trough to last ten thousand years. Why was that? . . . The only thing I can think is that there was some sort of promise in his heart. And I dont have no intentions of carving a stone water trough. But I would like to be able to make that kind of promise. I think that's what I would like most of all.[2]

But we no longer live in a world that allows us to make such promises, and as McCarthy's *The Road* (2006) would seem to suggest (it can be read as a companion piece to *No Country* in this regard), we will not be able to return to a world that allows for such promises either. In its closing sentences, *The Road* offers a moving reflection on this sense of loss: "Once there were brook trout in the streams in the mountains. . . . On their backs were vermiculate patterns that were maps of the world in its becoming. Maps and mazes. Of a thing which could not be put back. Not be made right again."[3] The world of McCarthy's novels, we might conclude, is defined by the same end of historical temporality and development that Rancière traces in our time.

Critics like Fredric Jameson suspect that the impossibility of imagining change in our time is related to the standardization of change and difference in contemporary capitalism. The end of the future, he contends, is connected to "the persistence of sameness through absolute difference."[4] This analysis, too, seems to be borne out by the contemporary novel. The protagonist of Benjamin Kunkel's 2005 novel *Indecision*, Dwight Wilmerding, a young resident of New York City, suffers from abulia, the pathological inability to make decisions. His illness, we learn, is a result of his "slow temporal metabolism," which is unable to efficiently digest "modern or postmodern life."[5] Dwight struggles profoundly with the fact that he is "unable to think of the future until [he] arrive[s] there" (1). The globalized world he is forced to inhabit appears to him utterly homogenizing, which leaves him unable to imagine life beyond a perpetual present. Dwight cannot help but wonder if there is really a substantive difference among various cell phone models, computers and other electronic gadgets, TV programs, contemporary political programs, and so on. Dwight is able to spot differences that technically are differences, yet he cannot find any differences that truly make a difference. This world in which true difference has been replaced by differences without significant consequences leaves Dwight unable to make decisions. After all, why make a decision where there is nothing at stake? The absence of difference in turn also erases the possibility of imagining a future qualitatively or categorically different from the present. The only futures Dwight can imagine lie in the past and were made possible by sociopolitical conditions that no longer exist. Dwight longs for life in Communist Romania, for instance, for a past in which the difference between the first and second world allowed people to make decisions that had clear stakes. This romanticized version of the past, Dwight reasons, still contained choices that were aimed at different possible futures. All the present affords him, however, are decisions that make no difference, which leaves Dwight with sense of living in a present that is defined by the "future collapsing in upon [him]" (7).

"Time, like mind, is not knowable as such," argues George Kubler in his 1962 classic *The Shape of Time*. "We know time only indirectly by what happens in it, by observing change and permanence, by marking the succession of events among stable settings, and by noticing the contrast of varying rates of change."[6] More recently, Marshall Brown has reiterated the importance of what is fundamentally a historical understanding of time: "History, being change, is difference."[7] But when difference itself has become standardized, nothing seems to change any longer, and we are unable to imagine the future as a time of promise, the exhaustion of history and of time itself seems inevitable. Time becomes unthinkable, and it collapses into a perpetual present. Novels such as Nathaniel Rich's *Odds against Tomorrow* (2013) examine our complicity in the collapse of the future. Mitchell Zukor, the protagonist of Rich's novel, a budding futurist, struggles with the consequences of his work. At one point in the novel, Mitchell realizes that "essentially a futurist [is] asked to prevent the future from happening." "The short term," he understands, is "all that matter[s]," which also means "that there [will] be no long term."[8] Plunged into an eternal present that cannot be mapped and which categorically makes long-term plans or future goals impossible, the protagonists of such novels move aimlessly through a largely unchanging world. Movement through this novelistic present is strikingly different from the walks of the modernist flaneur and the jouissance that the postmodern schizo experiences on his liberating strolls without destination. Movement in the contemporary novel is desperate, aimless, and frequently nostalgic, seeking to tread familiar ground and reexploring well-known paths in the hope of recovering a sense of linear progress and with it the futures and promises that lie at its end. Joshua Ferris's *The Unnamed* (2010) stages this terror of unavoidable, incessant movement without change. The novel's protagonist suffers from a condition that makes him unable to stop walking without intention or purpose, a condition that eventually claims his life. Unlike the modernist flaneur, Ferris's protagonist compulsively walks through the world without examination or reflection. Not a single step makes a difference, and his movement accomplishes little aside from taking him closer to death. Locomotion in Ferris's novel is devoid of purpose and without a sense of futurity; it is ceaseless movement through an unchanging, eternal now. The coinciding of aimless movement and absolute stasis thus binds novels like *The Unnamed* to novels such as Don DeLillo's *Cosmopolis* (2003). *Cosmopolis* centrally revolves around the current crisis of time and futurity, and at first blush, DeLillo's story of a billionaire asset manager stuck in traffic in his limousine on the way to a haircut appears to be yet another poignant example of the novel of the long now. And since we are not hard pressed to find contemporary novels that confirm theoretical discourse and represent our time as an era defined by unchanging presence and by the impossibility of development and change, we might therefore wonder: Is the engagement with time that we encounter in novels like *Cosmopolis* the mark of a literature of exhaustion?

In his essay "The End of Temporality," published in the same year as *Cosmopolis*, Jameson wonders, "After the end of history, what? No further beginnings being foreseen, it can only be the end of something else." This, Jameson reasons, presents a significant problem for art. After all, he writes, "modernism already ended some time ago and with it, presumably, time itself, as it was widely rumored that space was supposed to replace time in the general ontological scheme of things." Reiterating the well-worn suggestion that postmodernism is distinguished from modernism by the effacement of time in favor of space, Jameson argues that "time had become a nonperson and people stopped writing about it. The novelists and poets gave it up under the entirely plausible assumption that it had been largely covered by Proust, Mann, Virginia Woolf, and T. S. Eliot and offered few further chances of literary advancement."[9] But novelists did not stop writing about time. In fact, over the course of the past four decades or so, we have witnessed a new temporal turn in the novel that has intensified since the early 2000s. More recently, twenty years after his initial proclamation that we are unable to imagine the future as difference, Jameson has argued that the very disappearance of time becomes an important topic in our moment. But "the permanent present" Jameson writes, "means that no one can remember what the catastrophe was."[10] As a result, he continues, "there can be no thematic agreement about where we are now, and certainly no plausible forecast about futures, except to the degree that in that sense we don't have one." "The only remaining topic," he concludes, "is time itself, or rather this peculiar temporality of a present without a past or future." But the novel's return to the topic of time neither simply reiterates the exhaustion of time and futurity so widely associated with our moment nor confirms Jameson's claim that time no longer offers chances for literary advancement. Instead, the novel reveals the purported end of time as a limit of our imagination that results from a historical change in capitalism. By doing so, the novel allows us to understand the current crises of temporality and futurity not as the categorical end of time and the future but as the result of a change in the temporal regime upon which our material world rests. This change brings with it a crisis of imagination that demands to be confronted on the level of thought and imagination. The latter project has always been central to the work of the novel. Through its engagement with the temporal crises of our moment the novel formulates striking accounts of its possibility and indeed of its crucial importance in our time.

If we simply mapped the prevalence of the crisis of futurity as a plot point in the contemporary novel, it would not be difficult to conclude that the contemporary novel confirms the exhaustion of time, futurity, and change described by critics and theorists. However, if we examine in detail the ways the novel returns to the topic of time, and if we ask how the novel does so as literature—if we ask how novels engage with time specifically as novels—then we are able to trace the striking ways in which the novel, in Jameson's words, is able to tell us what the catastrophe was. Far from merely confirming the crisis, the contemporary novel forwards detailed accounts of the sources of the crisis of temporality, and it helps us imagine time differently, in ways that wrest hope and the possibility of change from the grip of a seemingly inescapable present. Novels like those of DeLillo, Rich, and Ferris show us that the perception of the end of change and promise is associated with a materially specific crisis of masculinity and a historical shift in the gendering of time in the context of which men struggle with the repetitive, standardized, and often timeless everyday that, as Rita Felski shows, was traditionally a site of confinement for women.[11] Similarly, while the present may not offer the forms of temporality and promise upon which the world of McCarthy's old men was built, novels such as Teju Cole's *Open City* (2011) offer us versions of a contemporary critical flaneur who examines the now as a time of temporal pluralism marked by the scars and continued presence of the history of colonialism and segregation and by the discontinuous temporality of migration. And as Andrew Hoberek argues, McCarthy's novels, too, develop complex interrogations of the relationship between time and the imagination. For the final lines of *The Road* do not offer accounts of utter exhaustion but rather reveal the complex, changed understanding of the "radically unfixed potential" that, Hoberek shows, "inhabits McCarthy's bleak narrative."[12]

No doubt, saying positive things about the status of the novel today is in many ways more rewarding than finding yet another way to declare its death. And yet the suggestion that the novel continues to be important in our time ultimately means little if it is not based on a detailed account of the kind of work the novel is able to do today. In this chapter, I forward one such account and show how exactly the novel is able to respond to the current crisis of futurity. "One of the greatest achievements of the novel," Peter Boxall argues, "is that it helps us to know time, and perhaps somehow to master it."[13] Yet if this is so, what exactly does it mean (for our understanding of both time and the novel) to say that a novel allows us to know time? And how might a novel allow us to master time? Moreover, if the novel indeed allows us to know and master time, is this something that only the novel can do or that the novel is able to do better than other forms of art or knowledge? Of course, I do not claim that this chapter can answer these questions definitively or exhaustively. But I propose a set of basic answers along with methodological suggestions that aim to contribute to our ongoing attempt to examine the novel's engagement with time and its status in our moment. This chapter is therefore not interested in the ways in which the contemporary novel may be said to reflect aspects of the temporal crisis or how it may represent this topic. Rather, I wish to examine how the crisis of a type of temporal thought gives form to the novel and how the novel today relates to time based on an understanding of how novels work. By focusing on the novels of DeLillo, one of the foremost practitioners of the time novel today, this chapter establishes a series of basic methodological propositions that will guide the examinations of the work of the contemporary novel in the chapters that follow. I argue that the possibility and value of the novel in our time lies in its ability to provide us with a direly needed critique that allows us to read time as a form of knowledge. The novel's critical function has throughout its history been wedded to its engagement with time as narrative and as a form of knowing ourselves and our relationship to the world. Today, the novel returns forcefully to its ability to generate critiques of temporal thought, an ability that was also of crucial importance for the rise of the novel as an art form, and it thereby renews its possibility and significance in the context of the current temporal crises. In short, by examining the relation between the novel and time, we see why reading novels matters and what is at stake in studying the work of the novel today. We should not lose faith in the novel, for the time in which we live, far from marking its exhaustion, is a time for the novel.

THE TIME OF THE NOVEL

Eric Packard, the protagonist of DeLillo's novel *Cosmopolis*, likes white paintings—for a peculiar reason. Eric, we learn in the beginning of the novel, "liked paintings that his guests did not know how to look at. The white paintings were unknowable to many, knife-applied slabs of mucoid color. The work was all the more dangerous for not being new. There's no more danger in the new" (8). Eric's paintings, which invoke Robert Rauschenberg's famous White painting series (1951), introduce a key problem in and for the novel: the problem of reading time. Rauschenberg argued that his White paintings should be understood as clocks.[14] John Cage, who aligned the logic of his famous *4′33″* with that of Rauschenberg's White paintings, in turn suggested that, like the silence of *4′33″*, the white canvasses create a neutral backdrop against which we are able to register and interpret the flow of the world.[15] Cage's performance and Rauschenberg's White paintings were at times combined in order to heighten the effect of the logic of each work. Much like the silence of *4′33″*, which amplifies and foregrounds the noise of the auditorium, Rauschenberg's paintings offer a static plane of whiteness that allows us to read temporality as the change of a world in flux. Eric's white paintings therefore raise a number of uncomfortable questions. What happens when the logic and function of the white painting is evacuated by the flow of history? What is the function of the white painting in a world that seems to be no longer in flux and in which time itself has come to a standstill? What present potential for the analysis of time may lie in an art form that was intimately connected to clock time, a form of time that, as we will see, *Cosmopolis* shows to have been utterly exhausted? In the context of the purported stasis of the contemporary world, which gives form to the lack of movement that defines DeLillo's novel, we must finally also ask: Is the novel as devoid of novelty as Eric's white paintings? Can the novel still tell time?

Jonathan Arac argues that "there was an age of the novel, and it has passed, though many novels are still written and are still worth reading."[16] Arac limits the novel's project to the development of a national consciousness and the development of print culture. Yet while these are no doubt important aspects of the novel's history, limiting his account of the novel in such a way allows Arac to make a large-scale proclamation about the current state of the novel that rests on a significantly eroded foundation: "The novel generally no longer does what it used to. In the United States now, and for some decades past." "Perhaps only in those cases in which new groups gain a powerful relationship to print," Arac concludes, "can the novel again seem fully consequential."[17] The rise of the novel, however, is also intimately connected to a temporal project and a philosophical change that we must revisit to appreciate how the novel developed as an art form that critically engages with time. This aspect of the novel's history in turn affords us important insights into the kind of work the novel is able to do in our moment. Examined from this standpoint, the novel still does precisely what it used to, and it does what it used to in a situation that endows the work of the novel with renewed urgency and importance.

If we revisit the conditions of the novel's rise, we quickly see that the problem of an enclosed, timeless world is not new to the novel. The shift from epic to novel, John Neubauer shows, is directly related to a problem of enclosure from which the novel aims to free thought. "The two most comprehensive theories of the novel [of the twentieth century]," Neubauer argues, those of Georg Lukács and Mikhail Bakhtin, "are infused with notions of homelessness."[18] And while every student of the history of the novel is likely familiar with Lukács's suggestion that the novel is "the literary form of the transcendent homelessness of the idea,"[19] the full extent of the temporal underpinnings of this argument remains underexplored. Lukács describes the epic as bound up with the "transcendental shelteredness" of the "closed world" of Greek antiquity. However, "the security of the Greek world became suffocating for later ages," Neubauer argues.[20] This situation of confinement generated an artistic crisis that was resolved by the novel's rise and the epic's decline. The decline of the epic and the rise of the novel can be understood as a historical shift, as the development of new narratives and new forms of knowledge in the attempt to come to terms with and make sense of a changed world. The epic is the form of a world in which, as Jameson argues, "meaning is inherent in all its objects and details, all its facts, all its events." As the literary form of immanent meaning, however, the epic finds itself ill suited to make sense of a world defined by constant change and developments, phenomena, and events that are no longer, as Jameson puts it, "meaningful in and of themselves" but require "outside commentary or explanation."[21] The novel arises in just this moment when the belief in a world structured by immanent meaning comes into crisis. At its heart, the work of the novel is a matter of critiquing, analyzing, and explaining a rapidly changing world. The rise of the novel therefore solves a problem of thought. The novel replaces the established understanding of the world as immanently meaningful, which under new historical conditions creates a sense of enclosure and confinement, with a view of the world that traces meaning in change and historical development, and examines both self and world as constantly in flux. The notion of the novel as the form of transcendental homelessness therefore expresses the novel's rise as a matter of its ability to give us a way to imagine the world beyond the confines of transcendental shelteredness. "Homelessness in the novel," Neubauer explains, "came to indicate that the world itself was out of joint."[22] And a world that is out of joint and no longer understood as being inherently meaningful is a world in need of critical analysis and explanation. It is a world that gives rise to and needs the novel, for the novel makes such a world thinkable and livable for us.

Lukács and Bakhtin trace the rise of the novel back to the same historical situation and conditions, yet they interpret the novel's relation to these conditions differently. While Lukács's account of the novel as the literary form of the transcendental homelessness of the idea is connected to a distinct sense of melancholia, Neubauer argues, Bakhtin's celebrates the novel's rise as connected to the "linguistic homelessness of the literary consciousness."[23] The novel's work for Bakhtin begins "by presuming a verbal and semantic decentering of the ideological world" in the context of which homelessness marks the 'fundamental liberation' from 'the hegemony of a single and unitary language' that leads to the novel's development."[24] What both Lukács and Bakhtin share, however, is a sense that the novel's project is a critical one. The novel carries out philosophical work, as its rise marks the emergence of a new form of knowledge that allows us to imagine and make sense of the development and the crises of the world. Crucially for our purposes, the novel's ability to do this kind of work and the shift from epic to novel are also bound up with a shift in our temporal imagination. Neubauer reminds us that Lukács's account of the transition from epic to novel relies on Goethe's and Schiller's idea that literature departs from the epic poet's "totally past" (*vollkommen vergangen*) narrative and instead narrates every event as "totally present" (*vollkommen gegenwärtig*). But whereas Goethe and Schiller associate this shift with drama, for Lukács this transition becomes the defining characteristic of the novel's rise and the exhaustion of the epic. In the epic, Neubauer writes, characters "do, of course, know of aging and death, but they experience the passing of time within 'the blessed timelessness of the divine world.'" The novel, on the other hand, emerges once this timeless home disappears, and Neubauer argues that we must understand the novel's commitment to temporality as its "constitutive principle."[25]

Timothy Bewes likewise argues that Lukács's observation that epic narrative has no strong sense of temporality is "one of the most compelling moments in his argument."[26] Lukács's theory of the rise of novel foregrounds the importance of the novel's development of a form of thought that seeks to register time in the flow and change of the world. The novel constitutes a form of thought aimed at the examination of the present as history, which indicates why the novel assumes such an important role not only as art but also as a form of knowledge in the context of the temporal crises of our time. After all, "only in the novel, whose very matter is seeking and failing to find the essence," Lukács writes, "is time posited together with the form."[27] While the immanence of meaning abolishes time in the epic, the novel traces time as a matter of the historical dynamism and change that results from a world in constant development. Their important and substantial differences notwithstanding, the theories of both Lukács and Bakhtin outline the centrality of the temporal shift from past to present as a central characteristic of the novel's rise, and both understand the novel's rise as a matter of the its constitutive departure from the timelessness of the epic. The world of the epic is completed and inherently meaningful, and the epic's narrators and singers relate events that remain eternally past and timeless. The novel, however, leaves behind the epic's temporal distance and "contemporizes" the world by treating it as unfinished; it aims to make meaning of the world not by trying to arrive at stable, essential meaningfulness but instead by tracing meaning in the world's constant change.[28] The rise of the novel therefore marks the development of an art form altogether committed to temporality and the desire to address itself to the changing present as ongoing social and historical change.

And yet, since the work of the novel is directly related to the transition from the timelessness of a world defined by immanence to the mobile temporality of an ever-changing, developing present, we might be tempted to conclude that this does spell doom for the novel in a moment when the mobile temporality of the world has seemingly come to a standstill. However, the novel's great importance lies not only in its ability to tell the time of a rapidly changing modern world. It also lies in the novel's ability to formulate new ways of telling time in situations of confinement and enclosure in which change has seemingly become impossible, and time and the flow of history appear to have stopped. J. M. Bernstein, for instance, reminds us that the significance of Flaubert's novels lies not in their ability to mediate the temporality of 1848 as a moment of great historical energy and transformation but instead in their ability to trace the sources of the "empty time" following the period of revolutionary upheaval, a time in which "action, change, history were impossible."[29] Bewes in turn argues for an understanding of the development of the novel as driven forward by a "problematic," by "the task of making a presentation in a situation where presentation has become impossible."[30] It is in moments of crisis, therefore, that the real work of the novel can be said to begin. Some of the most significant moments in the novel's development result from its ability to wrest new conceptions of time and a sense of possibility and change from the grip of periods of stasis in which other forms of knowledge struggle to make sense of new historical conditions. We begin to see, then, why the contemporary novel's renewed focus on time is so important. Today, the novel is called upon once more to try to fulfill the task that occasioned its rise, to give us new forms of telling time in a moment when our established ways of doing so have been exhausted by the flow of history. The novel answers this call by returning to the aspect of its rise, its ability to make time knowable to us, which we find in its purest form in the time novel. But the question remains how exactly the novel, given its rise and its constitutive commitments, might relate to the present. To determine how the novel responds to the particular crises of temporality that define our moment, we must examine how the contemporary novel thinks about time.

FORMS OF TIME

Stuck in traffic, Eric finds time to reflect on how the city that he observes through the windows of his limousine is marked by the transition into finance capitalism. Eric is frequently visited by members of his advisory team, including Vija, who offer analyses of the new forms of temporality that this stage of capitalism brings with it. Eric responds decidedly negatively to city spaces that defy or struggle to keep up with the transition into this new temporal regime, spaces that still bear the signs of previous moments in history and signal uneven temporal development. Remaining traces of the money economy in the midst of a world of virtual and abstract finance capital particularly bother him. "Real" money strikes Eric as "a form of money so obsolete [he] didn't know how to think about it." Eric considers himself to be part of the new future of finance. Money, by contrast, "hard, shiny, faceted," is connected to "everything he'd left behind or never encountered, cut and polished, intensely three-dimensional" (64). To Eric, the streets in which monetary transactions are still carried out register as "an offense to the truth of the future" (64), as frustratingly residual spaces and anachronistic remnants of times past in a present that is elsewhere fully defined by the temporality of financial futures. Looking at the city, Eric notes that he even dislikes the word *skyscraper*: "He took out his hand organizer and poked a note to himself about the anachronistic quality of the word skyscraper. No recent structure ought to bear this word. It belonged to the olden soul of awe, to the arrowed towers that were a narrative long before he was born" (9). Eric considers "the hand device itself . . . an object whose original culture had just about disappeared." "He knew he had to junk it," he concludes (9). What bothers Eric about anachronisms is their connection to a conception of time and a version of futurity that have been exhausted by the rise to dominance of the present stage of capitalism. Eric wishes the present to be temporally uniform and devoid of the temporal leftovers that, in his estimation, hinder the development of the time and the future to which he believes he belongs. Just like the objects he contemplates, different conceptions of time are affected by the flow of history and will eventually appear out of time as their original function is rendered obsolete. The lingering presence of residual conceptions of temporality bothers Eric, however, who wishes to move into the future without being burdened by any traces of the process of historical transformation required to get there.

Eric's analysis of time and *Cosmopolis*'s general approach to the crisis of temporality are significant insofar as the novel seeks to understand time as a matter of forms of temporal knowledge. In her 2015 book *Forms*, Caroline Levine argues that "if we are to understand the ways in which social experience is powerfully constrained and organized according to temporal forms . . . we would do well to adopt keen attentiveness to multiple patternings of time." Specifically, Levine emphasizes, we must understand "the rhythms of the world in a formalist fashion" and become "alert to the temporal organizing principles that govern social organizations and institutions."[31] *Cosmopolis*, I would argue, accomplishes precisely this task. DeLillo's novel examines time as form, which in *Cosmopolis* means understanding time as a form of knowledge that allows us to make sense of but also fundamentally shapes and helps establish the material structures to which it is dialectically connected. Specifically, *Cosmopolis* seeks to read time's recent history as the development of different ways of imagining time that correspond to and facilitate the development of different stages in capitalism. *Cosmopolis* thus foregrounds a material understanding of temporality that allows us to historicize time itself. And once we understand time in this manner, DeLillo's novel shows, we are also able to historicize and examine the material causes of the current crisis of temporality. *Cosmopolis*, that is, asks us to read time in time, and it thus allows us to understand the current crisis of temporality not as the categorical end of time but rather as the crisis of a particular form of temporal knowledge that arises under specific historical conditions.

No doubt, the suggestion that novels like *Cosmopolis* afford us ways to make sense of our struggle with the eternal now of our era by reading time in time will benefit from additional clarification. Traditionally, our imagination of time is based on what Adorno describes in *Negative Dialectics* as a "fetishistic inversion." Time is not an a priori but a man-made concept: "Not one is without the other."[32] But this relation is hidden by time's fetishistic inversion: we create time as a way of knowing and structuring the world and our existence in it, but we subsequently naturalize time and treat it as something external to us, an immutable force that is beyond our control or that ultimately controls us. The transformation of time into an a priori therefore means that we exempt time from time by severing time's relation to history. Instead of examining time as a series of forms of knowledge that change over the course of history and assume specific functions in their respective historical contexts, time becomes timeless insofar as time itself is not understood as moving through history or having a history of its own. And of course, this static, timeless understanding of time, which treats time as though it were inherently meaningful, is bound up with the epic's conception of the world. The novel, however, examines time, like the world, in its progress. In this way, the novel transcends our normalized engagement with time, which is largely preoccupied with the tension between natural time and the time of lived experience. This duality seems to produce meaningful insights whenever we reflect on the disjoints between the two sides that emerge when time bends and stretches, and when our subjective experience of time does not quite line up with the natural flow of time. Our focus on the time of lived experience moreover generates infamous problems that have long preoccupied art and theoretical thought alike. The most notorious of these problems is that of the vanishing present, the understanding of the time of the now as the imperceptible moment between past and future that is only imaginable in abstract terms. This understanding of time is also deeply embedded in language. According to the *Oxford English Dictionary*, time is the most frequently used noun in the English language. Everyday language contains a myriad of clichés and puns that revolve around time, several of which this book manages to avoid. Our temporal vocabulary is rife with expressions that revolve around time's experience and its individual perception: time flies when we have fun; time moves more slowly when we read a rather abstract work of literary criticism; and so on. But as long as we only examine time as a matter of either subjective experience or natural time (days and seasons or the cosmic time of the stars), time itself remains removed from history and time itself becomes timeless.

Cosmopolis, however, is interested in time's own temporality, in the historical development of our temporal imagination and its connection to both art and material reality. *Cosmopolis*'s examination of the present, by extension, does not focus on the difficulties it may pose for subjective experience. Instead, DeLillo's novel makes legible the temporal crises of our time resulting from a change in capitalism that brings with it a demand for new forms of temporal knowledge and exhausts our established temporal episteme. Moments when previously dominant forms of temporal knowledge begin to lose their usefulness inevitably result in significant crises, precisely because the function and success of temporal regimes depend on their ability to become intimately familiar to us. The success of a temporal regime is measured by the degree to which we come to treat it as a natural or even an a priori relation to the world. As a result, the exhaustion of a temporal regime means that we lose our established way of telling the time of our lives, making sense of our temporal relationship to the world, and knowing the logic of time according to which our world is structured. Our conception of time and indeed the majority of narratives through which we make sense of our environment, Kubler argues, are based on "borrowed ideas" and "traditional accumulations." Yet periodically, the temporal fabric of our existence is also subject to profound change. "From time to time the whole pattern shakes and quivers, settling into new shapes and figures,"

Kubler argues. Whenever this happens, we witness significant social and political crises, since the loss of a previously dominant form of temporal knowledge is tantamount to the loss of an established way of making sense of our world and of our lives in it. For this reason, the emergence of new temporal regimes inevitably gives rise to great bewilderment and a profound sense of insecurity and anxiety. "These processes of change," Kubler therefore argues, "are all mysterious uncharted regions, where the traveler soon loses direction and stumbles in darkness."[33]

Our struggle to make sense of time has a long history in art and philosophy. But instead of trying to grapple with the meaning of time as an abstract universal or wrestling with the age-old challenge that the vanishing present seems to pose, novels like *Cosmopolis* show that we may be better served by attempting to examine the history of our struggle with time itself. Such an examination allows us to understand time not as a static, transhistorical entity that continues to confront us with the same timeless problems and questions but as a form of knowing and describing the world that is under constant development. This in turn allows us to understand our moment of crisis, in which we stumble in darkness as we struggle to develop ways of telling the time of our moment in history not as the categorical end of time but as the result of a historically specific timequake. Instead of lamenting the end of time and the collapse of the future, we are thus called upon to examine the causes of this timequake and to formulate ways of addressing the new prevailing conditions of its aftermath. Jameson's original diagnosis of our crisis of temporality therefore indirectly indicates the required response. If the collapse of the future into the present is a matter of a weakness in our imagination, then it must also be addressed on the level of our imagination. Novels like *Cosmopolis* offer us precisely such an examination of our present and treat the crisis of temporality as a crisis of narrative and knowledge, not of time itself. When Vija suggests that "we need a new theory of time" because "time grows scarcer every day," she indicates that the crisis in our temporal imaginary is prompted by a specific historical transition. What, then, is this new historical moment that exhausts our established ways of telling time?

WHAT CAUSED THE DEATH OF THE FUTURE? THE MATERIALITY OF TIME

Vija argues that we must interrogate how capitalism changes our understanding of time in order to gain insights into the nature of the current crisis. The rise of capitalism, Vija knows, necessitated the standardization of a specific form of time that could support and stabilize its structure. "Clock time," she argues, "accelerated the rise of capitalism." What this means, she explains, is that "people stopped thinking about eternity. They began to concentrate on hours, measurable hours, man-hours, using labor more efficiently" (79). The rise of clock time occurred under specific historical conditions, served a set of historically specific functions, and introduced a specific way of knowing time, a time remade in capitalism's image. This change in the way humanity imagined time brought with it a profound philosophical change. Standardized clock time has become so ubiquitous and so definitive of our existence that we are tempted to conflate it with natural time itself. In his 2014 book *Speed Limits*, Mark C. Taylor argues, for instance, that the relation between clock time and industrialization clearly shows a coordinate of time's construction under capitalism that often remains invisible or that we treat as natural: time's linearity. But linearity is just one among many ways of conceiving of time. The association of time with linearity should also be understood as a way of understanding and indeed of structuring the world. Industrialization, for example, Taylor shows, "was coterminous with the emergence of the linearity of perception in which separate points are connected in grids to form a sense of space, and sequential moments are strung together in a series to create time."[34] Jimena Canales illustrates that the timeline itself has a fascinating history, emerging in the 1850s as a way to conceptualize time and historical progress along with the notion of "timekeeping."[35] Clocks, Canales shows, became known as natural objects and were directly associated with the "history of time," which indicates the degree to which we retroactively impose clock time onto history. The standardization of clock time thus also creates a parachronic understanding of time, since clock time is frequently imagined as expressing a natural, foundational measure of time. Yet in spite of the great force it exerts upon our lives, clock time and the standardized time of capitalism itself have been with us for only a relatively short time. In 2018, for example, the US Standard Time Act celebrated its one hundredth birthday.

Understanding time as a form of knowledge that is put to work in the context of specific material conditions, which it in turn supports, allows us to see not only that time has a changing history but also that time is as much a matter of knowing the world as it is a matter of world making. Time, that is, not only makes material structures in general and the development of capitalism in particular knowable to us; it also makes the rise of capitalism itself possible. In *Temporalities*, Russell West-Pavlov argues that the history of modern time has at every step been fundamentally molded by economics.[36] Since the establishment of Newtonian absolute time that was formulated in concert with the beginning of the Industrial Revolution, the modern sense of time has progressed through various temporal regimes. We must examine the historical progression of these temporal regimes "in connection to capitalism and its respective forms," West-Pavlov argues, because "both absolute time and capitalist production detached temporal and productive structures from the traditional matrix of nature, locality and social networks." "Indeed," he concludes, "it is possible that the capitalist system provided the primary contours of absolute time."[37] Newtonian absolute time allowed for the standardization and precise measurement of production, circulation, and trade, as well as the creation of social and cultural forms that supported their respective stages in capitalism. This creation of absolute standardized time also resulted in time's abstraction. Under capitalism, time is no longer primarily a matter of the duality of self and world, of the subjective experience of time and of natural or "cosmic" time. Instead, time becomes an abstract measure of capitalist relations, and this conception of time overwrites the temporality of natural rhythms and subjective experience. Work time, clock time, hours and minutes only have meaning in the context of capitalist production and insofar as such conceptions and units of time serve to stabilize the logic of capitalist valorization. Norbert Trenkle argues that the creation of "objectively measurable time that has been separated or dissociated from subjective time" occurs at the precise moment when "clock time and capital . . . become inextricably bound up with one another."[38] As a consequence, Trenkle argues, we must resist the simplified suggestion that clock time was invented along with the clock at a certain moment in history. The truth is more complex than this, and it lies not in the technological innovation that made possible more precise timekeeping but in a profound change in the way that we work, live, and imagine our existence in the world. After all, he suggests, the reason peasants did not measure the time of harvesting their fields in minutes is not because the clock had not yet been invented. They did not do so because the form of temporal knowledge that determines life under capitalism was absent from this historical context, but primarily because it made no sense in the context of precapitalist societies.[39]

The rise of capitalism required the development of a form of temporal knowledge that stabilized capitalist valorization, production, and basic operations such as wage labor. To function this way, as Barbara Adam shows, time first had to become "an abstract exchange value." In fact, she continues, the "common decontextualized value" upon which capitalism is founded is nothing other than time transformed into a "decontextualized, asituational abstract exchange value that allows work to be translated into money." Moreover, only a particular form of time could be adapted to capitalism, because "only the quantitative, divisible, time of the clock is translatable into money." In this sense, Adam argues, "clock time is the very expression of commodified time," since "only as an abstract, standardized unit can time become a medium for exchange and a neutral value in the calculation of efficiency and profit."[40] In *Translating Time*, Bliss Cua Lim proposes that "homogeneous time" (the standardized, abstract time of capital) should be understood as a capitalist relationship and a key index of reification. Though the mechanical clock emerged in the last decade of the thirteenth century, she shows, it was not until the rapidly modernizing nineteenth century that "a single standard time would be promulgated throughout the world."[41] Trenkle considers the establishment of the capitalist temporal regime one of the sharpest breaks with all precapitalist social orders,"[42] and Lim illustrates that this break and the attempt to homogenize time required immense effort to reduce the plurality of temporalities that up to this point defined our relation to time.[43] The reduction of temporal pluralism and the subsumption of temporal knowledge under capitalism is an important event in the history of time that reveals the crucial, functional connection between capitalism and abstract clock time and at the same time requires us to understand our relation to the material world decidedly differently. Under capitalism, as Marx famously observes, "time is everything, man is nothing; he is at most an incarnation of time."[44]

"The difficulty that faces all those who have tried properly to understand temporality," Boxall writes, "is that time seems not to have any material being, seems not to *exist* in the way that we are accustomed to understanding existence."[45] But if we replace the focus on time's striking ephemerality with an examination of time's material history, we are able to see that though time may not exist as a material being, more significantly, it assumes a direct function in the creation of the material world and makes the material world knowable to us. And precisely because this is so, because time and capitalism are intricately and necessarily bound up with each other, the present crisis of temporality should not be cause for dismay and disillusionment. Instead, it should serve as encouragement to tug at the fraying ends of the time of capital. Rather than focusing on time's baffling arrest, we ought to historicize and analyze the current crisis of temporality as an index of the temporal contradictions of the current stage of capitalism. We are confronted not with the end of time but with a transition in the history of capitalism that brings with it a crisis of the established temporal regime. As capitalism transitions into a new stage, it must develop a new form of temporality that is able to support its changed logic.

In his 2008 book *Capital and Language*, Christian Marazzi argues that we are witnessing a crisis of the very foundations of capitalist time, a "crisis of industrial time as homogeneous, abstract, chronometric, computable, objectifiable time, external to human beings and to things."[46] Capitalism, Marazzi argues, has shifted away from "'classical' Newtonian-Taylorist time" and toward what he simply calls "new times."[47] But what exactly are these new times? David Harvey argues that "contemporary finance capital, with the aid of information technology, has radically reconfigured spatio-temporality over the last forty years in ways that have disrupted other forms of capital circulation as well as daily life."[48] Cédric Durand similarly associates our current temporal crisis with the transition into dominant finance capitalism. Durand understands financialization as "a sign of autumn," because finance capital requires a logic of temporality that "appropriates our future" in the sense that fictitious capital, the driving form of capital behind financialization, "implies a growing pre-emption of future production."[49] The new time of financial, digital capitalism and the information economy have a profound effect on our imagination and knowledge. In the early 2000s, scholars such as Robert Hassan begin to argue that we are seeing the emergence of an "information ecology" that affects our lives as much as nature and the built environment and generates its own form of temporality: "network time." Hassan's book *The Chronoscopic Society* shows how this new form of temporality, a time of compression and acceleration, changes knowledge production and by extension society in dramatic ways.[50] As a consequence of this large-scale historical transition, Massimiliano Tomba argues, "an entirely new consideration of time and space is needed if we are to confront our contemporary world."[51] "To see things and selves radically otherwise," Christina Lupton and R. John Williams suggest, "may simply be a matter of thinking them differently in time."[52] But thinking things and ourselves differently in time is not all that simple. After all, time is a crucial element of what Marx described as capitalism's "phantasmagoria," those narratives about time and space that become standardized and deeply ingrained in our lives to reproduce capitalism's conditions of production. And any change to or crisis in this phantasmagoria creates significant challenges for thought and culture alike. Still, if we understand the temporal crisis of our moment as one of capitalism's foundational phantasmagoria, then we are able to seize it as a moment of opportunity and possibility. If we address the current crises of time as substantial tears in capitalism's temporal fabric resulting in social and political contradictions, then we are able to engage with these crises in a manner that warrants Lupton and Williams's optimistic suggestion that "the new politics of time may only just be getting started."[53]

The novel offers us a way of launching this new politics of time by allowing us to understand the sources of our crisis of temporal imagination and indicating alternative ways of conceiving of time. To be sure, our moment is not the first instance in which the novel has tasked itself with this important project. H. G. Wells's novels, for example, Boxall argues, examine "the way that narrative itself makes time present to us." The contemporary novel's examination of time is deeply indebted to novels such as Wells's *The Time Machine*, which, Boxall contends, displays the "power of narrative to overcome the experience of temporal disappearance."[54] The time novel today is the form most able to carry out just this project. The time novel examines the current crisis of time as a crisis of our temporal imagination, situates the crisis in the history of both time and capitalism, and furnishes us with a new form of temporal knowledge and new ways of reading our present. In what follows, I illustrate how DeLillo's novels work through some of the most substantial challenges of the new times for our imagination. We will see that the novel's significance in our moment lies to no small degree in its ability to reveal these challenges as problems of reading and interpretation.

THE IMPOSSIBILITY OF READING REAL TIME

Vija knows that the temporal logic of contemporary capitalism creates a problem: "It's cyber-capital that creates the future. What is the measurement called a nanosecond? Ten to the minus ninth power. . . . I understand none of this. . . . Time is a corporate asset now" (79). Vija argues that the "acceleration of time" in contemporary capitalism requires units of temporal measurement that are no longer thinkable, which in turn creates a problem of reading and interpretation. When Vija and Eric examine an "electronic display of market information" that "streak[s] across the face of an office tower on the other side of Broadway," they realize they are not witnessing something that is hard to read or, like Eric's white paintings, creates confusion about how it should be read. Instead, they gaze at information that ought not be read at all:

> Beneath the data strips, or tickers, there were fixed digits marking the time in the major cities of the world. He knew what she was thinking. Never mind the speed that makes it hard to follow what passes before the eye. The speed is the point. Never mind the urgent and endless replenishment, the way data dissolves at one end of the series just as it takes shape at the other. This is the point, the thrust, the future. We are not witnessing the flow of information so much as pure spectacle, or information made sacred, ritually unreadable. (80)

The time of the pure virtuality and fictionality of value in finance capitalism along with the information about value itself are systemically and necessarily unreadable. Inserting the time of reading and interpretation into this relation would constitute an obstacle to the logic of the system by introducing time into a relation that tends toward absolute immediacy and timelessness. The ideal way to relate to finance capital, therefore, does not quite correspond to the logic of "business at the speed of thought," which Bill Gates famously championed in the late 1990s.[55] Rather, Vija and Eric recognize that they are confronted with a logic of capital that should exist beyond the speed of thought but operates at the speed of immediate experience. *Cosmopolis* treats contemporary capitalism as fundamentally opposed to the temporal lag required by reading and critical interrogation. Actually reading the flow of the market would undercut the new system's foundational temporal regime. Reading and thought, insofar as they are aimed at the time of inquiry and analysis, must exist only as fictional aspirations in a system aimed at full immediacy and the abolition of time itself. In order to function, in other words, contemporary capitalism must not be read. The time of reading and analysis, by extension, constitutes a threat to this form of capitalism. And as indicated by the widespread struggle with the perceived new socioeconomic reality marked by a timeless present, capitalism's aim for immediacy and timelessness reveals itself as not only crucial to its structure but also one of the main contradictions of contemporary life.

Not surprisingly, the acceleration of time, in particular insofar as it results in a problem of interpretation, creates a problem for thought and culture alike. Through a reading of the movie *Speed* with which he concludes his 2003 essay "The End of Temporality," Jameson forwards an account of the end of temporality as a matter of the climax of speed. *Speed* for Jameson strikingly exemplifies the exhaustion of plot and time at the moment when the movie commits itself fully to the pursuit of "nonstop action."[56] Already in 1992, Jean Baudrillard notes that the acceleration of "technology, events and media, of all exchanges" has "propelled us to 'escape velocity,'" freeing ourselves from the "referential sphere of the real and of history." Baudrillard expresses this problem in familiar postmodern terms as a "problem of the real" that brings with it a loss of history: the real is possible only inasmuch as things can be "reflected and thus in some way endure and have some consequence." For history to exist, a number of conditions have to be met: "A degree of slowness . . . (that is a certain speed, but not too much), a degree of distance, but not too much, and a degree of liberation (and energy for rupture and change), but not too much." Together, Baudrillard argues, these conditions "bring about the kind of condensation or significant crystallization of events we call history."[57] But what Baudrillard examines as a problem for our conception of the real and of history reveals itself as an even more fundamental problem in *Cosmopolis*: the time of contemporary capitalism stands opposed to the temporality required by interpretation, reading, and critical thought.

A number of theorists have addressed this problem in recent years. Franco Berardi argues that the end of time at the climax of speed under contemporary capitalism creates a new reality that Marx could only anticipate as an abstract possibility, a potential future scenario in which the temporal logic of capitalism reaches both its climax and its internal limit and logical breaking point. Berardi writes,

> Marx spoke of a tendency, a limit point in the process of the valorization of capital: the impossible possibility that capital might circulate "without circulation *time*," at an infinite velocity, such that the passage from one moment in the circulation of capital to the next would take place at the "speed of thought." Such capital would return to itself even before

> taking leave of itself, passing through all of its phases in a process encountering no obstacles, in an ideal time without time—in the blinding flash of an instant without duration, a cycle contracting into a point.[58]

In *The Futurism of the Instant* (2010), Paul Virilio suggests that under contemporary capitalism "past, present and future contract in the omnipresent instant, just as the expanse of the terrestrial globe does these days in the excessive speed of the constant acceleration of our travels and telecommunications." Capitalism's new temporality, Virilio argues, "without any measurable duration—except in terms of milliseconds or nanoseconds," exhausts narratives of progress and results in a "sudden loss of memory" that carries with it a loss of imagination, which in turn contributes to the sense of the exhaustion of our "great progressive illusions."[59] Capitalism's new temporal regime, its commitment to immediacy, creates a crisis for thought and culture that expresses itself in the perception of the end of futurity and temporality. It is not surprising, therefore, that we can trace the emergence and rise of the notion of the end of the future in relation to the gradual transition into digital, real-time capitalism beginning in the 1990s. "No human language can withstand the speed of light," and "no meaning can withstand the acceleration of time," writes Baudrillard,[60] a problem that *Cosmopolis* examines as one of the most pressing philosophical and aesthetic challenges of our time. How, DeLillo's novel asks, might we come to terms with the moment when capitalism's commitment to immediacy removes the temporal lag and the critical distance that make interpretation possible, when capitalism's attachment to immediacy establishes a form of time whose units of measurement surpass our imagination and established modes of representation?

"Money makes time," Vija notes, adding "it used to be the other way around" (79). In fact, she argues, "money has lost its narrative quality the way painting did once upon a time. Money is talking to itself" (77). And while it will come as a great relief to many that trite remarks like "time will tell" and "money talks" may finally disappear as the phrases are emptied of even their last remainders of content by the historical transition in which we currently find ourselves, the fact that capital requires a form of time that has moved beyond the limits of narrative and interpretation is without doubt bad news. In *After the Future* (2011), Berardi argues that the twenty-first century marks the fulfillment and at the same time the exhaustion of twentieth-century notions of the future, along with its aesthetic role, at the moment when "speed is internalized" as part of the acceleration of psychic and cognitive rhythm.[61] In *The Uprising: On Poetry and Finance* (2012), Berardi traces the relation between capitalism's temporal immediacy and what he calls the "hypercomplexity" of finance, which together hinder attempts at critical evaluation due to the "disproportion between the arrival rate of new information and the limited time available for conscious processing."[62] Maurizio Lazzarato likewise considers capitalism's commitment to immediacy one of the defining characteristics of our present. "Above all," he writes, capitalism "has deprived [us] of the future, that is, of time, time as decision-making choice, and possibility."[63] The circulation of capital without time, which demands a structure that refuses to be read and interpreted, inevitably produces a crisis of imagination and language. Our established vocabulary, our traditional metaphors and analogies no longer allow us to come to terms with units such as the yoctosecond. The time of capital becomes unthinkable and unrepresentable. Real-time capitalism thus marks a new stage in the abstraction of time, a moment when time becomes decidedly less real and reaches the point of absolute abstraction. Capitalist real time is time made functionally and infrastructurally unreadable, and the expanding present, the omnipresent instant, can therefore be understood as a symptom of our struggle to come to terms with capitalism's presentist temporal episteme. The problems resulting from the unreadability of real time allow us to appreciate Mark McGurl's suggestion that we should understand the spread of real time as a new stage in the history of capitalist standardization and indeed as a new form of domination. "Real time," he writes, "looks not like Utopia but instead like a massive project of Western capitalist domination and deterritorialization."[64]

How, then, might we be able to read time and make sense of our existence when, as Vija argues, our lives are determined by the frenzied pace of a world that envelops us in its rhythm, that forces us to live its pace without the ability to examine it? Ours is not a time of reading or interpretation, she concludes, since "the frenzy is barely noticeable most of the time. It's simply how we live" (85). But how does the novel respond to a situation in which both time and capitalism have become so deeply defined by immediacy that they have become unthinkable and unreadable? We may begin to answer this question by reminding ourselves that the problem of immediacy is not a new one for literature. After all, immediacy poses more than temporal challenges for literature. Rather, the question of immediacy is involved in the crucial differences between our understanding of basic relationships such as that between self and world (the difference between an immediate, experiential relation to the world and a distanced, reflective, or mediated relation), between art and world (the difference between works of art that aim to represent the world in its immediacy and works of art that, through aesthetic distance, mediate the world), and between reader and text (the difference between the immediate experience of a novel and a mediated, hermeneutic engagement with it). Additionally, accounts of the differences between cultural and artistic mediums depend to no small degree on the distinction between a given medium's relation to the world and its relation to the reader. Does a photograph relate to an event more immediately than the event's literary representation? Does music establish a more immediate relationship to the listener than a novel does to the reader? Is the distinction between reading and experiencing a novel a distinction between a mediated or immediate relation to the literary text, and if so, how does this distinction determine the possibilities and limits of our critical choices?

One of the great contributions to our understanding of these relations can be found in the work of Walter Benjamin, specifically in his examination of the ways different mediums engage with the temporal rhythm of modernity. In *Dead Time*, Elissa Marder illustrates how deeply Benjamin is interested in the problem of immediacy and the "overwhelming increase in external stimuli that prevent the impact of particular experiences from becoming assimilated, processed, and remembered." Of particular significance for Benjamin, Marder shows, is the development of technologies "that are specifically designed to grasp particular experiences in their immediacy." In this situation, it seems curious that Benjamin would also develop a keen interest in lyric poetry, Marder notes. The explanation, she suggests, lies in the fact that Benjamin understands lyric poetry as a "highly mediated form of experience" able to articulate the changes in experience produced by the new historical context and its associated "temporal disorders." Lyric poetry makes meaning of a situation in which "'unmediated' communication cannot transmit the meaning of an experience."[65] Real-time capitalism raises the problem of immediacy for art with new urgency. The very logic of real time presupposes immediacy not only temporally but also as a relation to capitalism that makes reading and interpretation impossible due to the abolition of what McGurl describes as "the usual delay attendant to processes of mediation."[66] As a result, the immediacy of real-time capitalism creates significant problems for both art and knowledge. In this context, the oppositional character of the literary artwork and the possibility of literature lie in literature's function as a highly mediated form of knowledge. And while lyric poetry may have been the literary form that in Benjamin and Adorno's time offered a mode of resistance to "the reification of the world," in our time it is the novel that elevates this potential of literature to its highest form.

DeLillo's 2010 novel *Point Omega* allows us to explore the basic aspects of this account of the novel and extends *Cosmopolis*'s examination of the challenges that capitalist immediacy poses for interpretation. In *Point Omega*, the tension between the attempt to read time and the problem of immediacy is transformed into an aesthetic problem. That is, DeLillo's novel routes its treatment of the interpretation of time through its engagement with the ways we read film and, by extension, novels. In doing so, *Point Omega* is able to foreground the possibilities offered by novelistic reading for our attempt to address the current temporal crisis. Most of the novel's plot revolves around its protagonist, Richard Elster, an intellectual and disillusioned former adviser to the Pentagon during the Iraq War who moves to the desert to dedicate himself to the attempt to rediscover time and space. Elster's story is framed by two sections, titled "Anonymity 1" and "Anonymity 2." The framing sections are dedicated to an unnamed protagonist who visits the *24 Hour Psycho* exhibit at the Museum of Contemporary Art. *24 Hour Psycho*, an art installation created by Douglas Gordon in 1993, stages a screening of Alfred Hitchcock's *Psycho* slowed down to a screening time of exactly twenty-four hours. Through his engagement with the art installation, the protagonist of the novel's framing sections is made aware of the ways he reads this radically slowed-down version of Hitchock's film, which causes him to reflect on the kinds of interpretation invited by film and, by extension, time. He describes his first encounter with the installation as follows:

> The film's merciless pacing had no meaning without a corresponding watchfulness, the individual whose absolute alertness did not betray what was demanded. He stood and looked. In the time it took for Anthony Perkins to turn his head, there seemed to flow an array of ideas involving science and philosophy and nameless other things, or maybe he was seeing too much. But it was impossible to see too much. The less there was to see, the harder he looked, the more he saw. This was the point. To see what's here, finally to look

> and to know you're looking, to feel time passing, to be alive to what is happening in the smallest register of motion.[67]

The radical slowing down of Hitchcock's film results in the narrator's distantiation from the film and allows for the kind of detailed examination and interpretation that film's regular, unrelenting speed makes impossible. The slowed-down version of the film allows him to take time for interpretation. In fact, he reasons, the film's pacing trades in the form of time that structures film as a medium entirely for the time of interpretation, and the film's meaning becomes wholly attached to the kind of reading, the corresponding watchfulness, that this new temporal logic creates. The effect of the film, the protagonist notices, is that it "made him feel like someone watching a film" (11). The film's pacing opens it up to seemingly unlimited possibilities for reading and interpretation. Each scene, he notes later on, becomes an "abstract moment, all form and scale," and this new attention to the form of both film and time encourages critique and "bind[s] him to total alertness" (102). The temporal manipulation of the film creates an active, critical relation to both the object and the process of viewing, and the very act of not being able to sit down to watch the film strikes the protagonist as an aspect of the critical process: "Standing was part of the art, the standing man participates" (102). His viewing of the exhibit leaves the protagonist with the desire for more distantiation, more interpretation: "He wanted the film to move even more slowly, requiring deeper involvement of eye and mind" (115).

To create the preconditions for this attentiveness to time and interpretation, the installation must take the film to the very limits of its medium. The distantiation that makes time available for interpretation makes legible parts of the film and opportunities for examination and reflection that the speed and temporality of film ordinarily preclude. But what film can only accomplish via a radical act of slowing down that disrupts the very logic of cinematic temporal narrative, the novel offers as a quintessential aspect of its relation to time. Novelistic reading is connected to a discontinuous, nonlinear, and plural form of temporality that is dictated not by the medium as technology but instead by the pace of interpretation itself and as such stands opposed to the incessant flow and immediacy of the time of capital. We read novels, that is, by lingering and pausing on words and ideas, by slowing down and even stopping aspects of the narrative, by rereading and reconsidering passages and sentences. The novel asks us to a beat in order to make the rhythm available for interpretation, to pause and step back to critically examine the time of our lives as the time of a specific temporal regime, and in doing so it refuses the blind immediacy of capitalism's frenzy. The time of novelistic reading is defined by the interpretive process itself, and it is thus quintessentially wedded to distantiation and mediation, to the ability to take time for consideration, for critical analysis. In order to approximate the temporal and interpretive logic of the novel to which *Point Omega* draws our attention, however, *24 Hour Psycho* must radically manipulate the medial logic of film. Still, film is unable to replicate the time and interpretive depth of novelistic reading without breaking the temporal foundation of the medium, which is bound to flow. Watching a film the way we read a novel, after all, would require constant pausing, rewinding, replaying, zooming in on aspects of a shot or isolating parts of the dialogue, modulating the timing of individual scenes, and fully taking control of the film's pacing. At its most basic level, therefore, novelistic reading is a form of interpretation and temporality that stands opposed to immediacy, and it is in its refusal of immediacy in favor of mediated, critical interpretation that we can locate the novel's refusal of the logic of real-time capitalism. It is in this sense, then, that we can evaluate the protagonist's insight in the *Point Omega*'s concluding passages, in which another viewing of *24 Hour Psycho* causes him to conclude that "real time is meaningless. The phrase is meaningless. There's no such thing" (115). By tracing the relation among reading time, film, and the novel, *Point Omega* forwards a striking account of the novel's possibility for our attempt to read time and critique the temporality of the present.

"Time and the literary . . . information technology is said to have annihilated both," write Karen Newman, Jay Clayton, and Marianne Hirsch, pointing to the abolition of time in the context of the rise of "electronic communication, instant messaging, and information retrieval," which are technologies of simultaneity.[68] And while commentators such as Will Self, with no small sense of glee and (self-)satisfaction, base their latest declarations of the death of literature or the novel ("This time it's for real") precisely on such an account of the waning of literature in the digital age,[69] Newman, Clayton, and Hirsch argue that the literary in fact quintessentially refuses this tendency toward simultaneity. For "the literary," they write, "joins immediacy and the instantaneous with their opposite, duration and critique. . . . [I]t prolongs the moment for critical reflection, producing time for a re-reading of the present."[70] This rereading of the present is associated most strongly with the novel. As Jean-Paul Sartre argues in his essay "On John Dos Passos and *1919*," "Only in appearance is the past preterite the tense of the novel; we have to see it as a present *with aesthetic distance*."[71] And just like *24 Hour Psycho*'s excruciatingly slow pacing and Eric's largely motionless journey through the city drive forward the protagonists' engagement with time and interpretation, the interrogation of the act of reading that is the novels' true plot, the novel restores our attention to the forms of time and reading and makes our present readable. Today, the novel in a sense confronts the inverse of the problem that occasioned its rise: instead of overcoming epic distance and the timelessness of the epic's eternal past, the novel allows us to read our present in a manner that refuses its confinement to the timeless and unreadable immediacy of the eternal now.

By estranging us from the temporal regime of real-time capitalism and affording us a way of reading the present critically, the novel serves as a forceful counterpoint to the immediacy and presentism of real-time capitalism. "The work's distance from mere existence," in Adorno's terms, in this way "becomes a measure of what is false and bad in the latter."[72] The novel aesthetically distantiates us from the frenzy of lived existence, from our immediate relation to the present temporal regime, thereby facilitating an interpretive, critical relation to our present. Novelistic reading emerges in the situation as a political act, as a site for immanent critique of the logic of the capitalist now. Reading the time of our present novelistically makes legible the end of time and the crisis of futurity as a self-imposed limit of our temporal thought and thus constitutes what we can describe with Lukács as an act of "defetishization": returning reified thought to what it truly is, namely a form of thought that mediates a social and material problem.[73] It is in this way, then, that we can understand Boxall's suggestion that fictional narrative makes time knowable by "break[ing] time open, undoing those bonds that habitually tie us to the official passing of time."[74] The undoing of our cognitive bonds to the temporal regime of contemporary capitalism through novelistic reading allows us to read time as dehabituated historical form. This work of distantiation, which estranges us from time's immediacy and its pure experience to make it available for interpretation and critical interrogation, constitutes the crucial aesthetic and political potential of the novel today, which we find elevated to its highest form in the time novel. Revitalizing a key aspect of the novel's work that underwrites the conditions of its rise, the *Zeitroman* allows us to read time as a form of knowledge and narrative in history, which in turn encourages the development of new forms of telling time in our moment. The contemporary time novel thereby makes legible that which capital must confine to systemic unreadability and that which we tend to not recognize as readable in midst of our lived experience of the frenzy of contemporary capitalism.

It is thus possible to establish the beginning terms of a more precise understanding of the term *contemporary novel* and of the novel's contemporaneity in our time. Contemporaneity describes more than a simple matter of being present. As Peter Osborne reminds us, the term *the contemporary*, in particular if we use it to describe artworks that seek to establish a meaningful historical relationship to the present, expresses not only a presence in the now but a critical and analytical relationship to the now as history.[75] To merely be present means nothing more than to inhabit one's time. To speak of contemporaneity, however, is to describe a relation to the present that is grounded upon the refusal to live in the moment in favor of a position of distantiated reflection and critical interrogation. By way of distantiated, critical analysis, the novel subjects the temporal regime of real-time capitalism to immanent critique, and in this manner it fulfills Giorgio Agamben's demand for an active, critical conception of the contemporary: "The contemporary is he who firmly holds his gaze on his own time so as to perceive not its light, but rather its darkness. . . . The contemporary is precisely the person who knows how to see this obscurity, who is able to write by dipping his pen in the obscurity of the present."[76] DeLillo's novels show us, however, that the criticality of such contemporaneity is not a trait. Instead, it is a result of the interpretive mode—the form of reading that the novel models for us. And it therefore is not the contemporary but rather contemporaneity, understood as the interpretive relation to the present in a moment of immediacy and temporal confinement, that we find in and through the novel, which allows us "to perceive, in the darkness of the present, this light that strives to reach us but cannot," thereby showing us "what it means to be contemporary."[77]

HOW TO READ A MOMENT: THE NOVEL AS CRITIQUE OF THE LONG NOW

Cosmopolis's Eric struggles with the fact that he frequently finds himself "limited in perspective, thinking only about the moment itself" (50). At first blush, this may not seem like a significant problem. After all, "it is easy to live for the day," writes Bloch. "All lazybones do that."[78] But living for the day—or, to use the more common expression that today masks the contradictions of the presentist temporal regime of real-time capitalism, living in the moment—is not as easy as it may initially seem. "All nearness makes matters difficult," Bloch argues, since immediate proximity and lack of distance create big problems for representation and thought alike.[79] "The Here and Now stands too close to us," writes Ernst Bloch in *The Principle of Hope*, which means that it is easier to experience the here and now than to critically examine it. But "raw experience," he elaborates, merely "transposes us from the drifting dream into another state: into that of immediate nearness." As a result, "the moment just lived dims as such . . . and its nearness makes things formless."[80] Bloch here foregrounds the same tension between the moment's lived experience and analyses of the present's temporal forms that also guides the examination of time in DeLillo's novels. To address the problem, to ensure that a moment is not merely experienced but examined, Bloch suggests a solution that initially sounds as simple as living in the moment: we should take time. But taking time in this context is a matter of finding ways to replace our immediate relation to the moment, to replace pure experience with a critical, interpretive relation to the now. "Taking time," Bloch explains, "lets you gain distance from a thing in order to see it better."[81] Similarly, Henri Lefebvre foregrounds the limits of time's lived experience and argues that "when rhythms are lived, they cannot be analysed." "In order to analyse a rhythm," he concludes, "one must get outside of it. Externality is necessary.[82]

DeLillo's novels echo the accounts of Bloch and Lefebvre and examine the problem of immediacy as directly connected to the problem of approaching time mainly as a matter of lived experience. In the beginning sections of *Cosmopolis*, we learn that Eric struggles with insomnia. Reading poetry only exacerbates the problem for Eric, since poetry amplifies his restlessness. It alerts Eric to the nuances of every passing moment and causes him to consider aspects of life that ordinarily pass by unnoticed, purely immediate. "Poems made him conscious of his breathing," he observes, noting the degree to which poetry causes him to establish a different relationship to his environment: "A poem bared the moment to things he was not normally prepared to notice" (5). His attempt to read himself to sleep, he realizes, accomplishes the opposite: he "only grew more wakeful" (5). The only way for Eric to sleep is to take sedatives, which accomplish the opposite task from that of poetry. Unlike poetry, sedatives send him "inward in tight spirals" (6).

And while he is able to go to sleep by taking sedatives, they also cause a collapse into pure selfhood: "Nothing existed around him. There was only the noise in his head, the mind in time" (6). While poetry facilitates wakefulness and an attentive, analytical relation to the world, sedatives cause Eric to withdraw into full immediacy and collapse any sense of distanced examination of the world into experience and identity: "When he died he would not end. The world would end" (6). The opening passages of *Cosmopolis* establish experiential immediacy as the key obstacle to a critical examination of the present and an analytical, formalist relationship to time. Experience and immediacy, we see, leave Eric unable to examine time; he is only able to be in the moment. The remainder of the novel develops an alternative relation to time that also determines DeLillo's *Point Omega* and *Zero K* (2016). The way to deal with the temporal crises of our time is to embrace what Eric understands to be the more uncomfortable relation to the moment: the restlessness that emerges from the moment's distanced interpretation, the relation that DeLillo's novels facilitate through their focus on the differences between various modes of interpretation. And while poetry is able to create the same distanced relation to the now as the novel, the novel's own temporality of reading allows us to examine time as narrative and epistemic form.

Zero K, which I examine in more detail in the concluding section of this chapter, contains a section titled "Artis Martineau," in which the novel sets up its ultimate account of a critical relation to the present by revisiting the problem of experience for both art and interpretation. In this section, Artis, a character who suffers from a fatal illness, reflects on her inability to determine how to know time. And of course, the name Artis (Latin, "of art") further emphasizes the novel's inquiry into art's ability to make time knowable to us. "Time," Artis muses, "I feel it in me everywhere. But I don't know what it is. The only time I know is what I feel. It is all now. But I don't know what this means."[83] Artis initially suspects that it is impossible to know time directly, that we can only know or try to make sense of time's experience. But this line of thinking poses a problem, since time that is only experienced is immediate time—it is all now, all present. Additionally, Artis struggles with the tension between temporal experience and the vocabulary through which she describes and understands this experience. As the commentary that accompanies Artis's passages suggests, "*She knows these words. She is all words but she doesn't know how to get out of the words into being someone, being the person who knows the words*" (157 [emphasis in the original]). Time's experience offers a concrete relation to time, but it does not allow Artis to know time, for she is unable to distance herself from the temporal vocabulary through which she must articulate her experience. Thus, while DeLillo's novels are frequently critical of a relation to time that is determined by experience and by ways of being in time—approaches that the novels seek to replace with analytical and critical approaches to time—it is clear that trading in immediate experience for distantiated reflection is not an easy task. It means embracing an estranged, alienated relation to time and the world, a relation that registers for characters like Artis as estrangement from herself. More problematically even, she realizes that she must step outside of the language of experience that determines her relation to time—and trading in the temporal vocabulary of experience for one of distantiated, formal analysis, she fears, amounts to an abandonment of selfhood.

For this reason, I certainly do not wish to discount critical examinations of temporal experience or suggest that DeLillo's novels simply argue for the abandonment of a focus on experience tout court. After all, as Agamben stresses, "Every conception of history is invariably accompanied by a certain experience of time, which is implicit in it, conditions it, and thereby has to be elucidated. Similarly, every new culture is first and foremost a particular experience of time, and no new culture is possible without an alteration in this experience."[84] Analyses of temporal experience remain important, and they, too, offer important opportunities for historical analysis. And yet the great value of the approach to time of DeLillo's novels, an approach that underlies the contemporary time novel's approach to time more generally, is the way it illustrates that our understanding of time is incomplete if experience remains our sole focus. In particular in the context of the temporal crises of our time and under the conditions of real-time capitalism, the continued privileging of phenomenological approaches to time that focus on lived experience risks reifying capitalism's commitment to immediacy and supports the dismantling of the social in favor of the subjective and identity, which is one of neoliberalism's defining characteristics. Limiting our examination of time to the immediate experience of temporality hinders our ability to come to terms with the unreadability of the present and our struggle with the seeming omnipresence of the now—it consolidates a relation to time that Bloch describes as the "darkness of the moment."[85]

Likewise, since the idea of the collapse of the future into an eternal now is linked to the standardization of difference, we cannot maintain an innocent belief in the politics of difference. Today, difference is not contrary to the logic and rhythm of capital; it is capital's logic and rhythm. Under a system that standardizes and instrumentalizes difference, differences between temporal experiences merely give way to increasing uniformity and foreclosure. Replacing our attention to differences between historical temporal regimes with a focus on differences between temporal experiences ultimately consolidates the subjugation of temporal pluralism to a singularized present: the rhythm of real-time capitalism. The inability to imagine the future as difference results as much from the dominance of real-time synchronization, which overwrites competing social imaginaries of being in time, as from time's fragmentation into myriad individualized temporalities that together follow and replicate capitalism's presentism. The immediacy of real-time capitalism encourages us to focus on the individual, immediate experience of the moment in order to overwrite competing forms of temporality that become legible when time is critically examined as the foundation of social relations. The darkness of the moment, which is connected to our focus on time's experience, veils the fact that time comes to us mainly as form, as temporal regimes whose rhythms structure the time of our lives and thus function as tools of material production and social domination.

Reading a moment is different than experiencing it. DeLillo's novels emphasize the importance of reading the moment as the time defined by the presence of temporal regimes that become legible when we assume a distantiated, critical relation to the temporal rhythm of our now. While the focus on experience further compounds the problem of the purported end of time and futurity, the distantiation and externality afforded by novelistic reading allows us in turn to "take time" and trace the sources of our era's laments for lost time in the material conditions of the present. Such a formalist reading of the moment allows us to read the present as a time rife with competing temporal imaginaries that the dominant temporal regime of contemporary capitalism seeks to synchronize or overwrite. We are able to trace, in Levine's terms, a "social world where temporal structures often thwart or compete with another."[86] By staging the problem of reading time as an aesthetic problem, the novel allows us to critically examine the systemic unreadability of contemporary capitalism. To read the moment novelistically, in other words, is to refuse the darkness of the moment that results from the immediacy of real-time capitalism. Lupton and Williams argue that it seems as though "nearly every category of literary analysis . . . could be framed as a question of temporal experience."[87] And this is no doubt in some sense true. But if we wish to understand the specific work that the novel's engagement with time is able to do in the context of the temporal contradictions of the present, then we must address the central role played by the contemporary novel's critique of experience in this context. I examine the novel's critique of experience and its significance for contemporary literary criticism in detail in the next chapter. For the time being, I wish to stress that while philosophers like Agamben probe the separation of experience and knowledge in order to trace the destruction of experience in contemporary daily life, the novel shows us that the temporal crises of our time result in part from the opposite: from the vast privileging of experience over knowledge in approaches to time and temporality.

Since its rise, however, the novel has emerged as an art form that refuses to set apart or privilege experience over knowledge. Locating the novel's engagement with forms of knowledge in direct relation to the novel's ontology and function, critics like Bewes suggest that we should understand the novel itself not as a "closed art form" but instead as a "mode of thought." In this way, Bewes argues, we can "reconceptualize the novel not as bound to a static, rigidified, and historically limited form but as a situation, defined by the existence, and persistence, of a problematic. As such, the novel implies not only an object of enquiry but a mode of reading and of looking, a critical positionality."[88] But it should be added that we need not reconceptualize our understanding of the novel as much as we should revisit the novel's foundational engagement with time, the problematic that defines not only its rise but also its historical development and its continued importance in the present. The novel's work is directly connected to its critical interrogation of our attempts to know time. Guido Mazzoni argues that we should understand the rise of the novel as the rise of an "alternative model of knowledge," one that probes the "relations between literature and other forms of knowledge."[89] The value of the novel can therefore be said to lie in its ability to critically engage with and offer alternatives to established modes of conceptual knowledge and scientific and philosophical discourse. And since the novel is able to capture the world and make it knowable in ways that are not possible for other forms of knowledge, it assumes an important role in the context of our current struggle to develop forms of knowing time beyond the crisis of futurity that results from the historical exhaustion of our established temporal episteme. From this standpoint, we can develop a deeper appreciation of the emphasis DeLillo's novels place on the importance of understanding our struggle with time as a problem of interpretation, not experience. Additionally, these novels draw our attention to the different ways of making sense of time offered by literature in general and the novel in particular. By addressing time and its crises as an aesthetic problem and a problem of interpretation, the contemporary novel translates the exhaustion of temporality into thinkable terms, which allows us to historicize and critique time as a form of knowing and transforming the world.

And yet we must explore this suggestion in more detail. How exactly does the novel generate critiques of temporal knowledge? How can a novel model a relation to time that allows us to move beyond a focus on experience and also resolve the problems with which Artis grapples? Before turning to the answers offered by DeLillo's *Zero K*, it is important to remind ourselves once more that these questions are connected to well-established problems that play a central role in the historical development of the novel. In fact, the struggle to know the present differently, in particular in a situation in which we understand ourselves to be confined to a time to which we are unable to imagine alternatives, gives rise to some of the high points of the modernist novel's treatment of time. Revisiting the modernist time novel therefore allows us to trace the time novel's formal development into the present and thus to gain important insights into the ways authors like DeLillo deploy the time novel in the conditions of our present.

In his examination of William Faulkner's *The Sound and the Fury* (1929), Sartre notes that the reader "is at first struck by the oddities of its technique." "Why," he wonders, "has Faulkner broken up the time of his story and disarranged the fragments?" Upon further examination, however, Sartre argues, it becomes clear that Faulkner did not "first think in terms of an orderly narrative and then shuffle the parts like a deck of cards." Faulkner's technique is no mere "exercise in virtuosity" but instead a direct expression of Faulkner's "metaphysics of time," of Faulkner's deployment of novelistic form to make legible a problem of temporal thought. "He could not have told the story in any other way," Sartre concludes. Sartre understands *The Sound and the Fury* as a novel that aims to imagine time beyond simple chronology and linearity, a novel that moreover explores the complexity of the present itself. "Faulkner's concept of the present . . . is not a circumscribed or sharply defined point between past and future," Sartre argues. At the same time, however, while the novel affords us a more complex account of the present as a time that consists of multiple temporalities that do not neatly assemble into continuity, chronology, or a singular synchronized sense of time, Faulkner's attempt at imagining the present plurally also comes at a price. "Beyond this present," Sartre notes, "there is nothing, since the future does not exist," because Faulkner's present is defined by the horrific impression that "one present . . . drives out another present. It is like a sum that we compute again and again."[90] Faulkner's present, in other words, is marked by the same problem we see in heightened form in the present of DeLillo's novels. In *Cosmopolis*, the constant and immediate interactions of communication and finance absorb all futurity into an increasingly complex present. And just like the present's complexity in DeLillo's novels (or the present's volatility in the novels of Gibson) results in the abolition of time, the multiplicity of the present in Faulkner results in the sense that time itself is inconsequential. After all, Sartre notes, watches break and characters' sense of time disappear, yet this never matters, because time itself ceases to matter as a result of the endless proliferation of different presents. But the significance of Sartre's examination of time in Faulkner also lies in the connection of this essay to his larger attempt to determine how the novel allows us to know time and the present.

One characteristic of Faulkner's present, Sartre argues, is "suspension," a term Sartre uses to indicate "a kind of arrested motion in time." "In Faulkner," Sartre writes, "there is never any progression, nothing which can come from the future. The present does not contain in itself the future events we expect."[91] Suspension results in the present's timelessness, and it must therefore be distinguished from suspense, which makes possible both plot and futurity. In fact, Marc Augé argues, our interest in the future and our imagination of the relation between present and future are deeply connected to the mechanisms of narrative plot and in particular to the function of suspense. "We are interested in the plot of a play or film," Augé argues, "because it stages a problem whose resolution we expect." And precisely because we are awaiting the resolution of the problem, plot can be understood as a matter of a temporal relation that Augé describes as "suspended time."[92] It is suspense, the expectation of the resolution of a problem, that characterizes both plot and our understanding of futurity as a matter of change and difference. Futurity is bound up with the anticipatory consciousness that also defines plot, which is why literary critics with an interest in time, as McGurl argues, must in particular in the context of the present temporal crises take note of Peter Brooks's definition of plot as "the syntax of a certain way of speaking our [temporal] understanding of the world."[93] Yet given this relation between plot and our temporal imaginary, the abolition of futurity in a present defined by the replacement of suspense with suspension might suggest not only the end of time but also the end of plot. For if plot depends upon suspense, on the anticipatory deferral of the future that creates the preconditions for a present understood as a time of development and change, then suspension marks the moment when time and plot as futurity become unimaginable. *The Sound and the Fury* as well as *Cosmopolis* and *Point Omega*, which are centrally defined by deceleration and stasis, are thus written at the limit of plot and explore plot's breaking points. But how does a novel tell time in such a situation? If plot is the expression of our temporal understanding of the world, how might we make sense of time in a situation in which both plot and temporality seem to reach their limits?

Sartre is full of praise for Faulkner's work, noting that "Faulkner uses his extraordinary art to describe a world dying of old age, with us gasping and choking in it." And yet, because a present without future is absurd, he wonders why "Faulkner and so many other writers [have] chosen this particular absurdity." To find answers to this question, Sartre argues, "we must look for the reason in the social conditions of our present life."[94] This suggestion is important for our engagement with the time novel, but Sartre does not elaborate on it in his essay on Faulkner. However, he develops this line of argumentation in further detail through his examination of the significance of the modernist novel for thought and politics in the first half of the twentieth century. Though he considers Faulkner the better and more "subtle" writer, Sartre argues that the novels of John Dos Passos offer answers to the problems of thought with which *The Sound and the Fury* grapples. Sartre contends that the American social novel and in particular the novels of Dos Passos offer a way of transcending a limit of the imagination that he considers a symptom of and one of the most dangerous elements of the French intellectual landscape leading up to the outbreak of World War II. Confronted with the threat of imminent war, Sartre was deeply troubled by crises and moments of danger that, as Cristina Diniz Mendonca Crema shows, "revealed history" while simultaneously revealing the utter absence of "theoretical instruments for grasping" the present as history. Established forms of idealism and subjectivism, Sartre knew, offered no solution. What was required instead, Crema writes, was a form of thought that could be found in the American social novel, a form of thought, as Sartre puts it, "which was not merely contemplation" but was aimed at understanding "real history." The novels of Dos Passos, Crema argues, offered Sartre such a form of thought. Sartre praises Dos

Passos's *1919*, for instance, for its ability to trace the relation between "the order of the day" and "the movement of history" as that "between the particular and universal."[95] What Sartre finds in the work of Dos Passos, therefore, is an anti-idealist realism that is able to read the present as history and thus move beyond the static past resulting from the influence of antiquity and the focus on timeless universals that Sartre associates with the secularization of French writing in the seventeenth and eighteenth centuries.

In an important footnote to his essay "Situation of the Writer in 1947," Sartre concludes that such an anti-idealist realism, which leaves behind modernist subjectivism, must be a realism of temporality. He writes, "We have learned from Joyce to look for a second kind of realism, the raw realism of subjectivity without mediation or distance. Which leads us to profess a third realism, that of temporality." This realism of temporality stands directly opposed to the realism of subjectivity and immediate experience, for "without mediation," Sartre argues, "we plunge the reader into a consciousness" and "refuse him all means of surveying the whole."[96] In "For Whom Does One Write?" Sartre argues that the turn away from idealism requires a turn to the present, a turn that Sartre believes to be of the utmost political and artistic importance. For the writer, Sartre argues, the present is "his chance and he must not waste it." Instead of contemplating "eternal ideas," the writer must examine the present, which is not a matter of "turning away from the temporal" but, on the contrary, of "coming back to it incessantly and go[ing] beyond it in each particular circumstance."[97] Here Sartre echoes Bloch's assertion that "all historical concerns want to and can live only in the now-time of history,"[98] adding that it is the novel, and specifically the novelistic realism of temporality, that affords us the ability to read the now-time as history. Sartre's account of the significance of a realism of temporality that replaces experience and subjectivism with the attempt to read time as history allows us to highlight an important aspect of the time novel, an aspect that is also a central component of the time novel's work in our moment. DeLillo's novels, as well as the forms of novelistic realism discussed in the next chapter, can be understood as a continuation and revitalization of a tradition of the time novel that finds its origins not in the better-known sources of the form associated with authors like Proust or Joyce but rather in the treatment of time found in the American social novel. What we see here, too, is another example of the close relation between the time novel and the social novel that already characterizes the German *Zeitroman*'s earliest forms, which emerged in close relation to the *Gesellschaftsroman*. The novelistic realism of temporality that Sartre describes assists thought in transcending established ways of narrativizing time insofar as it gives concrete form to Adorno's demand to examine time in time.

Novelistic examinations of time and their engagement with capital's tendency to replace time's plurality and mediation with standardization and immediacy give rise to particular formal and stylistic strategies. "The novel unfolds in the present, the way that life does," Sartre notes in his discussion of the work of Dos Passos, adding that the novel's temporality is a "staging device" that makes possible its processes of distantiation.[99] Sartre's notion of a novelistic temporal "staging device" has a history in modernist literary criticism, one that reemerges today in novels like DeLillo's. A central aspect of Hans Robert Jauß's work on Thomas Mann and Marcel Proust is the idea of *Zeitgeruest*, the temporal architecture or, more literally, temporal scaffolding of narrative. No doubt, scaffolding is too literal a translation here, and we may more accurately imagine the logic of this relation as the importance of the steel skeleton for modern architecture, whose architectural and historical significance resembles that of the novel's temporal skeleton. Similarly, A. A. Mendilow reminds us that Mann was fond of the notion of "time coulisses": staging competing sets of temporalities in the present to generate a sense of temporal depth and complex temporal relations.[100] In *Cosmopolis*, Eric's examination of time is bound up with reflections on the temporality connected to city space and architecture, on the time coulisses that surround him:

> He slid open the sunroof and thrust his head into the reeling scene. The bank towers loomed just above the avenue. . . . They looked empty from here. He liked that idea. They were made to be the last tall things, made empty, designed to hasten the future. They were the end of the outside world. They weren't here, exactly. They were in the future, a time beyond geography and touchable money and the people who stack and count it.[101]

But of course, the future of finance is also Eric's present, one that continues to be interrupted by what Eric perceives as remnants of past times, objects, people, places, and styles that he understands as vestigial objects, "degenerate structures." Eric senses that the particular form of time and the future he recognizes in the bank towers is designed, which is to say it is a particular form of thinking of time and futurity, a specific temporal regime, bound up with a particular form of capitalism that aims to leave behind previous versions of itself while also overwriting competing senses of time and futurity in order to solidify the temporal standardization on which capital rests. The temporal evenness that Eric encounters throughout the novel, instances of temporal depthlessness in which there is no longer a sense of competing temporalities, therefore is a result of the influence of finance capital and its aim to flatten and make uniform the temporal regime of real-time capitalism—and of course, Eric's opposition to any object or space that does not conform with this new temporal regime, anything that does not seem fully contemporary, ultimately supports capitalism's aim to instrumentalize, flatten, and standardize temporality. Reading the present may thus be understood as the commitment to reading the tensions and contradictions between our moment's competing temporal regimes.

In this way, we are able to appreciate more fully Thomas Mann's suggestion that *The Magic Mountain*'s temporal architecture requires "zweierlei Zeit," a duality of time. In his discussion of Mann's account of the *Zeitroman*, Jauß notes that from the beginning this duality of time may develop in two critical directions. The first direction provides the basis for Günther Müller's distinction between *Erzählzeit* and *erzählte* Zeit, which in turn finds its way into the work of Paul Ricoeur as the distinction between "narrated time" and "the time of narration."[102] The focus of this distinction, however, remains on the linguistic and purely narratological—on the attempt, therefore, to illustrate the temporal multiplicity of the novel's ability to narrate time. As Ricoeur shows at length in *Time and Narrative*, the time of reading constitutes one important dimension of the novel's temporal structure. Yet a second trajectory emerges from Mann's suggestion, one that Katrin Stepath describes as a focus on *Systemzeit*, the time of the system or systemic time.[103] *Systemzeit* is a measure of what we have throughout this chapter come to understand as the temporal regimes that define a moment in history, and *Systemzeit* is what Jauß understands to be at stake in Sartre's call for a "réalisme de la temporalité." If our interest lies in the narratological distinction between novelistic times, Jauß suggests, then Joyce's *Ulysses* illustrates the problematic undoing of this distinction, which highlights the consequences of the congruency of "objective time and poetic time" in a novel that collapses all distance into full immediacy.[104] *Ulysses* constitutes in this sense one of the most striking examples of the dialectic of temporal immediacy and modernist subjectivism.

Yet if we wish to engage with the historical and political specificity of time, then we must turn toward the realism of temporality, which, Jauß argues, is bound up with an emphasis on the impossibility of an immediate relation between the "musical-real" time of the world and "internal-imaginary" time. In this form of realism, a given character's experience of time is not an end in itself but merely the initial recognition that opens the door to an examination of the relation between historical consciousness and the historicization of changing forms of temporality. In this way, novels like *Cosmopolis* and *Point Omega* take plot and our relation to time beyond the limits of experience, for in these novels the plot is driven forward by the self-reflexive engagement with our struggle to interpret time and the analysis of time as a form of reading. These novels further connect the question of reading time to examination of our attempts to read art in general and literature and novels in particular. DeLillo's realism of temporality provides us with an examination of how we know the world and allows us to see that each way of knowing is also a form of temporal knowledge shaped by the temporal regimes of social life and of our world's material structures. The contemporary significance and political possibilities of the tradition of the time novel that reaches from Mann and Dos Passos to novelists like DeLillo lie in its ability to foster forms of knowledge that transcend the immediacy and subjectivism of real-time capitalism. In this way, the time novel creates the preconditions for the development of a new temporal vocabulary for our time and thus for the transcendence of the limits of capitalism's eternal now. After all, as Agamben suggests, "the original task of a genuine revolution . . . is never merely to 'change the world,' but also and above all to 'change time'."[105]

DEEP PRESENCE

Boxall understands the suggestion on part of the narrator of DeLillo's novel *The Body Artist* (2001) that we "have lost our bearings in this newly passing, postmillennial time" and that "we no longer know how to measure the now" as a call for an account of time that privileges the time of the planet over the time of human experience.[106] Similarly, Lupton and Williams suggest that "in recent years, time has become a prism through which many material, ontological, and even institutional categories are turned anew," which they understand in part as a matter of "literature's ability to explore deep time" and of critical approaches that "'read' whole libraries of data . . . in a time period no human being could ever hope to replicate."[107] And yet, while there is much to be said in favor of paying more attention to matters of deep time or long-term thinking, in particular in a moment in which short-term thinking and immediacy serve as convenient ways of refusing to engage with the climate emergency we all face, it is also important to foreground that authors like DeLillo do not simply turn to deep or natural time to replace the focus on immediacy and experience. Rather, the strongest version of the critique of temporality offered by novels like *Point Omega* and *Zero K* does not remain confined to the traditional duality of experiential and natural time. Instead of taking the critique of experience as an occasion to embrace the other side of this duality, the time of nature, DeLillo's novels strikingly take us beyond this duality and toward historical time. This move requires foregrounding the importance of *Systemzeit* as an alternative third way that allows us to historicize our understanding of time itself and locates the solution to time's purported exhaustion not in deep time but instead in a different relation to the moment: deep presence.

Zero K, for instance, returns repeatedly to the confusion that results from life in the compound where the novel's narrator, Jeffrey, visits his father, which is located underground and sealed off from the outside world. Jeffrey suffers from frequent confusion and often loses track of time, a confusion that the novel formally expresses in its discontinuous structure, which causes the reader to lose track of the relation between narrated time and the time of narration as much as Jeffrey loses track of the relation between natural and experienced time. Time itself, he notes, loses meaning. "Time compressed, time drawn tight, overlapping time, dayless, nightless, many doors, no windows" (115): this is how Jeffrey reflects on the time he spends in the compound. For time to have meaning, he begins to realize, it cannot be just the time of immediacy and experience. What he needs to solve this problem is "a window to look out of" (115). Finally having found a window, Jeffrey describes his changed relation to time: "I stepped back gradually and watched the view reduce itself within the limits of the window frame. Then I looked at the window itself, tall and narrow, top-ended by an arch. A lancet window, I thought, recalling the term, and this brought me back to myself, to a diminished perspective, something steadfast, a word with a meaning" (116). Jeffrey is therefore interested not so much in natural time as in the window itself, the changes in his standpoint, and those frames that determine his attempts to read the world, frames that continue to change his perception of an object. Time, Jeffrey realizes, becomes knowable neither through his experience nor directly through nature but instead through his reflection on the frame. Rather than suggesting that we should read our world in deep time since we now live, as Lupton and Williams put it, in "a time of big clocks,"[108] novels like *Zero K* stress that a simple shift toward natural or deep time alone cannot address or allow us to move past the crises of historical time and of time conceived as a form of thought and a form of narratively constructing our world.

After losing virtually his entire fortune speculating on the yen, Eric leaves his limousine and begins to walk. Toward the end of *Cosmopolis*, we find Eric wandering the city aimlessly, struggling with the same lack of purpose that prevents Dwight from making decisions: "He stood in the street. There was nothing to do. . . . The moment was empty of urgency and purpose. . . . How could he take a step in any direction if all directions were the same?" (180). In the novel's closing passages, Eric encounters a disaffected employee who intends to shoot him. Confronted with the threat of imminent death, Eric is able to look neither at the gun pointed at him nor at the shooter. Instead, he is mesmerized by a beetle "moving in its specialized slowness," in what strikes Eric as an "old dumb leaf-eating arcadian pace" (205). In the final moments of his life, Eric finds himself reminded of the tension between his experience of time and the natural time he contemplated earlier in the day while receiving an echocardiogram: "He felt the passion of the body, its adaptive drive over geologic time, the poetry and chemistry of its origins in the dust of exploding stars. How dwarfed he felt by his own heart. There it was and it awed him, to see his life beneath his breastbone in image-forming units, hammering on outside of him" (44). But Eric ultimately realizes that his true interest does not lie in the external time of nature. He hopes instead for time's very abolition: "He'd always wanted to become quantum dust, transcending his body mass, the soft tissue over the bones, the muscle and fat. The idea was to live outside the given limits, in a chip, on a disk, as data, in a whirl, in radiant spin, a consciousness saved from the void" (206). This, Eric thinks, would be "the next natural step" in capitalist evolution, which, he reasons, has become the same as human evolution: "It would be the master thrust of cyber-capital, to extend the human experience toward infinity as a medium for corporate growth and investment, for the accumulation of profits and vigorous reinvestment" (207). And yet Eric cannot determine how he might trade in his physical existence for such a future, since, like Artis in *Zero K*, he is unable to make sense of himself and of his relation to time without reference to the body: "His pain interfered with his immortality. . . . He'd come to know himself, untranslatably, through this pain" (207). Like the final paragraphs of DeLillo's *White Noise* (1985), the closing sections of *Cosmopolis* reflect on death via a transition to present-tense narration, and the novel ends with Eric waiting for the shot to sound in a moment suspended in complete presence.

The tension between natural time and the time of lived experience on one hand and the systemic time of capital on the other returns as a crucial aspect of both *Point Omega* and *Zero K*. The abolition of time through geologic time is a matter of great interest for the protagonist of *Point Omega*, Richard Elster. Elster travels to the desert for a work assignment and realizes that instead of serving as a counterpoint to the present's instantaneity, deep, geologic time further contributes to time's abolition: "Time falling away. That's what I feel here. . . . Time becoming slowly older. Enormously old. Not day by day. This is deep time, epochal time. Our lives receding into the long past. That's what's out there. The Pleistocene desert, the rule of extinction" (71). Instead of offering a corrective for or critique of the crises brought about by real-time capitalism's standardization of immediacy, deep time functions as an escape from the problems posed by the speed of capital and replaces the abstract immediacy of the capitalist present with the concrete immediacy of nature. Deep time must therefore be carefully set apart from the currently pervasive nostalgic attachments to concrete, natural immediacy that are literalized through trendy attempts to "get back in touch with nature."

In *Zero K*, the tension between the time of lived experience and the deep time of nature returns in the context of billionaire Ross Lockhart's quest to defeat death and therefore time. Ross's son, Jeffrey, visits his father in a mysterious desert compound in a remote area of southern Kazakhstan. Jeffrey discovers that his father has invested large sums of money in a project called the Convergence, a cryopreservation project that promises immortality. Ross and his terminally ill wife, Artis, are among those who have purchased the service offered by the Convergence. Immortality, Ross hopes, will not only allow him to be reunited with Artis at some point in the future but will also allow him to overcome the limits of his current existence—temporally, physically, and intellectually. "There are philologists designing an advanced language unique to the Convergence," he informs Jeffrey. "People will learn it and speak it. A language that will enable us to express things we can't express now, see things we can't see now, see ourselves and others in ways that unite us, broaden every possibility" (33). This new language formulated for an entirely new, timeless existence, Ross suggests, makes it possible to develop "another way to think and live" (34). The abolition of time offered by the Convergence, however, as Jeffrey gradually realizes, is distinguished directly from deep time, which cannot offer help to those who have "fallen out of history" (129). In a conversation with one of the researchers at the Convergence, Jeffrey asks, "Is the desert where miracles happen?" Jeffrey receives a bemused but telling answer: "Such a quaint response to ideas that attempt to confront a decimated future" (128). While deep time contains the tendency to contribute to the effacement of historical time, the Convergence seeks to perfect this tendency in the complete abolition of time. Its subjects will become "ahistorical humans" for whom time, in particular linear chronological time, no longer has meaning, and who will "speak a new language" that offers "new meanings, entire new levels of perception" (130). The group embraces timelessness as the way to resolve humanity's most fundamental problem of knowledge, which means that the Convergence, at its most fundamental, replicates the same problem addressed in *Cosmopolis* and *Point Omega*. Its dream of abolishing time is a dream of immediacy, of the final atonement of subject and object, self and world. The Convergence seeks a relation to the world that no longer requires mediation—"no similes, no metaphors, no analogies" (130). The Convergence offers not simply timelessness but full knowledge and immanently meaningful existence. Put differently, the Convergence offers a return to the world as conceived by the epic, the very world whose impossibility the novel makes legible. The problems of thought that the Convergence poses in *Zero K* are the same problems that underwrite the novel's ontology and function as an art form that affords us a way of knowing the world historically. The value of the novel is reiterated through the impossibility of the philosophical project of the Convergence, and in this way *Zero K* advances a striking account of the possibility and fundamental necessity of the novel in our time.

DeLillo's novel, however, also grapples with the lure of immediacy. The dream of the world offered by the Convergence is appealing and comforting, not least because it promises a radically simplified relationship to the world. Especially in moments when he feels overwhelmed by his visit to the desert compound, Jeffrey, too, voices the desire to escape the troubles of a world that is not inherently meaningful. "I didn't want interpretation," Jeffrey notes. He prefers a relation of immediacy, of pure experience: "I wanted to see and feel what was there, even as I was unequal to the experience as it folded over me" (133). But, Jeffrey ultimately learns, his escapist desire for immediacy is simply another version of the immediacy and complete contraction to the self offered by the Convergence. The project's promise to be "outside the narrative of what we refer to as history" is a project that is fundamentally "pledged to an inwardness, a deep probing focus on who and where we are" (237). One of the project's coordinators therefore announces to those who are about to undergo the procedure that they will experience a transition into complete identity: "You are about to become, each of you, a single life in touch with only yourself" (237). At this point in the novel, Jeffrey has become keenly aware of the problems with the relation to the world promised by the Convergence. DeLillo's novel returns to the same question repeatedly: "What's the difference between eyes closed in a lighted room and eyes closed in a dark room?" *Zero K* offers a simple but important answer, one that is bound up with Jeffrey's recognition that the dream of a life in which he is only in touch with himself does not offer solutions to his struggles: "All the difference in the world" (200). If immortality abolishes death and therefore time, but also the need for interpretation and mediation, then life, DeLillo's novels shows, depends upon the threat of death as much as it consists of the permanent struggle with interpretation, the world's lack of inherent meaning, and the need for analogies and metaphors that allow us to make sense of the gap between self and world. Indeed, it is this very gap between self and world, the constant struggle to make sense of our relation to a changing world, that ultimately defines life. And it is in this way, by giving us ways of making sense of such a relation to the world, that the novel allows us to understand what it means to live in time.

Over the course of the novel, Jeffrey develops a different relation to both time and the world. He no longer seeks to escape the struggle with the moment. Instead, he finds hope in trying to interpret it. "Know the moment," Jeffrey decides. "This was all I needed to take me day to day and I tried to think of these days and nights as the hushed countermand, ours, to the widespread belief that the future, everybody's, will be worse than the past" (200). DeLillo's novel thus ultimately refuses the deep time of nature in favor of an interpretive relationship to time that seeks to lend the moment deeper presence. By exploring the moment's multiplicity, by reading the temporal plurality of the present, Jeffrey is able to recover a sense of hope and possibility. Futurity in turn lies precisely in such a critical, interpretive relation to the present, one that is modeled by the form of the novel itself. Gradually, Jeffrey begins to understand that deep presence allows him to transcend the "thinness of contemporary life" and understand that "ordinary moments make the life" (107). Reminding us of Sartre's suggestion that the novel is a present with aesthetic distance, the final sections of *Zero K* shuttle back and forth between past- and present-tense narration as Jeffrey reflects on what it means to assume a deeper, critical relation to the moment. Jeffrey turns his attention to "things people do, ordinarily, forgettably, things that breathe just under the surface of what we acknowledge having in common," and he expresses his desire for "these gestures, these moments to have meaning" (209). Jeffrey develops a moving sense of intimacy with the moment, embracing its presence and welcoming the problems of interpretation posed by quotidian life. DeLillo thus returns here to the very commitment to the moment that already marked *Underworld* (1997), DeLillo's lengthy meditation on the importance and beauty of the quotidian, the overlooked, and the unexamined complexity and meaningfulness of the everyday. *Zero K* offers this deep, interpretive relation to the moment as an antidote to the crises of time and thought that result from the impression of the timelessness of the now. What *Zero K* describes as "nonmoments in time," moments in which "time is suspended" and the moment itself is opened up for examination, offer us ways to see beyond the focus on the end of plot and change due to time's suspension (235). The novel works not just via suspense and plot but through the suspension of time itself—through the creation of nonmoments of reflection and interpretation. The novel is the art form of the nonmoment, a form of knowledge that opens up time for critical interrogation in moments of its arrest.

In the closing passages of the novel, Jeffrey remembers watching the cryopreservation procedure being performed on Ross. Jeffrey struggles in particular to come to terms with one moment. Leaning closer to Ross, who is sliding every deeper into anesthetic stillness while his naked body is lying on a slab as he is prepared for immortality, Jeffrey seems to catch a few faint, final words: "Gesso on linen" (251, emphasis in the original). "I think this is what I heard," Jeffrey notes, only able to recall that "gesso was a term used in art, a surface or medium" (251). Gesso on linen. A white painting. *Zero K* offers us those answers to the problem posed by the white painting, which *Cosmopolis*'s Eric is tragically unable to find. The application of a layer of white gesso, Jeffrey knows, prepares the canvas for painting. DeLillo's novel thus traces the artistic engagement with time not in the novelty of forms but rather in the importance of a medium, as a relation of mediation that can create the preconditions for both thought and art. The function of the novel today, therefore, is not a matter of its struggle against time's passing and its desire to remain novel.[109] Instead, the novel's function and value lie in its ability to serve as a medium for thought that allows us to know our time differently and to create ways of telling time beyond the confines of the long now. Sometimes, as Ross notes in the beginning of *Zero K*, new ways of thinking and living do not require new ideas. Instead, they can also be brought about by ideas that are "approaching full realization" (8). The time novel itself is not a new form, but it is a novel form whose current function and significance can be understood in just such a way: in the context of the temporal crises of the present, the time novel is approaching full realization. *Zero K* concludes not with a search for novelty but with an argument for the importance of finding a sense of deep presence in a different relation to the time of the recurring and the quotidian.

Sitting on a bus at sunset, Jeffrey is struck by the effect the fading of the light has on his surroundings. "The streets were charged with the day's dying light," Jeffrey observes, "and the bus seemed the carrier of this radiant moment" (273). Absorbed by the sun's shimmer on his hands, Jeffrey is suddenly "startled by a human wail." Turning around, he sees a woman and a boy at the rear of the bus. The boy is on his feet, "facing the rear window . . . pointing and wailing at the flaring sun" (273). Jeffrey is reminded of an exchange with his father: sitting in his office as Ross tells him that "everybody wants to own the end of the world." But, Jeffrey wonders, "is this what the boy was seeing?" (274). Upon reflection, Jeffrey concludes that "the boy was not seeing the sky collapse upon us but was finding the purest astonishment in the intimate touch of earth and sun." And it is in this way that *Zero K* leaves us with a passionate argument for the recovery of time from the threat of the world's end. Hope lies not in novelty or in the idea of paradise. Rather, Jeffrey knows, we may find the source of time and hope in the little boy's pure astonishment and delight and in our ability to establish a relation of deep presence to the moment. Jeffrey returns to his seat and faces forward. "I didn't need heaven's delight," he concludes. "I had the boy's cries of wonder" (274).

CHAPTER 2

How to Read the Present

Writing in keeping with the times is not the same as writing according to life.
—Ernst Bloch, *The Utopian Function of Art and Literature*

Toward the end of Gary Shteyngart's *Super Sad True Love Story* (2010), which is set in New York City in the not too distant future, we find the novel's middle-aged and romantically challenged protagonist, Lenny, sitting on the couch in his apartment with his girlfriend, Eunice, reading a novel while waiting for war and catastrophe to end the world as they know it. Throughout the narrative, Lenny struggles to establish a deep, intimate bond with his girlfriend. Reading together, at the end of the world, he hopes, may offer him one more chance at creating a truly romantic experience. Much to his chagrin, however, the novel he has selected, Milan Kundera's *The Unbearable Lightness of Being*, is not the kind of novel that makes for good romantic reading. "I wanted him to get to the plot," Lenny exasperatedly notes, "to introduce actual 'living' characters . . . and to leave the world of ideas behind."[1] Kundera's novel, Lenny realizes, is "a novel of ideas set in a country that meant nothing to [Eunice]," and as a result, it keeps her at a distance—Eunice is unable to get into it. Lenny wishes that, instead of grappling with ideas, the novel engaged with the experiences of characters, which would lend their reading a sense of emotional immediacy. Kundera's emphasis on ideas, however, keeps Eunice and Lenny at a distance and does not allow for the deeply emotional experience for which Lenny had hoped. He wants "this complex language, this surge of intellect, to be processed into love." "Isn't that how they used to do it a century ago," he wonders, "people reading poetry to one another?" (275). The failure of Kundera's novel to facilitate emotional intimacy is exacerbated by the fact that Eunice turns out to be a bad reader. "I never really learned how to read texts," she explains, "just to scan them for info" (277).

Lenny's struggle with the novel is as tragic as it fascinating, since it contains an account of reading that is instructive for this chapter's examination of the novel's treatment of time and our ability to know, read, and interpret time. The scene in Shteyngart's novel revolves around three discrete ways of approaching a novel. Mining a novel for information does not qualify as reading—it is simply Eunice's default mode of relating to a text, and it is what she does because she never learned how to read a novel. Experiencing a novel stands opposed to reading insofar as reading is aimed at ideas and necessitates a relation of critical distance that makes reading, defined as interpretation, possible. Lenny's hope, however, is that the novel may create an immediate relation between the emotions of its characters and the experience of its readers, thereby assisting Lenny in his struggle to introduce true emotion into his relationship with Eunice. In short, Lenny does not wish to read the novel with Eunice as much as wants to experience it with her. The fact that he has chosen a novel of ideas, however, which demands to be interpreted and focuses primarily on problems of knowledge and thought and not on the experiences or emotions of characters, means that the attempt to experience it inevitably produces an unsatisfactory result.

In this chapter, I show that the contemporary time novel attaches its interrogation of the self-imposed limits of our imagination, which results in the perception of a crisis of temporality and underwrites our struggle with concepts such as presence and contemporaneity, directly to the distinction between reading and experience. The contemporary time novel rejects subjective experience in favor of an examination of time as a form of knowledge in history. As in Shteyngart's novel, this distinction becomes a formal problem that in turn illustrates the relationship between the time novel and the novel of ideas. The latter relationship is particularly notable since, as Adam Kelly argues, the novel of ideas has a difficult standing in American literary history and, in his estimation, remains a rarity even in contemporary American literature. In fact, Kelly suggests that one of the main contributions of David Foster Wallace to American fiction is his commitment to the novel of ideas in the context of a national literature that is otherwise mainly interested in experience. Kelly here returns us to a tradition of Americanist literary criticism, originating with Philip Rahv and Lionel Trilling, that criticizes American literature for its "experiential bias."[2] In his essay "The Cult of Experience in American Writing," Rahv describes American literature as defined by the "long-standing national habit of playing hide-and-seek with experience." For Rahv, the work of Henry James is indicative of one of the central differences between American and European literature. For European writers, Rahv argues, experience served "as the concrete medium for the testing and the creation of values, whereas in James's work it stands for something distilled or selected from the total process of living . . . a self-propelling autonomous 'presence' inexhaustibly alluring in its own right." "Since Whitman and James," Rahv continues, "the American creative mind . . . has found the terms and objects of its activity in the urge toward and immersion in experience. It is this search for experience, conducted on diverse and often conflicting levels of consciousness, which has been the dominant, quintessential theme of the characteristic American literary productions—from Leaves of Grass to Winesburg, Ohio and beyond." By highlighting its preoccupation with experience, Rahv suggests, we are able to foreground "some of the peculiarities of American writing," most significantly its "unique indifference . . . to ideas generally, to theories of value, to the work of the speculative and problematical." "Everything is contained in the American novel," Rahv concludes, "except ideas."[3] From the standpoint of Rahv's account of the American novel, therefore, Lenny's problem could have been easily avoided. Instead of selecting a European novel, he should have chosen an American one.

Although it is no doubt in some ways needlessly isolationist given the history of literary flows and exchanges between Europe and the United States, Rahv's account of the American novel, as Kelly shows, is far from unusual.[4] Lionel Trilling's essay "Reality in America," published in the same year as Rahv's essay, associates American culture centrally with "the chronic belief that there exists an opposition between reality and mind and that one must enlist oneself in the party of reality."[5] Indeed, "as late as 1981," Kelly argues, "Mary McCarthy was still mourning the absence of ideas from the American novel, and criticizing writers under the sway of James for suppressing their instinct to build fiction around abstract concerns." In recent years, Kelly shows, critics like Mark McGurl return to this argument and extend it from the American novel to realist fiction more widely conceived. "All of the ideas in realist fiction on the Jamesian model," McGurl writes, "are made subservient to the experience of thinking them. For all the intelligence exerted in their articulation, they are never valuable or interesting in and of themselves.'"[6] What matters for our examination of the contemporary American time novel, however, is less the question of the transhistorical accuracy of this critical lineage than the fact that, as I show in this chapter, the critique of experience and the emphasis on the importance of the novel's engagement with ideas constitute central aspects of novels that address the temporal contradictions of our moment. In such novels, our ability to find answers to the crisis of futurity and the struggle with an omnipresent now depends upon our ability to distance ourselves from experience and instead examine the idea of time itself.

In this way, as I illustrate by reading novels by Ben Lerner, Charles Yu, and Jennifer Egan, the time novel confronts the limits of our temporal imagination and begins the process of developing new ways of telling time, offering us new conceptions of temporality that allow us to make sense of our present moment in history. The time novel can be understood as a novelistic form that carries out the basic operation of immanent critique: it generates analyses of thought in time. The distinction between reading and experience in *Super Sad* corresponds to the distinction between interpretation and experience that underlies the account of reading time and the present forwarded by Lerner's novel *10:04* (2014) and Yu's novel *How to Live Safely in a Science Fictional Universe* (2010). The commitment to an examination of time that privileges form over experience is connected to the distinction between reading and experience that novels like *10:04* and *How to Live Safely* foreground as central to our ability to engage with the present. The contemporary time novel understands its own project as connected to an intriguing argument about the distinction between experience and reading: the experience of time and a novel does not amount to an interpretation of either.

Moreover, character development in the contemporary time novel is a result of the development of an idea and its critique: characters only develop insofar as they are able to formulate a new account of an idea, a new imagination of time. The function of the unnamed narrator in Don DeLillo's *Point Omega* and in novels such as *10:04* and *How to Live Safely*, for instance, is to express this subordination of character to idea. It is not the unnamed narrator's experience or subjectivity that matters in the novel. Rather, the unnamed character only matters inasmuch as he serves as a conduit for the novel's engagement with the idea of time, which creates the momentum that advances the novel's plot. It is in this sense that we can gain a deeper understanding of the suggestion that the time novel develops in connection with a range of novelistic forms, including the historical novel, the social novel, the novel of ideas, and the artist's novel. The time novel provides us with a critique of ideas in time. It interrogates the historical development of temporal knowledge and the formation and historical specificity of ideas of time, and it develops its critique through a confrontation with art itself. Novelists like Lerner examine the struggle to make sense of time in our moment in history in connection with the methodological challenges of interpreting artworks. Moreover, novels like *10:04* treat our (in)ability to read the present historically as a distinction between reading and misreading. The novel's critique of subjective experience is not only central to its ability to engage with the temporal crises of our time, but insofar as this critique is also directly connected to the novel's account of (mis)interpretation, it also has important consequences for our understanding of the work of literary criticism today. The time novel formulates a theory of reading that offers us a way of making sense of the present and also makes a strong case for the novel itself: it shows why we should read novels today. Novels like those of Egan and Yu, for example, outline a way of reading and "inhabiting" the present that embraces its temporality as the time of risk. This commitment to the present as risk is connected to a renewed embrace of the social and the communal, which in turn suggests that we may understand futurity not only as the consequence of our ability to read the present historically but also as a gift that can and should be given to others.

READING VERSUS EXPERIENCE

To Kundera, Lenny's struggle with his novel would likely not come as a surprise. After all, Kundera argues that the future of the novel lies in its ability to engage with time, and in order to allow the novel to do so, he suggests, contemporary novelists must "broaden the issue [of time] beyond the Proustian problem of personal memory to the enigma of collective time," to "overstep the temporal limits of an individual life, to which the novel had been hitherto confined."[7] But abandoning the focus on experience and instead examining the idea of time in history is not only a tricky proposition for the American novelist. More problematically perhaps, reading time without making reference to subjective experience requires us to depart from how time has largely been understood in Western thought: as a matter of the tension between lived time and natural or given time. In particular, modern philosophies of time, as Daniel Couzens Hoy shows, locate the source of temporality in analyses of our relation to time's passing. "Hegel's critique of sense-certainty, Husserl's analysis of protention and retention, Heidegger's ecstasies, James's notion of the dawning and fading of each moment of consciousness, Merleau-Ponty's notion of the identity of time and the self, Nietzsche's *amor fati*"—all of these approaches to time, Couzens Hoy stresses, analyze time first and foremost as a matter of lived time.[8] Similarly, Couzens Hoy illustrates that the work of Gadamer, Foucault, Bergson, Deleuze, and Derrida centrally revolves around "existential strategies" that may allow us to come to terms with the fleetingness of the present. As a result, it is not surprising that we witness a significant philosophical crisis in a moment when the present has seemingly ceased to move and thereby exhausts one of the foundations of the vast majority of approaches to time in Western thought. Leaving behind our established methodology for temporal analysis in an effort to explore new ways of imagining time is one of the most significant struggles of contemporary thought. We see, therefore, once again the immense value of the work of the time novel in our moment, for the time novel has tasked itself with precisely this project. The time novel provides us with a direly needed alternative to the dominance of phenomenological approaches to time by modeling a way to read time as form. The time novel shows that a focus limited to temporal experience is not able to trace the sources of the current crisis of temporality in contemporary capitalism. In fact, it is in part due to the continued predominance of phenomenological accounts of time in the context of real-time capitalism that the problem of the eternal present emerges in the first place. The time novel radically reconfigures our temporal imaginary, however, and allow us to read the purported end of time as the self-imposed limit of thought that results from the inability of established conceptions of time to make sense of the transition into real-time capitalism.

Literary criticism faces a possibly even greater challenge. The majority of recent literary and cultural criticism that is part of the new temporal turn is influenced by phenomenological approaches to time. Moreover, some of the major developments in literary criticism since the early 2000s are also characterized by a turn toward immediacy. Strikingly, at the very moment when the time novel forwards an approach to time that understands experience as a misreading of time that must be refused in favor of distantiated interpretation, we also witness literary criticism turning away from hermeneutics in favor of approaches that are aimed at immediacy and experience. Since the early aughts, literary criticism has been defined by a renewed interest in the fundamental categories of our discipline. Critics have asked how we read now, how we argue now, and how we may formulate a literary criticism for the twenty-first century.[9] One important aspect of these new disciplinary debates has been the rise of critical approaches that share either a suspicion of hermeneutics or the conviction that we ought to replace hermeneutical approaches to literature with approaches aimed at an immediate relation to the literary work.[10] In the effort to formulate a literary criticism for the twenty-first century, critics begin to turn toward immediacy and create the preconditions for the rise in popularity of, for example, the affective turn or the postcritical turn. However, the critique of immediacy, in various senses of the term, constitutes a central aspect of the contemporary time novel. As literary criticism begins to ask how we read now, the time novel starts to forward striking accounts of how the novel may allow us to read the Now. At the same time as literary criticism develops an ever greater interest in methodologies that explore immediate relationships to texts and objects, that is, the time novel emphasizes the importance of formulating critiques of experience and immediacy. And since we are witnessing a new temporal turn in literary criticism, it seems important to determine where this temporal turn stands in relation to two opposing sides: the time novel and literary criticism's interest in immediacy.

The work of Hans Ulrich Gumbrecht merits particular attention in this context. After all, Gumbrecht's work is directly associated with the notion that we live in a present without time. The account of our time as an "ever broadening present" underwrites the basic logical propositions of a range of Gumbrecht's essays and books, including *After 1945* (2013) and *Unsere Breite Gegenwart* (2010).[11] In the very moment when novelists like Gibson and DeLillo begin to foreground the value of the novel in historicizing the time of the present and refusing interpretive immediacy in order to avoid being paralyzed by the impression of the end of time in the present, Gumbrecht argues for a literary criticism aimed at an immediate relation to its object of inquiry, a relation that Gumbrecht describes as "presence." In *Production of Presence: What Meaning Cannot Convey* (2004), Gumbrecht outlines a conception of "presence" that is decidedly not a temporal concept. "The word 'presence' does not refer . . . to a temporal but to a spatial relationship to the world and its objects," Gumbrecht explains. He replaces the temporal idea of presence with a spatial one, because, he reasons, "something that is present is supposed to be tangible for human hands, which implies that, conversely, it can have an immediate impact on human bodies."[12] The physical tangibility of Gumbrecht's idea of presence and the nostalgic undertones of the desire to get back in touch with the object stand in stark opposition to the time novel's critique of immediacy. Gumbrecht's notion of presence anticipates recent critical approaches that seek to move beyond interpretation as a method of making meaning. To be sure, Gumbrecht certainly does not propose a simple replacement of meaning with presence. Instead, he argues for a "relation to the things of the world that could oscillate between presence effects and meaning effects."[13]

In his 2008 essay "Reading for the *Stimmung*? About the Ontology of Literature Today," Gumbrecht extends this argument and proposes a mode of reading formulated in relation to what he understands as our "need and desire for a certain degree of touch with the physical world." When we read literature for *Stimmung* (mood or atmosphere), Gumbrecht reasons, it can deliver that which "many of our contemporaries are longing to feel . . . when they read literature . . . the softest touch of the material world."[14] In *Atmosphere, Mood, Stimmung: On a Hidden Potential of Literature* (2012), Gumbrecht reiterates his long-standing conviction that the function of literature is not to describe or represent but to "make present."[15] Reading, on this account, is less a matter of interpretation than it is a matter of experiencing *Stimmungen*. The turn to presence in Gumbrecht's work is intended to solve a problem. According to Gumbrecht, literary criticism is in crisis because it has lost touch with both literature and the world. He takes aim at two schools of criticism in particular that he believes to be dominant today—if not directly, then by way of lasting influence. Each, he proposes, delivers a damaging understanding of the ontology of literature. By proposing "that any kind of world reference through language is impossible," deconstruction, Gumbrecht argues, absorbs "all possible functions of literary reading under the one and only view that it produced the ultimate and irrefutable experience of the impossibility of world reference through language." Cultural studies, which he understands to be "sheltered by the epistemological (or should one rather say ideological?) convictions of Marxism," is in Gumbrecht's estimation "empirically optimistic" (insofar as it "never harbors any doubts about its own capacity or the capacity of literature to access the 'real world'") and "epistemologically careless" (because it has no good account of the relation between literature and the real world). Gumbrecht believes that literary criticism will be under threat "as long as it dwells on these two positions that, in the form of contrast and tension, tend to neutralize each other." To confront this threat, Gumbrecht proposes *Stimmung* as a solution, as a "third position" that allows us to move beyond the limiting influence of the two dominant positions.[16]

However, more significant than the question of whether the problem that Gumbrecht identifies can be solved by a focus on *Stimmung* (and leaving aside for now the question of whether Gumbrecht forwards a truly convincing account of the state of contemporary literary criticism) is the fact that Gumbrecht's proposed solution does not solve a problem as much as it exacerbates a crisis. One wonders: What can be gained by introducing an atemporal conception of presence in a moment purportedly marked by a crisis of temporality and by omnipresence? What exactly is the work that an atemporal idea of presence does in the context of the current crisis of futurity? Of course, one might argue that the timeless present and Gumbrecht's call for an atemporal relation to objects go hand in hand. But since the latter further confirms the former, and the current crisis of temporality marks one of the most significant problems of our era, the timelessness of the present should be understood as a historically specific problem that requires solutions. Immediacy and atemporal presence, however, only further compound the problem. The underlying commitments of Gumbrecht's turn to presence in the age of the broad present give us important insights into the stakes of examining the tension between immediacy in recent literary criticism and the time novel's critique of immediacy. In the attempt to formulate an account of reading that is in touch with material reality and the real world, Gumbrecht reproduces the very problem that the time novel illustrates as the foundational cause of our inability to read the time and material logic of our world today. Gumbrecht's remedy for a literary criticism that has lost touch with the real world, in other words, can only seem a solution inasmuch as the idea of reading for presence and immediacy is able to sever its relation to the problematic role of immediacy in the real world. Moreover, insufficiently historicized arguments in favor of reading for immediacy are not only out of touch with the challenges posed for thought, art, and politics by the real world today, but they are also out of touch with the important ways in which literature itself engages with the problems of presence and immediacy under the conditions of real-time capitalism. Gumbrecht's attempt to save literary criticism therefore becomes particularly problematic when it bills itself as a literary critical method. Most of Gumbrecht's arguments apply not to literature specifically but rather to a range of cultural media and art forms. In fact, the specificity of literature or the novel matters less in his analyses than broader arguments about how we relate to the world. And while the contemporary time novel insists upon its current value and possibilities precisely by foregrounding the specific forms of imagination and reading that the novel can produce, Gumbrecht's account of reading flattens the differences between the registers of reading that are bound up with various literary genres and art forms. In the attempt to develop a literary criticism that is in touch with the real world and more in touch with literature itself, therefore, Gumbrecht's turn to immediacy severs the relation to both.

Gumbrecht is far from the only critic who turns to immediacy and reading practices focused on experience to solve contemporary literary criticism's problems. In fact, Gumbrecht's work indicates some of the most significant recent changes in literary criticism. But while it is important to examine how facets of recent literary criticism such as the affective turn might relate to the problems immediacy poses for art, thought, and politics today, the most troubling version of the turn to immediacy rests on a distinct sense of disciplinary nostalgia and conservatism. Charles Altieri, for instance, shares not only the general terms of Gumbrecht's solution but also the underlying account of literary criticism's crisis. In the same year that we saw the publication of Gibson's *Spook Country*, whose protagonist finds herself confronted with objects that signal a "terrible contemporaneity" while struggling to make sense of artists who fully embrace the present by turning to "mimetic literalism," Altieri issues a call for a return to approaches aimed at exploring "the difference between what art can do by virtue of its 'meaning' and what it can do by virtue of emphasizing its sensuous being as something over and against meaning."[17] Altieri's investment in sensuous experience is connected to the nostalgic longing for a kind of literary scholarship that was able to offer a more immediate sense of literary experience. Specifically, Altieri proposes a return to "the imperative to instruct and delight," which, he argues, may allow us to "break binary oppositions like materialism and idealism," returning us to the good old times of literary criticism and leaving behind a moment when "most theorists would rather run with the new than attempt to reconstruct the old."[18] Carolyn Lesjak argues that recent defenses of reading often rely on a logic that marks a new "disciplinary conservatism" in literary criticism. Arguments for forms of reading that are aimed at what is "apprehensible via the senses," Lesjak suggests, are the result of a general belief in the need to advocate for "a return to the pleasures of a kind of reading that theory has supposedly made impossible." And this new conservatism comes with a familiar temporal problem. Through its opposition to ideology critique, the much-discussed practice of "surface reading," Lesjak argues, "hopes to freeze time, to stay in the present in its appeal to the commonsensical, to a thing's face value."[19]

Arguments in favor of a literary criticism whose reading practices are nostalgically aimed at good old immediacy in order to save literary criticism from materialist and deconstructive approaches fail to address the contemporary novel's own struggle against immediacy and are, at the same time, strikingly unaware of their own historical, methodological, and political functions in the age of immediacy. Altieri's critique of materialist criticism, which occasions his essay, therefore ultimately undercuts itself. Altieri sets out to show how "the prevailing forms of materialist criticism . . . prove far less capacious and far less promising than do traditional understandings of literariness for articulating the distinctive roles literature can play in social life."[20] But precisely by studying how the novel struggles against immediacy and searches for new forms of imagination to help us think beyond the social and political impasses of our time originating in specific material conditions, we can formulate a criticism appropriate for our time, one grounded in a rigorous understanding of literariness. To propose presence and immediacy as a way forward for literary criticism in an era defined by crises of thought and imagination that directly result from the multifaceted challenges posed by immediacy is, to replace nostalgia with an old German joke, "wie Löschpapier aufs Feuer werfen."[21] Without a historical account of time and our temporal imagination and by further collapsing all time into immediacy, presence indeed rises to the defining condition and ultimate limit of thought and art in our time, and like contemporary capitalism, this presence champions immediacy as an instrumental relation to the real world and the literary text.

Rahv argues that the American novelist "exhibits a singular pattern" that defines the American novel, a pattern "consisting, on the one hand, of a disinclination to thought and, on the other, of an intense predilection for the real: and the real appears in it as a vast phenomenology swept by waves of sensation and feeling."[22] But today this description applies more readily to literary criticism than to the novel. And given Rahv's admittedly somewhat hamfisted account of the American novel and the much more nuanced and persuasive account of the relation between character and ideas in the Jamesian tradition of American realism that McGurl outlines, the fact that the contemporary American time novel conceives of its possibility in our era as directly wedded to the critique of experience and the turn toward examinations of ideas in time constitutes an important event in the history of the American novel. Lesjak argues for the value of a Jamesonian account of reading that "maintains an emphasis on the value of narrative (via Ricoeur's notion of "narrative intelligence" and Hayden White's idea of "emplotment") and its unique capacity to hold multiple temporalities together," which, Lesjak argues, means to read for the ways in which narrative is able to "make time and history appear."[23] We find precisely such a form of reading and narrative in the contemporary novel's account of its own relation to time. After all, novels like Yu's *How to Live Safely* not only suggest that the Present-Indefinite is bad for art. Yu's novel also shows that we need a time machine to allow us to explore time itself—and novelistic narrative is this time machine. The unnamed narrator of *How to Live Safely* travels through time and thereby writes a narrative: the novel that we are reading. And traveling through time by way of narrative allows him to navigate a world made by narrative, in a time machine that "runs on a state-of-the-art chronodiegetical technology: a six-cylinder grammar drive built on a quad-core physics engine, which features an applied temporalinguistics architecture allowing for free-form navigation within a rendered environment, such as, for instance, a story space, and, in particular, a science fictional universe."[24]

The aim of my argument here is limited to the time novel and thus to only one facet of the contemporary novel—albeit, I would suggest, a very important one. Still, there are, of course, just as many contemporary novels that make a good case for mood, sensuousness, and immediacy as there are novels that critique experience and immediacy. Likewise, I should foreground once more to avoid potential misunderstandings that I do not wish to suggest that literary critical approaches with an investment in immediacy, sensuousness, and experience have no merit in the current moment. But I do want to argue that a number of problems emerge when experience and immediacy are our primary or, even worse, our sole analytical framework for examining today's temporal crisis. The critique of immediacy in the contemporary time novel reveals that our ability to tell time experiences a crisis when interpretation is conflated with experience or we lose sight of the possibility of reading time as form in history. I certainly do not wish to circumvent fascinating recent debates about the relationship among experience, affect, and interpretation.[25] Instead, I propose here a way to reframe the debate by focusing on how the contemporary novel itself understands what it means to read a novel in the present. A greater appreciation of the novel's own account of its function in the present and its ability to develop solutions for the crises of imagination that define our time allows us to develop literary critical approaches that are formulated in concert with the novel's own theories of reading. In this way, we are also able to generate some answers to a pressing question for contemporary literary criticism: What is the point of reading novels today?

The strongest contemporary accounts of reading that focus on affect and other forms of immediacy formulate analyses of the possibility of literature in close connection with the particular historical and sociopolitical conditions of the present. The strength of such analyses arises in part from their rigorously developed understanding of the relation between immediacy and the material logic of our moment. Rachel Greenwald Smith's 2015 book *Affect and American Literature in the Age of Neoliberalism*, for example, shows that recent American literature's engagement with emotions stands in polar opposition to neoliberalism's often damaging emphasis on the individual.[26] Greenwald Smith's examination of the American novel's treatment of the relation between feeling and form provides an important parallel to the examination of the relation among time, interpretation, and form that we find in the contemporary time novel. Similarly, Sean Grattan's 2017 book *Hope Isn't Stupid: Utopian Affects in Contemporary American Literature* develops an understanding of affective reading that is finely attuned to the specific material and historical conditions of the present.[27] While the time novel shows that we must explore the plurality of temporalities that together make up our present in a moment when capitalism seeks to collapse all forms of temporal knowledge into a singular sense of presence and experiential synchronicity, Grattan argues that it is of the utmost importance to wrest a hopeful plurality of feeling and affect from a present in which the term *austerity* names not only an economic and sociopolitical strategy but also an affective one: a reduction of feeling in an austere world in which hope is branded as naive and unrealistic. Literature, Grattan illustrates, can model for us richer ways of "belonging" than the impoverished modes of existence mapped out for us by neoliberal capitalism. It is worth defending hope, Grattan argues passionately and persuasively, and literature offers one way of doing so. Here, Grattan develops an account of the function and importance of literature today that complements the possibility of the time novel to model for us new ways of telling time and of imagining our relation to the present. What aligns *How to Read a Moment* with projects such as Greenwald Smith's or Grattan's, therefore, is the conviction that literature in general and the novel in particular are able to formally engage with the pressing sociopolitical and philosophical crises of our time in ways that generate answers and solutions unavailable to other modes of thought or knowledge. Greenwald Smith and Grattan develop their analyses based on a firm grasp of the material and social challenges produced by the current stage of capitalism, and it is my aim to follow the admirable example their scholarship sets for us.

Let me conclude this section by returning to the history of the novel. The contemporary time novel's critique of experience and the form of temporal reading it formulates based on this critique are not unique to our moment. Rather, they mark an important stage in the novel's overall historical development. To appreciate the full significance of the contemporary time novel, that is, we must locate its treatment of the tension among time, form, and experience in the context of the novel's historical development, which is itself driven forward by the novel's changing engagement with this very tension. Here, it is helpful to revisit Hans Robert Jauß's theory of the novel, which illustrates the significance of the novel's relation to time for its rise and historical development.[28] The novel's ability to resolve the problem of the epic's timelessness, Jauß argues, is bound up with what he describes as "Balzac's Geniestreich" (stroke of genius): the development of the realist novel away from the model of the singular novel and toward the novelistic cycle (*Zyklus*).[29] The form of the novelistic cycle is in turn perfected by Proust, Jauß argues, in whose work the continuity of narration both on the level of the event (external time) and on the level of consciousness (internal time) is perpetually interrupted and undercut by the discontinuity of Marcel's memory. In Proust, time appears as "moi successifs," through the development of identity that is bound to the schism between time and memory. But while, as Jauß argues, the "experience [*Erfahrung*] of time" comes to function "as the immediate object of novelistic reality," in particular in the context of modernist subjectivism, as in Proust and Joyce or in the context of the novel's interest in the psychology of temporality, time itself tends to disappear from the everyday in the modernist novel. Just as, in McGurl's account, ideas in the realist novel in the Jamesian tradition only matter insofar as they shape and are mediated by a character's experience, time in the modernist novel is not examined in itself but is largely a matter of the perception of time's passing, of the changes in the present that, as Jauß shows, "are felt via individual shocks registered by the subject."[30] As a consequence, time is not examined objectively, and the modernist novel by and large lacks a conception of *Systemzeit*.

And yet it is precisely this significant distinction between the novels of Proust and Joyce and the novels of Mann and Musil that represents a further development in the novel's engagement with time. Whereas the narrator of Mann's *Buddenbrooks* (1901) still wonders whether it is possible to "narrate time itself . . . in and for itself," Jauß suggests, working out answers to this question becomes Mann's central task during the twelve-year composition of *The Magic Mountain*.[31] For Jauß, this question signals a break with the novelistic tradition of nineteenth-century Germany, which continues to exert its influence in the beginning decades of the twentieth century. By attempting to address time itself in *The Magic Mountain*, Mann moves beyond the temporality of the family chronicle. It is no longer the relation between the fate of a family before the backdrop of a particular historical moment, Jauß argues, but time itself, detached from matters of pure content, that becomes the novel's main interest.[32] Jauß's account of the novel's turn to examinations of time itself therefore provides us with an account of the rise of the time novel as a particular stage of the novel's overall development crucially shaped by its relation to time and the temporal imaginary. In contrast to the novels of Proust and Joyce, Mann's *The Magic Mountain* can be understood as one point of origin for the true time novel understood as a novel that aims to examine time as form in itself. And insofar as the novel's development is fundamentally connected to its engagement with time, Mann introduces a kind of novel built on the dialectic of temporal and novelistic form. Simply put, the time novel's examination of time as form is always bound up with and made possible by an examination of the novel's own historically specific possibility.

In order to treat time not as the experience of the protagonist but in and through itself, Jauß shows, Mann juxtaposes the temporal perspective of "the flatlands" (historical time and the time of the novel's narrator) with Castorp's gradual "hermetic enchantment into timelessness," which aims to express the protagonist's gradual escape from time as "an objective process." One of the main artistic strategies that Mann deploys to this end is the same strategy we encounter in the contemporary American time novel: the "standing now," the nunc stans in which time arrests and expands.[33] The juxtaposition of historical time and the standing time of the protagonist's subjective experience stands opposed to the treatment of time in Joyce's *Ulysses* (1922). In *Ulysses*, Jauß contends, time is the "unmediated mirror of [the protagonist's] consciousness" and as such no longer the object of narration but instead its "subject and the 'donnée immediate' of novelistic reality."[34] This difference comes with important limitations for the Joycean time novel, and it is of crucial importance for the contemporary time novel, for whenever the engagement with time is confined to immediacy, we witness the collapse of plural, competing temporalities into a broad spectrum of presence with which the novel can only engage on the level of the character's experience. As we have seen throughout this book, the time novel comes to us in threefold form: as a direct engagement with history to reconstruct the internal picture of an epoch, as in *Kahlschlag* literature; as an examination of time as subjective experience (modernist subjectivism and postmodernism's interest in temporal experience); and as an examination of time itself in history, which is to say as a critique of time as a form of knowledge, as a narrative that makes (meaning of) the world. The latter version of the time novel extends into our present, in the context of which its commitment to the critique of immediacy and experience assumes a vital role in the novel's ability to address the problem of time's separation from history and in which temporal immediacy poses a profound challenge for our ability to examine time as form. The contemporary time novel's commitment to reading time historically and developing a critique of the limits of temporal knowledge today thus constitutes a further development of a tradition of the time novel that originates in the work of Mann and Musil, in contradistinction to the phenomenological time novels of Proust and Joyce. In other words, the contemporary, formalist time novel, following Mann, treats time as a problem of standpoint. The phenomenological time novel treats time as a matter of point of view.

INTERPRETIVE IMMEDIACY: SEEING EVERYTHING AT ONCE

The unnamed narrator of Ben Lerner's novel *10:04* (2014) is a young writer in the process of turning a well-received short story that he published in the *New Yorker* into a novel. When asked by his agent how he plans to expand upon the short story, the narrator regrets his initial answer: "'I'll project myself into several futures simultaneously,' I should have said, 'a minor tremor in my hand; I'll work my way from irony to sincerity in the sinking city, a would-be Whitman of the vulnerable grid.'"[35] Ultimately, the narrator delivers on his Whitmanian aspirations. In the early passages of the novel, however, he is largely preoccupied with the possibility that the city in which he lives may indeed sink. The residents of Lerner's New York City live in constant fear of the expected arrival of a major storm that could plunge the city into chaos. Yet the narrator is not so much scared as he is thrilled by the prospect of an approaching storm that, forecasters suggest, "may be historical." He reflects on his exhilaration in the face of potential destruction and finds that he is "excited by foreboding and something else, something like the feel of a childhood snow day when time was emancipated from institutions, when snow seemed like a technology for defeating time, or like defeated time itself falling from the sky, each glittering ice particle an instant gifted back from your routine" (18). A big storm or a major environmental catastrophe signals a disruption of the rhythm of the everyday to the narrator. Such events strike him as a way to temporarily pause the hectic rhythm of life and step outside the temporal uniformity of the quotidian. The big storm never hits, however, and everyday life continues in its regular rhythm, which, as the narrator observes, deprives the present of the sense of history that large-scale destruction seems to promise: "Another historic storm had failed to arrive, as though we lived outside of history or were falling out of time" (230).

Lerner's novel asks how we might recover history and a sense of temporal development in our present. Historic storms, it becomes clear, are not the solution. Big storms and natural catastrophes are the adult equivalent of childhood snow days: they offer only momentary reprieves from the relentless rhythm of the everyday. Rather than setting time and history back in motion, they circumvent the problem by affording us ways to temporarily avoid the time of routine. More troublingly, however, the hope for historic storms compounds the present's stasis insofar as the responsibility for changing the conditions of the present is displaced from humanity onto nature. Instead of conceiving of history as the temporality that results from the actions of people in the present, the residents of New York City look to heavy weather to provide the catalyst for large-scale, historic change. By understanding historic change as resulting from (or requiring) natural disasters, we grant ourselves absolution from the responsibility for change: we imagine historic change as events that happen to humanity as opposed to events that humanity brings about. The fascination with natural disasters and apocalyptic destruction, events that create change in a situation in which mankind struggles to address and resolve its problems, is therefore involved in creating the impression of an ahistorical and static present. The idea of a historic storm is also connected to a distinct sense of escapism and nostalgic longing, to the wish for a return to simpler times made possible by the destruction of the present world. Accordingly, Judy Wajcman argues that calls for "deceleration" are an "inadequate intellectual and political response" to the temporal crises of our time. After all, she writes, "wistfully looking back to an idealized slower time and mourning its passing has long been the preserve of conservative political theory."[36] To wish for the arrival of a catastrophic natural event that helps us slow down or interrupt the present in order to solve the problems posed by real-time capitalism is as sensible a solution as getting a lobotomy to solve the problems posed by cognitive capitalism.

But if slowing down or escaping the time of the present is not the answer, then what is a suitable intellectual and political response to the time of the long now? If the time of our present is defined by immediacy, and if the speed and indeed the structural logic of real-time capitalism result in systemic unreadability, then it might seem that we need a way of seeing or reading the present that is designed for the age of immediacy. While purchasing supplies to prepare for the arrival of a big storm, the narrator of Lerner's novel has a striking experience. The narrator gazes at a jar of instant coffee and has a revelation:

> I held the red plastic container, one of the last three on the shelf, held it like the marvel that it was: the seeds of the purple fruits of coffee plants had been harvested on Andean slopes and roasted and ground and soaked and then dehydrated at a factory in Medellin and vacuum-sealed and flown to JFK and then driven upstate in bulk to Pearl River for repackaging and then transported back by truck to the store where I now stood reading the label. It was as if the social relations that produced the object in my hand began to glow within it as they were threatened, stirred inside their packaging, lending it a certain aura—the majesty and murderous stupidity of that organization of time and space and fuel and labor becoming visible in the commodity itself now that planes were grounded and the highways were starting to close. (19)

As he examines the object in his hands, the narrator reads not only the coffee can's label but also, in an instant, the entirety of the system of production and commodification that underlies the object in his hands. The social and material relations that the commodity ordinarily masks become apparent to him. This experience raises two problems of reading. First, for a brief, magical moment, the narrator is able to read the totality of capitalism. Second, the narrator is able to grasp the totality of social and material relations that ordinarily constitute the unreadable content of a commodity through his immediate connection to the object itself. Instances of longing for magical solutions to two notorious obstacles to reading—the unreadability of the totality of material relations and the impossibility of immediacy in interpretive processes—are not unique to Lerner's novel.

Dwight, the protagonist of Ben Kunkel's novel *Indecision*, responds to the timelessness and lack of change that characterize his life in New York City by nostalgically idealizing life in Communist Romania. But while the desire to travel back in time does not offer him a solution to the challenges of life in the present, Dwight does find an answer to his problems by leaving New York City and traveling to Ecuador. On a jungle tour, he meets Brigid, a young Belgian woman. Deep in the Ecuadorian jungle, high on a potent local drug, Dwight and Brigid have a conversation that radically changes how he engages with the present. Brigid asks Dwight to consider an imaginary fruit: "When you eat from this fruit then whenever you put your hand on a product, a commodity, an article, then, at the moment of your touch, how this commodity came into your hands becomes plainly evident to you. . . . We will feel it" (216). Dwight considers the potential implications of such a way of seeing the world and its objects while eating a *tomate de árbol*—and is suddenly struck by the sense that he is able to see the world in just the way described by Brigid:

> It was like flying over water and then when you looked down to the ocean the skim of mirror was yanked off, so that the water became transparent, and there the sea was, filled with what you knew had always been there: the rubbery gardens and drowned mountains, the creatures from plankton up to nekton, the swimming bodies and unburied skeletons, and now you—or I—I saw it all at once. And so in this fucked-up San Pedrified way the entire world system of neoliberal capitalism disclosed itself to me. (217)

The dream of interpretive immediacy, of "seeing it all at once," also features prominently in Yu's *How to Live Safely*, which I examine in more detail later in this chapter. In Yu's novel, the (once again unnamed) narrator travels through time and describes the act of "gliding into the present" as follows: "Sliding into the time corridor, you can see it all, the spiky skyline, high and low points in the overall texture and layout of the past and future of this place . . . an entire day's worth of movements, an entire day all at once, not a blur, not an average, but the totality of the day" (57). It seems, then, that it is this way of reading the present, seeing it all at once and being able to read the totality of capitalism or of time itself, should provide us with a mode of interpretation that allows us to make sense of the time and logic of the omnipresent instant. But the problem with the dream of interpretive immediacy lies not just in the fact that it is only a fictional relation to the present, a thought experiment that requires magical coffee cans, mystical fruits, or time travel. The actual problem with this much sought-after solution is that it ultimately collapses back upon itself. Immediacy, these novels shows, is not the solution. It merely reifies the problem, particularly in a moment in history built upon a temporal regime that tends toward immediacy. By engaging with the idea of interpretive immediacy, with the dream of being able to see it all at once, novels like those of Lerner, Kunkel, and Yu grapple with the challenges of a time and a mode of capitalism in which everything seems to happen at once. It is crucially through its engagement with the problem of immediacy that the time novel is able to offer us a different way of reading the time of the present.

The problem of immediacy and its relation to the desire to see it all at once is not a new one for the novel. In fact, it is a central aspect of Thomas Mann's account of the *Zeitroman*. Mann argues that one of the central features of the time novel is its engagement with the problem of the *nunc stans*, the standing now. The idea of the *nunc stans* has a long history that features prominently in the philosophy of time. From Boethius's "now that remains" and Saint Thomas Aquinas's "simultaneous whole" to Hannah Arendt's "standing now" and Jorge Luis Borges's "Aleph," the *nunc stans* is generally understood to mark the opposite of the *nunc fluens*, the moving now. The concept expresses a relation between time and the present that locates the source of the time itself in the present's flow. The basic logic of the relation remains unchanged since Boethius's suggestion that "Nunc fluens facit tempus, nunc stans facit aeternitatum":[37] the present that moves, passes, and changes creates time; the present that stands still creates eternity. The idea of the *nunc stans* associates the phenomenon of a present that no longer changes or passes with eternity and the end of time itself. The eternity that results from the *nunc stans* is associated with divine knowledge of the world: knowing and seeing at once all that is happening, all that has happened, and all that will happen. Absolute, immediate knowledge collapses time into the perpetual, standing now. This notion of eternity is therefore not a matter of eternal life, which would absolve us from death and aging and permit us to watch history unfold before our eyes. Instead, the eternity of the *nunc stans* is marked by the absolute stasis and lack of development that results from a situation in which we are able to see everything at once. This is, after all, the famous problem of Borges's Aleph: it is precisely the desire to see it all at once, to catch a glimpse of the totality of life and of the world, that cancels out time, history, and any possible notion of change.[38] It is also for this reason that the time and structure of real-time capitalism, in which everything happens at once, is connected to systemic unreadability and the perceived stasis of time. And just as the structure of real-time capitalism cannot be read without erasing the very logic that stabilizes it, the tension between immediacy and the desire to see it all at once creates a crisis for both knowledge and representation. The temporal and interpretive problem posed by the desire to see everything at once finds expression in the famous problem of Borges's Aleph: the Aleph can be neither narrated nor imagined. Thus, while the idea of seeing it all at once initially seems to promise a way to read the totality of capitalism—the relation to the now for which the protagonists of Lerner's and Kunkel's novels search—it ultimately reproduces the very relations of immediacy with which the novels' protagonists struggle. Immediacy, Kunkel's novel humorously suggests, does not lead to difference, the true object of Dwight's search; it leads back to—or more accurately, it is unable to leave—the plane of identity. Instead of understanding the totality of the world, Dwight ultimately only sees himself: he finds out who he truly is. And as he is surprised to discover, his true self is a democratic socialist. While excited to finally have discovered who he really is, Dwight is also tearful, since he feels "definitely a little apprehensive about the hard study of political economy that [he] would have to do" to fully develop and further confirm his "undeniable" intuition regarding his identity (217).

The dream of interpretive immediacy, of being able to see it all at once, is therefore an aspect of the long-standing desire for the atonement of subject and object, of self and world, of the desire to know the world fully and to grasp the thing in itself. In our time, as the novels of Lerner and Kunkel show, the desire for interpretive immediacy begets merely another version of the immediacy that underlies our struggle with the eternal now: it reproduces the present as *nunc stans*. And yet the narrator's encounter with the *nunc stans* in Lerner's novel sets in motion a development that ultimately leads to a solution to the problem of our seemingly ahistorical present. Throughout the remainder of the novel, the narrator confronts the problem of the present's ahistoricity as a problem of interpretation. Lerner's novel asks which interpretive methods might offer us ways to read the present historically. Through his critical engagement with art and its interpretation, the narrator is able to examine the value and limits of different interpretive methodologies. Lerner's novel suggests that the question of how we make sense of art affords us insights into the differences between interpretive strategies that in turn allow us to see the possibilities and limitations of our temporal imaginary and thus produce readings of the present. In this way, through its self-reflexive interrogation of the relation between art and reading, Lerner's novel offers us a concrete example of what it means to understand the novel not only as a form of knowledge (it presents different ways of reading, telling, and knowing time) but as a critique of knowledge (it reveals our relation to time as the result of different forms of temporal knowledge and allows us to see their historical limits).

We can trace this logical development in Lerner's novel by examining the narrator's changing relation to time. The narrator continues to reflect on the interpretive methods invited by different art forms, and he ultimately develops an account of the parallel relation between interpreting an artwork and making meaning of time. Still reeling from his experience with the container of instant coffee, he notices that even familiar photographs on his girlfriend's refrigerator are "no longer entirely familiar" (19). The photographs seem different, "as if the image were newly indeterminate, flickering between temporalities" (20). Later that same evening, the narrator rewatches his favorite movie, *Back to the Future*, and notices a similar flickering between temporalities, which also signals a difference in meaning. Key scenes in the 1985 movie acquire a strikingly different meaning when read in the context of the present. "In the movie," he notes, "they lack plutonium to power the time-traveling car, whereas in real life it's seeped into the Fukushima soil; *Back to the Future* was ahead of its time" (22). In addition to the changes in meaning that the temporality of an object may produce, the narrator also reflects on the significance of the mid-1980s for our understanding of time and in turn for his development as a writer. He recalls sitting in a classroom decorated with "letters to Christa McAuliffe in exaggerated cursive, wishing her luck on the *Challenger* mission, which was only a couple of months in the future" (14). His sense of the moment's resignification through memory is heightened by the fact that he also remembers "build[ing] a diorama of the future with a boy" who, he now knows, "will hang himself" (14). He remembers 1986 as the year that marks the death of his innocent belief in the future. In fact, the *Challenger* catastrophe signals to him the end of American society's ability to look at the future with optimism. Temporal imaginaries and conceptions of the future, he realizes, have shelf lives. They are exhausted by historical events that make it impossible to maintain ideas of the future whose meaning has been radically changed. The narrator remembers particularly vividly Ronald Reagan's desperate attempt in the aftermath of the *Challenger* disaster to keep alive the techno-optimism of the space race and the association of the future with technological innovation and scientific discovery that had crashed along with the spacecraft. He recalls a particular passage of Reagan's address to the nation:

> And I want to say something to the schoolchildren of America who were watching the live coverage of the shuttle's takeoff. I know it is hard to understand, but sometimes painful things like this happen. It's all part of the process of exploration and discovery. It's all part of taking a chance and expanding man's horizons. The future doesn't belong to the fainthearted; it belongs to the brave. The Challenger crew was pulling us into the future, and we'll continue to follow them. (15–16)

Reagan's speech and its continued appeal to the narratives of techno-optimism that it attempts to preserve signify for the narrator a moment of historical transition, a time when the future crashes into the present and we struggle to develop new narratives of the future. He decided to become a writer, the narrator remembers later in the novel, because the *Challenger* disaster signaled the beginning of a new moment in history: "The dawning of our era of live disasters and simulcast wars" (10). The immediacy of the experience of the *Challenger* disaster on live TV strikes the narrator as a poignant indication of the logic of this new era. "I don't have a single friend who doesn't remember watching it as it happened," he tells us, recalling the significance of the live television event that signaled the crash of the future into the present. Everyone watched the event, he notes, "not as a replay later when you knew the shuttle was doomed, but when you expected the shuttle to disappear successfully into space and instead saw it engulfed in a giant fireball, saw the branching plumes of smoke as its components fell back to earth" (111).

The significance of the simulcast event also foregrounds the narrator's interest in the problem of immediacy and the ways in which art and culture are involved in creating and maintaining an era's dominant temporal regimes. Art allows the protagonist to reflect on how we make meaning of time in the age of immediacy. As in DeLillo's *Point Omega*, the examination of the relation between temporal and artistic interpretation in Lerner's novel is determined by the narrator's visit to a twenty-four-hour video work. The narrator of *10:04* visits Christian Marclay's *The Clock*, which, he tells us, is "a twenty-four-hour montage of thousands of scenes from movies and a few from TV edited together so as to be shown in real time; each scene indicates the time with a shot of a timepiece or its mention in dialogue; time in and outside of the film is synchronized" (52). By synchronizing the respective clock times of the montage and everyday reality, the installation allows the protagonist to examine the relation between clock time and the rhythm of the quotidian. Moreover, the installation illustrates that the centrality of clock time in our lives depends upon the work of culture and different cultural mediums and technologies. One of the work's most striking aspects for the narrator is its ability to reveal the temporal regimes that underlie real time. "Marclay had formed a supragenre that made visible our collective, unconscious sense of the rhythms of the day," he notes (52). By confronting him with the question of how "The Clock can be integrated into an overarching narrative" (52), the installation alerts the narrator to the temporal ties that bind individual temporality to an overarching temporal structure embedded in material reality that is reinforced by the temporal work of culture. "I'd heard The Clock described as the ultimate collapse of fictional time into real time," the narrator recalls, "a work designed to obliterate the distance between art and life, fantasy and reality" (54). But after viewing the work himself, he develops a different reading of the montage. His relation to the work, he notes, is one of distantiation: "I watched time in The Clock, but wasn't in it" (54). The effect of this distantiation is strikingly similar to the manner in which the narrator of *Point Omega* describes his relation to *24 Hour Psycho*. Just like DeLillo's narrator, who believes he is seeing "pure time," the narrator of Lerner's novel finds that the distantiated view of time in *The Clock* leaves him with the impression of "experiencing time as such" and "not just having experiences through it as a medium" (54). This initial recognition of a form of distantiation draws his attention to a second one: "When I looked at my watch to see a unit of measure identical to the one displayed on the screen, I was indicating that a distance remained between art and the mundane" (54). In the same way that art establishes a critical relation to his own relation to time, it defamiliarizes him from his relation to the quotidian and allows him to read the rhythms of the everyday.

But already this first step in the novel's effort to determine what kind of interpretive relation to the present can afford us a historical reading of time may strike some as suspect, since it relies centrally on the idea of aesthetic distance. The notion of aesthetic distance, as Jacques Rancière reminds us, is frequently associated with Kantian logic and thus with a distinctly ahistorical usage that also serves to "conceal social reality" and thus marks "the site *par excellence* of the 'denegation of the social.'"[39] However, there is a different account of aesthetic distance, Rancière emphasizes, in which we can locate a politics of the aesthetic that is at its heart a "politics of the resistant form."[40] This notion of distantiation originates in the work of Bertolt Brecht, and it is, Rancière argues, the precondition for "critical art."[41] This notion of aesthetic distance is the logical foundation of the relation in Lerner's novel between art and the world on one hand and art and time on the other, and it establishes the methodological basis for a historical reading of time. When Rancière speaks of *distanciation* as the precondition for critical art, he refers to the Brechtian *Verfremdungseffekt*, a term that is traditionally translated into English as "estrangement or alienation effect." In the beginning sections of Lerner's novel, the narrator recounts several instances of estrangement that set in motion his reflection on the relation between interpretation and reality in the remainder of the novel. When examining a pair of safety scissors, he notes that his relation to the object is marked by a "vertiginous sensation like a transient but thorough agnosia in which the object in [his] hand . . . ceases to be a familiar tool and becomes an alien artifact, thereby estranging the hand itself, a condition brought on by the intuition of spatial and temporal collapse" (13–14). Such moments of estrangement facilitate the narrator's continued interrogation of our methods for making meaning of objects and the world, and the novel's engagement with time is routed through this framing analysis of our interpretive methods. The narrator's critical examination of thought itself and of time as the often invisible temporality of the everyday requires estrangement, which, he notices, art can facilitate. Distantiated reading and interpretation in *10:04* is made possible by and underscores a sincere belief in the importance of aesthetic distance for art's function and our interpretation of art. Art's critical possibility and its ability to model a form of critical thought that interrogates knowledge originate in the distance between art and the mundane, the distance that allows the reader to transcend the limits of a purely subjective experience of time. The narrator recognizes that *The Clock* transports him outside of time, and this estrangement from time in turn provides him with a distantiated reading of clock time and the temporal rhythm of everyday life. The narrator is thus able to examine how time itself is shaped by temporal imaginaries that, he understands, have histories of their own insofar as they arise under specific historical conditions and are ultimately exhausted by the flow of history. The temporal distance between readings of the movie *Back to the Future* generates differences in meaning. More significantly, however, these differences in meaning draw attention to the temporal development of our understanding of time and futurity itself, and in this way the novel sets into motion a historical critique of time as a form of knowledge.

The commitment to distantiation as the counterpoint to interpretive immediacy in novels like *10:04* utilizes a strategy that we associate more readily with speculative fiction, which, through cognitive estrangement, allows us to see our world through strange eyes, making legible aspects of life that we ordinarily do not notice.[42] In this sense, *10:04*, as well as the novels of DeLillo, can be understood as aiming at cognitive estrangement from time in order to make time itself legible as narrative. In turn, time is understood as a form of knowledge whose meaning and ability to make meaning of the world depend upon historical context. To read our present historically is to examine it through strange eyes. But Lerner's novel also foregrounds the importance of developing such a distantiated, critical view of time by rejecting interpretive immediacy and a focus on the subjective experience of time. We can understand this historicizing relation to time with Peter Boxall as a relation of "presence" that stands opposed to the pure presentism of the long now. Boxall reminds us of Mark Currie's important suggestion that "presence requires a kind of self-distance." "Fiction itself," Boxall argues, "does not protect us from this fact, but emerges from it. . . . [F]iction itself comes into being as it registers the difference from self that is part of every narrative reflection—the distance that is the job of narrative both to open, and to close."[43] In Lerner's novel, self-distance serves as an important precondition for a historical reading of time. However, *10:04* goes even farther than suggesting that the focus on time's subjective experience limits us to an immediate relation to temporality which does not allow for a historical reading or critique. The novel in fact argues that the subjective experience of time constitutes an interpretive error when it is understood as establishing a meaningful relation to time. Confusing the interpretation of time with its experience, the novel suggests, causes us to misread time. Rather than making meaning of time, that is, subjective experience imposes only the semblance of meaning onto its object. If the meaning of time is understood to lie in the historical development of time as a form of knowledge, then temporal experience is not meaningful.

10:04's interest in the difference between a meaningful reading of an object and a reading that projects meaning onto an object where there is none is one of the central aspects of the short story the narrator published in the *New Yorker*. The short story, "The Golden Vanity," is inserted into the novel itself and formally mediates and sets into motion the process of aesthetic distantiation that underlies the development of the novel. It is narrated by a young male writer who is only identified as "the author." In the short story, the author meets his friend Hannah in a crowded barroom. Initially, he is not able to recognize her, since, he explains, he is "bad with faces" (68). His inability to recognize a familiar face, however, gives rise to a conversation with Hannah that causes him to question how we recognize or make meaning of faces. Hannah asks him "if he ha[s] ever seen the satellite image of that rock formation in Mars—one of those standard textbook images used to illustrate pareidolia," instances in which "the brain arranges random stimuli into a significant image or sound: faces in the moon, animals in the clouds" (69). Pareidolia is an interpretive operation that locates meaning where there is none. The infamous rock faces on Mars that Hannah references are, of course, not faces. They only look like faces and are only meaningful to those who seek to read them as evidence of (former) life on Mars. Just as my claim that a passing cloud I observe while lying on my back in the grass looks like a bunny does not offer a meaningful reading of the cloud, reading Martian rock formations as faces and cultural traces of an extraterrestrial civilization does not constitute an interpretation of the rock formations. Instead, it is an imposition of subjective response onto the cloud or the rock formation that mimics an interpretive act.

This distinction matters in *10:04*, because the novel's argument for a historical reading of time is predicated upon the rejection of interpretive immediacy, which it equates with a mode of reading that reproduces the very conditions under which the impression of a timeless present emerges. As in the case of the desire to see it all at once, the notion of a timeless present and our inability to imagine alternatives to the eternal now emerge when we replace distantiated critiques of time in history with time's immediate experience—even if the latter purports to register historically specific phenomena. To read time historically, *10:04* suggests, we must avoid pareidolic readings of time. This is not to say that Lerner's novel categorically rejects the value of experiencing art and time. Rather, the value of *10:04* for our moment lies to no small measure in its conviction that our ability to understand the contemporary crisis of temporality as a crisis of our imagination depends upon an examination of time as a form of knowledge whose historical development is marked by periodic moments of crisis. Art, *10:04* shows, can model for us an interpretive relation to time that allows us to understand the meaning of time and its ability to establish meaningful relationships with the world as a result of the specific function assumed by forms of temporal knowledge at different moments in history. If we are interested in determining the meaning of time, especially in an era in which both time and history are said to have ended, then we can look neither to time's experience nor to natural time. We must read time in and as history, for only this interpretation of time will be meaningful.

THE RISK OF PRESENCE

Yu's *How to Live Safely in a Science Fictional Universe* offers us an account of the attempt to make meaning of time that is strikingly similar to that of *10:04*. The tension between the interpretation of time and temporal experience drives the plot and structures the logic of Yu's novel. *How to Life Safely* illustrates the continued significance of the distinction between the focus on subjectivity and temporal experience that Sartre associates with the time novels of Proust and Joyce and the realism of temporality that he locates in the work of Dos Passos. However, as Yu's novel illustrates, the latter tradition of the time novel is not limited to realism. It also extends to and is further developed in speculative fiction.[44] Stuck in the "Present-Indefinite," the unnamed first-person narrator of Yu's novel embarks upon a journey through time with two interrelated aims: he wishes to determine the meaning of time, and he also hopes to find his missing father, the "structural engineer" who invented time travel (5). Shortly after inventing time travel, the narrator's father disappeared, and he has since been lost in time. To the narrator, his father's loss also signifies the loss of linear time, a temporality that strikes him as more comforting than the alienating present in which he is currently stuck. He mourns the loss of the order, comfort, and sense of routine provided by linear time, and he nostalgically associates the time of his father with the ability of standardized clock time to bring stability to his life: "The workweek was a structure, a grid, a matrix that held him in place, a path through time, the shortest distance between birth and death" (35). Now that time has been disconnected from the structures that formerly stabilized it, the narrator finds that he is increasingly sympathetic to the goals of his father, who "searched for systems of thought, for patterns, rules, even instructions" (37). His father's research, we learn, aimed to identify a single, universal system to stabilize time: time's "ultimate origin" (48). The narrator's nostalgic longing for linear temporality and order in the novel's early sections initially assumes that time has a natural origin. Discovering time's origin, he hopes, may help him recover a sense of temporal progression and futurity in his life. And so for the narrator of Yu's novel, too, it initially seems as though finding a way to again imagine the future in the Present-Indefinite requires a retrospective gaze: he must find his lost father and, by doing so, recover a lost sense of time that would allow him to formulate a linear conception of change and progress. His ultimate desire is to leave behind "the Now" and find a "life without the risk of Now," because "Now," he suggests, "is overrated. Now hasn't been working out so great for me" (22). To escape from the Present-Indefinite, the narrator thus decides that he must gain some perspective. To do so, he resolves to travel to "the center of the universe," New York City, which, he hopes, will provide him with perspective: "Only it's not in space. It's perspective in time" (57).

However, the perspective in time that the narrator finds resembles the totalizing gazes of the protagonists of Lerner's and Kunkel's novels. As he arrives in New York City in his time machine, he is able to see everything at once. This ability, however, does not provide him with the insight into time that he had hoped to gain. Instead of leaving behind the Now, he finds himself confronted with timeless omnipresence. And yet his failure to gain perspective through the attempt to see it all at once also yields an important insight. He begins to understand that the solution to his problem lies in a different way of relating to the Now: not to escape from the present but to truly live in time. But to truly live in time, the narrator knows, is a profound struggle: "This is what it feels like to live in time. The lurching forward, the sensation of falling off a cliff into darkness, and then landing abruptly, surprised, confused, and then starting the whole process again, falling into each instant of time and then climbing back up only to repeat the process" (63). Yu's novel understands the absence of change and the struggle with the Present-Indefinite as the consequence of a limit we impose on our temporal imagination and a direct result of the narrator's initial unwillingness to understand presence as a matter of embracing the Now as risk. Ultimately, the narrator learns that there are two ways of living in the Now: the passivity and escapism of his original position of being stuck in the Present-Indefinite and the active embrace of risk that is the mark of true presence. The latter option, he realizes, offers the solution to timelessness. Instead of escaping the present and nostalgically longing for past futures, we must address the challenge of the Present-Indefinite by inhabiting the present actively, as risk. In the final pages of Yu's novel the protagonist urges us to embrace this way of understanding and living in the present, encouraging us to "step out into the world of time and risk and loss" (233).

Embracing the present as risk, the narrator learns, requires us to embrace the loss of past, stable notions of time as well as a certain loss of selfhood. Distance from the self allows the narrator to read and inhabit the present as risk. After a lengthy temporal journey that includes several encounters with himself in different moments in time, the narrator ends up in the same place and time where he began his travels, facing the dilemma with which the story opened, and he shoots himself. "All of that self-storytelling just comes down to this, the most simple of all situations," he explains when once again confronted with his future self, whom he cannot help but shoot:

> The story of a man trying to figure out what he knows, teetering on the edge of yes or no, of risk or safety, whether it is worth it or not to go on, to carry on, into the breach of each successive moment. It's a survival story, too, the story I have been telling myself. Is he friend or foe, this strange person in front of me, enemy or ally, only, in this case, both sides, all sides, they all happen to be the same person, and that person is me, and the answer, in all cases, appears to be foe. I am my own most dangerous enemy. (225)

Self-distance in Yu's novel can be understood as a dialectical negation of the self and recognition of the impossibility of an immediate relation between self and world that in turn allows us to conceive of selfhood and our understanding of the world as a matter of constant development. The perpetual struggle with the unbridgeable gap between self and world, not the ability to see it all at once, creates the temporality that we call history. After all, he notes, limiting our examination of time to experience and the self is "just dandy and fuzzy and self-affirming, except that none of it solves the problem. . . . How many times will I have to destroy myself before I learn, before I understand . . . I am my own limit, and that limit is the present" (228). The ultimate realization that the present ought to be inhabited and understood as risk also allows him to solve the problem of inevitably having to shoot himself. Shooting himself is not a problem, he realizes. It is the answer. Shooting himself means leaving himself behind while simultaneously discovering himself anew, abandoning the idea of a stable, static sense of self and thereby re-creating himself as a developing, historical subject who is able to inhabit the moving present. This notion of self-distance in turn allows him to understand the meaning of time, which lies in time's own perpetual movement and change—and the meaning of time becomes legible to us when we interpret the present as history. The final confrontation with himself leads to a moment of insight: "At the moment I understand it, he does, too, we're both on the verge of it, and so by the time I finish my sentence, he sees, and I see. He knows and I know and he knows I know, and I know he knows. . . . He shoots me . . . and in a sense, one of us dies, and in a sense, we both do, and in a sense, neither of us does" (229). The act of shooting himself marks the narrator's recognition of the need to fully embrace the risk of the Now and seek the meaning of both self and time in those instances when self and time transcend themselves in the confrontation with their limits: "It just happens to be the most excruciating pain that I have ever felt in my entire life, and it feels really good" (231).

The critique of subjective experience in the context of the interpretation of time forwarded by novels like *How to Live Safely* has important consequences for our understanding of literary critical approaches to time and the novel. While the work of Fredric Jameson is indispensable for a literary criticism invested in questions of form and history, Jameson's oeuvre also has limitations that are instructive for our purposes here. Mitchum Huehls shows that Jameson's examination of the contemporary crisis of temporality provides us with important ways to engage with the "fervent cult of presentism" that characterizes our time. However, Huehls argues, Jameson's overall analysis remains limited by his simultaneous rehabilitation of "long-denounced concepts such as lived experience, the subject, and even humanism."[45] Huehls shows that DeLillo's *White Noise* offers us an alternative to this focus on the subject, since it allows us to read temporality as wedded to the "formal production of meaning."[46] Huehls's reading of *White Noise* underscores the importance of the turn away from experience in favor of form for our understanding of the novel's engagement with time. The contemporary time novel shows that our ability to read the present historically depends on an approach to time that privileges form over subjective experience. Through its account of presence as an active relation to the Now as history, novels such as *How to Live Safely* extend a mode of temporal critique that we find, for example, in Pierre Bourdieu's account of the incompatibility of the time of subjective experience and historical time, defined as the time of practice. And insofar as it examines time as form, which is to say as a form of knowledge that is also a form of world making, the time novel understands its own work in just this way: as a form of practice. "The production of time that occurs in and through practice has nothing to do with an experience (in the sense of *Erlebnis*) of time, even if it presupposes an experience (in the sense of *Erfahrung*)," Bourdieu writes in The Rules of Art.[47] In Minima Moralia, Adorno makes this argument even more pointedly: "Considerations which start from the subject remain false to the same extent that life has become appearance. . . . Subjective reflection, even if critically alerted to itself, has something sentimental and anachronistic about it: something of a lament over the course of the world, a lament to be rejected not for its good faith, but because the lamenting subject threatens to become arrested in its condition."[48]

READING TAKES TIME; OR, THE MEANING OF PAUSES

Walter Benjamin reminds us that historical analysis is particularly important in the context of "a present which is not a transition, but in which time has come to a stop." In fact, Benjamin argues, instances in which time ceases to flow bring with them not only crises but also opportunities for thought. After all, he writes, "thinking involves not just the flow of thoughts, but their arrest as well." Moments when both time and thought stop create a "configuration pregnant with tensions."[49] The narrator of Lerner's *10:04* is fascinated by such moments of arrest. He plans to arrive at a performance of *The Clock* at a particular time, precisely *10:04*, "to see lightning strike the courthouse clock tower in *Back to the Future*" (52). The time *10:04* designates for the narrator one moment in which time's arrest creates the preconditions for a reflection on time and history itself, for examining the narratives upon which our understanding of temporality and futurity rests. The narrator's interest in Benjamin's treatment of time and in the lightning strike on the clock in 1985's *Back to the Future* at *10:04* invokes Benjamin's account of the shots that were fired at a clock during the July Revolution of 1830.[50] For Benjamin and for the narrator, the stopped clock marks not the end of time but the end of a historical period; it designates a momentary suspension of temporality that is pregnant with anticipation. Time's arrest offers the possibility for transition into a new historical situation, and the momentary pause in the flow of time makes possible the critical engagement with the Now out of which new forms of thought may arise. Instead of bringing about a dead end for thought and temporality, the paused present affords us precisely that time—those nonmoments, in DeLillo's terms—that make possible a reflection on time itself and thus encourage the creation of new forms of telling time. For the narrator, the performance of *The Clock* provides him with a more complex, dynamic way of understanding the time of the present, and he recognizes, at *10:04*, "acutely how many different days could be built out of a day" (55). This understanding of the plural present in history, which sets in motion the narrator's attempt to read time in history and ultimately develop a new idea of futurity, returns us to Benjamin's suggestion that time arises from history itself, for "the nourishing fruit of the historically understood contains time as a precious but tasteless seed."[51]

The suggestion that pauses are as important for our understanding of historical time as the flow of temporality also determines the engagement with the "goon" that is time in Jennifer Egan's 2010 novel *A Visit from the Goon Squad*. One of the novel's protagonists, the music producer Bennie, nostalgically longs for a lost past. In the past, Bennie is convinced, music was better—and it was better because it was not perfect: "Bennie knew that what he was bringing into the world was shit. Too clean, too clear. The problem was precision, perfection; the problem was digitization, which sucked the life out of everything that got smeared through its microscopic mesh. Film, photography, music: dead. *An aesthetic holocaust!*"[52] Bennie understands the perfection of music in the digital age as a sign of the end of music's historical development—the end point of an aesthetic project whose life was directly connected to the lack of perfection. Perfection erases the sense of progress, development, and innovation that Bennie loves about prior moments in music history. Bennie longs specifically for the music of the 1970s, which he views as the last decade during which the gaze of music was still directed forward. From the beginning, however, it is clear that Egan's novel centrally revolves around a critique of nostalgia as an inadequate response to the present. *Goon Squad* locates the source of these nostalgic longings historically, in the conditions of our time, and urges us to assume a different intellectual relationship to the present. One of the novel's other protagonists, Jules, anticipates the novel's ultimate answer to this problem in a conversation with his sister Stephanie about their struggle with the present and their sense that they are unable to imagine a positive future. Jennifer, Jules notes, keeps "thinking of the old days" because she feels "like everything is ending." "If you asked me this morning, I would have said we're finished. . . . All of us, the whole country—the fucking world," Jules comments on his own view of the future, "but now I feel the opposite." "So, what's the answer?" Stephanie inquires, to which Jules responds, "Sure, everything is ending . . . but not yet" (132).

Jules's understanding of the present as the time of the "not yet" mirrors the logic of the closing sentences of *How to Live Safely*, in which the novel's narrator explains what it means to inhabit the present as risk: "Move forward, into the empty plane. Find the book you wrote, and read it until the end, but don't turn the last page yet, keep stalling, see how long you can keep expanding the infinitely expandable moment. Enjoy the elastic present, which can accommodate as little or as much as you want to put in there. Stretch it out, live inside of it" (233). But the not yet of the paused present is not just a matter of deferring the end that gives rise to time itself. It also contains a utopian dimension inasmuch as the not yet of the expandable moment harbors the latent potential that lies in the present. Yu's novel offers us a way of understanding the purported absorption of the future into the present as a historical moment in which we need to think time and the future differently. In this moment, it is of vital importance to understand utopia and futurity as a matter of change and agency in the present, as a project of reclaiming the moment and expanding it precisely through the act of actively inhabiting the Now. Yu's novel closes with a final page that reads: "[this page intentionally left blank]" (234). The writing and reading of the unblank blankness of the final page of *How to Live Safely* marks an opening in the present that arises from the commitment to living in the Now unsafely, embracing the present as risk.

Like Yu's novel, *Goon Squad* suggests that the way to respond to the challenges of our time in a way that does not succumb to nostalgic or escapist desires is to inhabit the moment. As in Yu's novel, this requires stalling and pausing. One of the most memorable characters in Egan's novel, a young boy named Lincoln, has a peculiar hobby of central importance to the logic of *Goon Squad*: he collects and catalogs pauses in music. Lincoln enjoys long pauses in songs because they seem to toy with the sense of an ending and thereby ask us to reflect on time itself. Lincoln also "loops the pauses in each song," so that they "last for minutes" (246). A particularly notable chapter in *Goon Squad* takes the form of a PowerPoint presentation that illustrates the intricacies of Lincoln's hobby. Egan has explained that PowerPoint offers interesting opportunities for the interrogation of time, since "PowerPoint itself is a form structured around moments separated by pauses." The value of pauses, according to Egan, is that they help us become aware of time passing "in the moments where it seems to have stopped."[53] The pauses in Egan's novel, especially in the PowerPoint chapter, transform the present stillness of our time into an opportunity to read time itself. The insertion of the PowerPoint chapter and the engagement with pauses in Egan's novel return our analysis to the temporal possibilities of the novel form and novelistic reading, which are structured around pauses that allow us to read time in and of itself. While pauses that disrupt music work in contradistinction to the regular logic of the medium and stand out as notable exceptions to the expected rhythm of music, instances in which novels cause us to pause and linger in order to engage with an idea, a sentence, or a word disappear because they are the very foundation of novelistic reading. Novels like *Goon Squad* and *Point Omega* illustrate that novelistic reading is based on a relation between interpretation and temporality that music and cinema can only approximate by disrupting the fundamental temporality of the medium itself.

Novelistic reading allows for a relation to time that refuses the logic of the temporal regime of real-time capitalism. Philosophers including Byung-Chul Han have been calling for just such a relation to time. Han argues that the current crisis of temporality is a consequence of erasing the "possibility of contemplation" and the "ability to linger" from our lives.[54] So-called "strategies for deceleration," he adds, do not provide solutions to the problem. They in fact hide it. What is required instead is a revitalization of what Han describes as the *vita contemplativa*, a way of life aimed at contemplation and examination.[55] Han argues that contemporary capitalism disrupts our ability to lead an examined, contemplative live. Consumer culture in particular, he shows, causes us to unlearn the art of contemplative lingering, since capitalism's constant imperative to consume abolishes the sense of duration required by contemplative lingering.[56] Simply reducing the speed of the present, however, does not transform the current state of things. After all, Han stresses, both slow food and fast food stand in the same relation to consumer capitalism: they are made to be consumed.[57] Moreover, the fragmentation of historical time in our era, which Han describes as leading to the creation of "atomized time," further erodes the possibility of contemplative lingering.[58]

The novel offers us precisely such a possibility for lingering and thus a way of reading the present that stands opposed to the incentive to experience the immediate present upon which the logic of real-time capitalism rests. Moreover, as we see in the novels of Lerner, Yu, and Egan, the lingering facilitated by novelistic reading is not merely contemplative but in fact critical insofar as these novels draw our attention to pauses as a relation to the present that makes it possible to historicize the present and time itself. Understood from this standpoint, being stuck in traffic on the way to a haircut is not entirely bad as long as it leads to a critical examination of the present, as in the case of DeLillo's *Cosmopolis*. Pauses and lingering are not about moments of simple disruption that momentarily absolve us from the time of the quotidian. Novelistic lingering, *10:04* shows, is not like a snow day. It gives way neither to nostalgia nor to escapism. Instead, it facilitates a critical relation to the moment as history, and it encourages us to dwell critically on contradictions of the present that otherwise remain unexamined. It is no accident, thus, that those contemporary novels offering us some of the most striking analyses of time in history, including the novels of Gibson, DeLillo, Lerner, Yu, and Egan, but also those of John Wray, Ruth Ozeki, Rachel Kushner, and Paul Harding, are all what we might call novels of interpretation.[59] The discontinuous and variable temporality of novelistic reading, which is connected to pauses and lingering, facilitates the cognitive estrangement associated with the time novel's critique of the present. The novel's encouragement to linger and pause is aimed at distantiation from the present and thereby sheds light on the darkness of the moment. Han argues that beauty itself experiences a crisis in our time, for beauty is not just to be experienced but must be examined if we are to uncover beauty's meaningfulness. Immediate enjoyment, however, does not allow for a full conception of beauty, which only discloses itself to us through temporal delay. Beauty lies not in the momentary shimmer of a thing, Han argues, but in its afterglow.[60] The significance of contemplating a beautiful sentence likewise becomes apparent by lingering on the beauty of the idea it contains, through the afterglow of its intellectual impact on us, which encourages us to continue to pause, to examine, to critique. This understanding of novelistic reading in the context of the contemporary time novel allows us to add another facet to our understanding of the time novel's contemporaneity. For the contemporary, Boris Groys argues, "is actually constituted by doubt, hesitation, uncertainty, indecision—by the need for prolonged reflection, for a delay." "We want to postpone our decisions and actions in order to have more time for analysis, reflection, and consideration," and that, he concludes, "is precisely what the contemporary is—a prolonged, even potentially infinite period of delay."[61]

COMMON TIME AND THE GIFT OF FUTURITY

The engagement with the "goon" that is time and with the crises of futurity and hope experienced by the characters of *Goon Squad* is mediated by the formal composition of Egan's novel. Egan sets up the chapters of the novel to move between temporalities, adding layers of complexity by switching between narrative tenses. Narrated through particular scenes from the lives of a range of different characters, the novel's individual chapters are structured around competing temporalities. Chapters set in the present are narrated in past tense as long as the novel tries to establish the logical link between our present and the past for which the characters nostalgically long. Chapters set in the future are narrated in future perfect (in periodic conversation with simple present tense) and convey the sense that the future is preestablished by the problematic temporal relation to the present. But as Egan's novel shows, the source of the nostalgia that the characters experience is not just a matter of aging and a general longing for better, earlier, youthful times. It also reveals the fundamental ways in which our temporal imagination is gendered and in turn shows that conceptions of gender are deeply bound up with processes of temporalization. One important aspect of Egan's novel is that *Goon Squad* highlights a problem we have encountered in a variety of contexts throughout this book: time is not neutral, but it is gendered, and as we see in more detail in the next chapter, it is also racialized. Indeed, time serves as a crucial tool for maintaining essentializing gender narratives. As has become clear by now, the current crisis of temporality is largely experienced and described (in the contemporary novel and possibly in much commentary) by white (wealthy) men. Novels like Egan's thus provide a counternarrative to this version of the present and also lay bare the connection between systemic time and historically specific gender divisions and structures of segregation and exclusion.

Sasha, for instance, one of the novel's central characters, serves for men in the novel as a medium for nostalgia, a mere gateway to the past, existing in their minds as perpetually past, static in time, and thus a way to recover their youth. At the end of the novel, Alex and Bennie try to visit Sasha at what they believe to be her apartment. Giddy with anticipation, Alex and Bennie ring the doorbell. Waiting for Sasha to answer the door, Alex wonders if she will recognize him and longingly conjures up a scenario that he hopes will play out once the door opens: "Alex imagined walking in to her apartment and finding himself still there—his young self, full of schemes and high standards, with nothing decided yet. The fantasy imbued him with careening hope" (339). For Alex, meeting Sasha is not about reconnecting with a former partner or learning more about Sasha's life. It is solely about rediscovering himself, and it is only through the nostalgic recovery of the anticipation and futurity of his youth that Alex is able to find a sense of optimism. But no one answers the door: "He pushed the buzzer again, and as more seconds passed, Alex felt a gradual draining loss. The whole crazy pantomime collapsed and blew away." "I don't know what happened to me," Alex remarks helplessly, "I honestly don't." "You grew up, Alex," Bennie responds, "just like the rest of us." And so, faced with a closed door, the men find themselves standing on a street at night, listening to dogs barking, trucks passing, "and the hum, always that hum"—"the sound of time passing" (339–40). Egan's novel balances sympathetic portrayals of sad men who are unable to deal with growing up, who cannot find hope or a way forward in life, with striking, incisive critiques of the gendering of time and the temporalization of gender, as it highlights how women are forced to serve as bearers of male nostalgic projections.

Elsewhere, I show in great detail how deeply and problematically the range of declarations of a crisis of futurity and the idea of a long Now are bound up with narratives of masculinity and paternalism.[62] Novels like Egan's draw our attention to how time is gendered, how gender distinctions are temporalized, and how historical moments become (retroactively) gendered. Novels like *Goon Squad* and Rachel Kushner's *The Flamethrowers* (2013) thus serve an important function in the context of the temporal crises of our moment. Kushner's novel is a dazzling blend of artist's novel, social novel, historical novel, and time novel. And it is precisely through its combination of novelistic forms that *The Flamethrowers* is able to engage with the relation between our imagination of time and futurity on one hand and gender on the other. Moving between different characters, settings, and time periods, between

Nevada and New York, the United States and Brazil, early twentieth-century Italy and 1970s Italy, Kushner's novel traces the development of a young female artist against the backdrop of the rise and fall of conceptions of futurity and the political projects with which they are bound up. Following the waxing and waning of young people's excitement for and interest in the future, from Italian futurists to radicals and artists of the 1970s, Kushner's novel presents a prehistory of the temporal crises of our time, anticipating and, crucially, historicizing the crash of futurity that began to influence culture, politics, and thought in the 1980s. And yet, while the complex formal structure expressing the temporal shifts traced by the text could be read as a linear narrative of the fall of modern conceptions of futurity, Kushner's novel also shows that such a linear understanding of temporality is deeply bound up not only with crises of temporality but also with the gendering of time. The novel undercuts the diagnosis at which it may superficially seem to point by illustrating the limits and origins of a linear conception of temporality and futurity that, from its beginning, was connected to the temporal exclusion of women. The future, it shows, is often understood as the domain of men, and crises of futurity or outright denials thereof are well known to women, who are confined to the role of negative other of this form of temporality.

The narrative of the novel's central character, the young female artist Reno, is juxtaposed with flashback narratives that take us to the early twentieth century and the exploits of Valera, racer, builder, and lover of early motorcycles and grandfather of Reno's boyfriend, Sandro. While grandfather and grandson are decades and continents apart, their attitudes and beliefs about time and women are strikingly similar. "A young woman is a conduit," Sandro tells Reno, "all she has to do is exist." "You have time," he elaborates, "meaning don't use it, but pass through time in patience, waiting for something to come."[63] Throughout the novel, Reno struggles with problems of presence, timelessness, and an uneasy relation to futurity. Kushner's novel, however, does not present this just as an individual problem or in relation to Reno's art only; rather it traces Reno's temporal crises to the origins of twentieth-century conceptions of futurity that continue to underwrite Sandro's beliefs. Riveted by the speed of modernity he finds exemplified in the emergence of the motorcycle at the beginning of the twentieth century, Valera moves to Milan, "the capital of the new" (78). Ecstatically pursuing the thrill of speed and the ideology of progress, Valera and a group of fellow young motorcyclists hasten toward a future full of promise and excitement, a time brought about by speed that, the young men note, gives them "at last, divinity in the form of the straight line" (78). The idea of futurity and change pursued by the young men is, however, developed in direct relation to the distinction between the time of men and the time of women. "Women were trapped in time," Valera notes. While he finds himself "chang[ing] only for the better," he understands women to be standing still in the time of the quotidian, carrying out only repetitive work related to child rearing and domestic labor. Men, Valera believes, "move at a different velocity," and once they feel their velocity, he concludes, "all they had to do was release themselves from the artifice of time. Break free of it to see that it had never held them to begin with" (79). Like Sasha in the imagination of the men of *Goon Squad*, women in the context of the origins of futurism exist as the negative other of the futurity that is the time of men. And while men, in Valera's mind, can break free from time in a manner that allows them to change and race toward the future, women remain trapped in time, in the timelessness of the everyday, in the perpetual present to which they remain confined not just as a result of social norms but in order to prop up the excited futurity and thus the temporalized masculinity of futurism. Novels like *The Flamethrowers* and *Goon Squad* historicize the current crisis of futurity and reveal the ways it is bound up not only with current matters of gender and sexuality but also with the long historical connection between conceptions of time and futurity on one hand and constructions of masculinity and femininity on the other. Kushner's hard-boiled feminist time novel reveals that the limits of our temporal imagination and our conceptions of categories like futurity, change, progress, or linearity are deeply interwoven with the limits that traditional conceptions of gender and sexuality impose upon our imagination—and of course, this dual limit, as Kusher's novel shows, constitutes the very real limits of social and political transformation as well as art.

In the work of male authors, too, we encounter a clear awareness of the ways conceptions of futurity, progress, and presence are connected to the troubling centrality of the white, male individual subject. Like *Goon Squad*, Lerner's *10:04* replaces the focus on the individual with an ultimate turn toward a politics of community that continues the process of undercutting autofictional form rooted in the turn to the unnamed narrator. Since contemporaneity also marks a coming together in time, novels like *Goon Squad* and *10:04* locate the ultimate solution to the problem of a timeless present in the historical reading of time that becomes possible and gives rise to a new idea of futurity when we linger in common to reclaim the present as the temporality of community. The protagonist ("the author") of the short story "The Golden Vanity" in *10:04* has an important experience that, together with the unnamed narrator's viewing of *The Clock*, centrally shapes the new understanding of time proposed by Lerner's novel. Walking through Brooklyn Heights, "the author" has a revelation:

> Some conspiracy of brickwork and chill air and gaslight gave him the momentary sense of having traveled back in time, or of distinct times being overlaid, temporalities interleaved. No: it was as if the little flame in the gas lamp he paused before were burning at once in the present and in various pasts, in 2012 but also in 1912 or 1883, as if it were one flame flickering simultaneously in each of those times, connecting them. He felt that anyone who had ever paused before the lamp as he was pausing was briefly coeval with him, that they were all watching the same turbulent point in their respective present tenses. (67)

In the flicker of the gas lamp, the protagonist reads the possibility of a form of contemporaneity across time, and this sense of transtemporal contemporaneity leads him to develop a new understanding of community, one that shapes the remainder of Lerner's novel. The ties that bind, he realizes, need not only emerge from a sense of contemporaneity understood as being together in time in the present. They also originate from the connection between common social and political projects whose urgency and power to unify reverberate across time and chronology. Contemporaneity across time emerges from recognition of the latency of a given present's turbulence, out of which a sense of history and futurity can emerge. Contemporaneity across time therefore replaces the simple idea of contemporaneity as a matter of inhabiting the same moment with a sense of affiliation and commonality that arises from an understanding of the present as history.

Alexander Nagel and Christopher Wood propose that such an understanding of time is a mode of thought not available to "the historian who interprets the work of art as a token within a system of symbolic exchanges," but instead is available only to art itself. Art, they argue, creates "the possibility of a conversation across time."[64] Art is able to create a form of reading time that imagines contemporaneity nonsynchronously in order to foreground the historical commitments that may afford us a more profound understanding of what it means to be in time. *10:04* foregrounds the value of understanding contemporaneity as a common relation to the present as history as an antidote to the paralyzing influence of the temporal crises of our time. The development of "the author" and of the narrator of Lerner's novel depends upon this understanding of contemporaneity, which puts the individual fully in the service of the idea pursued by the novel. The narrator of Lerner's novel thus becomes "a contemporary" in the sense outlined by Giorgio Agamben: "The contemporary is not only the one who, perceiving the darkness of the present, grasps a light that can never reach its destiny; he is also the one who, dividing and interpolating time, is capable of transforming it and putting it in relation with other times."[65]

The replacement of the subject or individual with the contemporary in Lerner's novel as a way to retemporalize time and history in the present and art in history goes hand in hand with a passionate argument for the importance of the politics of community for our time. Looking at Manhattan's skyline at night, the novel's narrator realizes once more that the answer to the problems posed by the temporal crisis of the present is not to be found in a turn to the time of nature, since natural time and the even the change resulting from historical storms ultimately reinforce the perceived timelessness of the present. The Manhattan skyline, on the other hand, creates a feeling of great elation in the narrator:

> It was a thrill that only built space produced in me, never the natural world, and only when there was an incommensurability of scale—the human dimension of the window tiny from such distance combining but not dissolving into the larger architecture of the skyline that was the expression, the material signature, of a collective person who didn't yet exist, a still-uninhabited second person plural to whom all the arts, even in their most intimate registers, are addressed. Only an urban experience of the sublime was available to me because only then was the greatness beyond calculation the intuition of community. (108)

We encounter here another version of the not yet, one that locates futurity in a politics and temporality of community and collectivity. Throughout the final sections of the novel, the narrator comes to the conclusion that art itself facilitates this orientation toward a future community. His friend Alex provides the narrator with an important impulse that helps him come to this realization. When he discusses with Alex his plans for extending his short story into a novel—which, he suggests, will be a novel that revolves around a character who falsifies an archive—she argues that he should refrain from writing such a "a novel about deception." Such a novel would misunderstand and misrepresent the true problem and the solution that is actually needed today: "I feel like you don't need to write about falsifying the past. You should be finding a way to inhabit the present" (137).

Toward the end of the novel, the narrator of *10:04* sets out to follow Alex's advice and writes precisely such a novel to determine a way to inhabit the present—the book we are reading. *10:04* concludes with a scene in which the narrator and Alex, who are expecting a child together, stand on Brooklyn Bridge and gaze at the city, looking into the future. And it is now with great sincerity, as opposed to irony, that the narrator turns to Walt Whitman to explain his vision of inhabiting the present in a way that develops a communal imagination and politics of futurity: "I thought of Whitman looking across the East River late at night before the construction of the bridge, before the city was electrified, believing he was looking across time, emptying himself out so he could be filled by readers in the future" (193). Much like the protagonist of Yu's novel, who understands that he is his own limit, the limit that is the present, the narrator of Lerner's novel transitions from an isolated, presentist "I" to a communal, historical "we" aimed at the future. David Carr argues that the work of G. W. F. Hegel is immensely important in its ability to give us a form of thought that understands temporality in relation to "the narrative character of we." Hegel, Carr argues, helps us conceive of a "communal subject that is genuinely plural" through the anticipatory recognition of a common relation to history. This notion of futurity and commonality, Carr suggests, "turns on the notion of a common project."[66] This common project that begins with the ability to read the present historically expresses itself in the final turn to the anticipatory "we" in Lerner's novel. It also gives rise to experiments with second-person plural narration in novels like Joshua Ferris's *Then We Came to the End* (2006), which, with a striking degree of historical awareness that anticipates the economic crash of 2008, deploys the "narrative character of the we" to examine a moment of severe crisis in contemporary capitalism from the standpoint of the precarious workers of finance capitalism. Lerner traces this turn from "I" to "we" as a precondition for our ability to read time historically. The sense of historical temporality as a communal project, which Carr describes as "the communal event of the present," thereby stands opposed to a broad present marked by capitalism's fragmentation of the temporal demos into myriad individual temporalities.[67] History, the narrator realizes, emerges not from historic storms but from the turbulence of contemporaneity understood as the time of a communal project.

The famous "I" of Whitman's *Leaves of Grass*, which ultimately stands in the service of the "we" of the democratic experiment of the United States, becomes the model for a way to inhabit the present in a manner that formulates the idea of the subject as always in the service of the anticipation of a communal project and a coming community. In this way, futurity emerges precisely out of a changed imagination of the present: "I'd been hard on Whitman during my residency, hard on his impossible dream, but . . . we made, if not a pact, then a kind of peace. . . . I resolved to dilate my story not into a novel about literary fraudulence, about fabricating the past, but into an actual present alive with multiple futures" (194). This account of the present, the narrator tells us, locates futurity in "the process of exploration and discovery" that is aimed at a "form of collectivity that can stand as a figure of its possibility" (239). In the novel's last sentence, switching to present tense, the narrator leaves us with a section taken from Whitman's "Crossing Brooklyn Ferry" adapted for our time: "I am looking back at the . . . city in the second person plural. I know it's hard to understand / I am with you, and I know how it is" (240). The critiques of individuality and subjective experience and the turn to a politics and temporality of communality that allows for a historical reading of the otherwise timeless present constitutes a common aspect of the contemporary time novel. In fact, as illustrated by novels such as Peter Dimock's impressively rich and evocative novel *George Anderson: Notes for a Love Song in Imperial Time* (2013), the contemporary time novel attaches the project of telling the time of our present historically to a renewed commitment to equality. The narrator of Dimock's novel, Theo Fales, seeks to transcend the "historylessness" that the novel understands as "now the condition of everyday life" by finding "a historical method" that allows him to imagine time in a new way. "In the vision I had two years ago," he tells us, "I came to the end of myself and found other people standing there—and knew that the present was a gift of time in which to sing a true history of equal historical selves."[68]

The arresting suggestion that we ought to understand the present as a gift, as time containing a futurity conceived as possibility that we can create for and extend to others, also underlies the understanding of time for which Egan's *Goon Squad* argues in one of the novel's most moving passages. Scotty, a former rock musician, who, as a result of a series of bad choices, is now virtually penniless and spends his days fishing New York's East River, encounters a former friend who has since become a record executive (Bennie). After a meeting in his office, out of a sense of pity and obligation to their past friendship, Bennie gives Scotty his card. Bennie suggests that he is willing to listen to any new music Scotty may want to send his way, offering him a second chance at a career in the business. The morning after his meeting with Bennie, Scotty leaves his regular fishing spot after having contemplated his next steps. He notices a young junkie couple in his path, walking in the opposite direction. "They were huddled up against each other, looking haggard and sexy the way young people can for a little while, until they just look haggard" (106). Scotty stops the couple and inquires if they are musicians. "He's awesome," the girl responds. Scotty carefully removes Bennie's card from his pocket and hands it to the girl. "Call this man," he urges the couple. "He runs a record label. Tell him Scotty sent you. . . . He's my buddy." "I really hope you will," Scotty emphasizes in an effort to convince the couple, but he feels helpless, because, he knows, he can "only do this once," he'll "never have that card again." "He'll call," the girl finally replies. "I'll make him" (107). Egan's novel shows that nostalgia is as much a turn away from the present and toward the past as it is a turn to the self. Scotty, however, realizes that the opportunity represented by the business card may be best used not as a way to restore his own career, to make the old new again, but as a gift that can be put to better use by others. Recovering a sense of possibility and transcending the limits of the self may also require the ability to understand the present in the way Scotty does, *Goon Squad* shows, as a time that may be rife with possibility—not possibility for us but instead for others. This account of futurity, understood as a gift from which not we but others may benefit, constitutes one of the most stirring aspects of Egan's novel. After all, how dare we continue to profess our inability to imagine a better future after having paused to consider the afterglow of the beauty of this passage in Egan's novel and the utterly profound joy that Scotty finds in understanding how easy and rewarding it can be to create futurity by conceiving of it as a gift?

> I nodded and turned, leaving the junkies behind. I walked north, forcing my eyes to see as far as they could see. . . . "Hey," I heard behind me, two ragged voices. When I turned,

they called out, "Thanks," both at the same time. It had been a long time since anyone had thanked me for something. "Thanks," I said to myself. I said it again and again, wanting to hold in my mind the exact sound of their voices, to feel again the kick of surprise in my chest. (107–8)

CHAPTER 3

The Tenses of Race

The Privilege of Contemporaneity and the Unequal Distribution of Presence

It has always been one of the primary tasks of art to create a demand whose hour of full satisfaction has not yet come.
—Walter Benjamin, "The Work of Art in the Age of Its Technological Reproducibility"

In his 2014 essay "The Future as Form," Marcial González draws our attention to an important and underappreciated aspect of the contemporary US ethnic novel: its formal mediation of "a migration . . . across the temporalities of history." Of central significance to this engagement with the multiple temporalities of history, González suggests, is the question of the status of the future, in particular in a moment that González describes, in reference to Fredric Jameson's work, as marked by an "immense privileging of the present."[1] The African American time novel has been engaged in precisely such an inquiry into the temporalities of history for over three decades now. In fact, the African American novel's rearticulation of established notions of time, history, and contemporaneity provides us with an important counternarrative to the presentism frequently associated with contemporary culture. Already in 1984, Samuel Delany's novel *Stars in My Pocket Like Grains of Sand* forecasts the temporal crisis that has since become one of the defining problems of our moment. The novel's temporal backdrop is the persistent threat of what it identifies as "Cultural Fugue": an epistemological singularity brought about by a world whose complexity overwhelms thought itself, a situation that leads to the complete destruction of civilization in the absence of an alternative imagination of the future. Cultural Fugue is the point of crisis at which "the socioeconomic pressures . . . reach a point of technological recomplication and perturbation where the population destroys all life across the planetary surface."[2] José Muñoz argues that the great value of Delany's work lies in its ability to foreground the centrality of one of the most pressing projects of our moment: "A critique of the totalizing and naturalizing idea of the present."[3] One might add to this point that in particular Delany's deployment of the neo-slave narrative in novels like *Stars in My Pocket* foregrounds that denials of futurity are a fundamental aspect of the history of systematic exclusion, domination, and segregation. Those who have historically been denied a future, Delany's novel stresses, are affected decidedly differently by anxiety-laden proclamations of crises of futurity on the part of the dominant culture. In our moment, too, the fear of the end of change, time, and the future registers starkly differently with those who have faced racial segregation and exclusion and have historically been denied both a sense of futurity and integration into the cultural contemporary. As one character in Delany's novel poignantly puts it, "You know . . . for Cultural Fugue to take place, you have to have a culture." (72).

The notion of a uniform global contemporary, a largely homogeneous long now, is deeply problematic. To be sure, analyses of the temporal crises of our present are important to illuminate the sociopolitical and cultural consequences of the historical transition into real-time capitalism. And yet simply reiterating the by now ubiquitous association of our era with a general crisis of futurity runs the risk of furthering the temporal flattening envisaged by real-time capitalism: we forget to ask which alternative temporal imaginaries and which conceptions of futurity and notions of what it means to be together in time the dominant temporal regime of our time must exclude or erase to maintain the fiction of a singular, totalizing form of contemporaneity. In this chapter, I argue that we must investigate how the construction of a singular notion of contemporaneity, or indeed the suggestion that our time is marked by a crisis of time and futurity—though the latter may in many instances be aimed at a critique of capitalism and contemporary racism—serves as an enabling fiction of our imagination of social and racial difference. The singularization of the contemporary serves as a central mechanism not only of real-time capitalism but also of the homogenization of our social and racial imagination, and as such it is directly bound up with mechanisms of racial segregation, cultural exclusion, and historical erasure. In recent years, however, African American novelists have laid bare the historical relation between racialization and temporalization in works that provide us with striking counternarratives of our present.

The omnipresence of the contemporary today, these authors show, is decidedly not a novel phenomenon. Rather, it is but one example of a long history of crises of temporality that are well known to those who have suffered from mechanisms of exclusion, segregation, and domination that are directly bound up with the strategic denial of presence and futurity. By placing the concept of the contemporary and its current crises in the context of the historical development of the American racial imagination, African American novelists like Colson Whitehead and Kiese Laymon also recover a form of futurity that is absent from other aspects of contemporary culture and thought, one that emerges through a prospective, anticipatory understanding of the present as plural and heterochronous.

Lloyd Pratt's work shows that temporal homogenization has always been deeply involved in the attempt to form a unified, singularized conception of what it means to be American. In *Archives of American Time*, Pratt reveals the direct relation between temporal homogenization and the attempted "consolidation of U.S. national and racial identity" in the nineteenth century.[4] And yet, Pratt argues, "the print and reading revolutions that distinguish this period did not come close to achieving the homogenization of time with which they have sometimes been associated in American literature, American literary studies, and U.S. history."[5] Rather than participating in the construction of a singular racial and national identity through the construction of unified American time, literature assumed an important role in resisting this project. In fact, Pratt argues, to no small degree because literature "super-added certain specifically literary temporalities to those already circulating in the extraliterary settings of nineteenth-century America," this period in American history ought to be understood more correctly as marked by the failure of temporal unification, as a time that that was ultimately "deeply inhospitable to the consolidation of national and racial identity." Pratt is fascinated by the kind of literature that "deepens the period's temporal repertoire," by the kind of writing that "supplements the orders of time that emerged from industrial manufacture [and] slave economies" and showed that American temporality should be understood "not as a teleology of progress or transcendence but as a superimposition and coexistence of heterogeneous times."[6] Real-time capitalism, as we have seen, amplifies the pursuit of temporal homogenization in ways that surpass and ultimately seem to exhaust previous temporal regimes and forms of temporal thought. In this moment, the historical relation between time and our social and racial imagination on one hand and literature's ability to super-add temporal pluralism to a purportedly unified sense of contemporaneity on the other are more important than ever. If literature of the nineteenth century notably refused time's singularization and, in Pratt's terms, pluralized time and thus resisted the push toward temporal purification, then we must ask if and how literature is still able to carry out this task in our time, in an era when real-time capitalism appears to structurally implement the purification of time as the temporal order of our present.[7]

Given the widespread notion that our era is defined by a totalizing sense of presentism, it might seem as though the long-standing aim to singularize and homogenize time may finally have been achieved. The suggestion that presentism is the definitive temporal regime of our moment, however, can only be maintained if we solely focus on sites of homogenization—and if literary criticism focuses mainly on those works of literature, often works that represent white (male) middle- or upper-class experiences of our present, readily confirming the crisis and underwriting that which capital seeks to standardize and homogenize. In other words, limiting our examination of the present to, say, the novels of Richard Russo—narratives that mourn the loss of ordered futures and life narratives that novels like *Empire Falls* (2001) or *Bridge of Sighs* (2007) associate with industrial capitalism, responding with nostalgia to the rise of a new stage of capitalism and its associated social and temporal order—elevates a limited set of conditions to the status of a universal narrative about our time.[8] The African American novel, however, refuses such overly general accounts of the temporality of our moment. The African American time novel in particular lays bare the complicity of the idea of the omnipresent now with a long-standing aim of racial domination, and it locates current forms of presentism in the history of the attempted unification of our racial and national imagination, which has been fundamentally involved in the struggle for American time. The forms of temporal multiplicity found in the contemporary African American *Zeitroman* disrupt attempts at formulating a singular, homogeneous national and racial identity and remind us that, today as much as during the period that Pratt describes, the singularization of time is bound up with the singularization of racial and national identity.

In what follows, I show that contemporary African American novelists formulate a strikingly different understanding of two terms that have been widely discussed in recent criticism and theory, terms that are also directly implicated in the crises of our temporal vocabulary resulting from the temporal crises of our moment: *the contemporary* and *contemporaneity*. The African American time novel allows us to unearth the historical and logical complexity, as well as the uses and limitations, of these concepts. Because the idea of the contemporary is dialectically bound up with the creation of a particular sense of sociability, and contemporaneity is a fiction of being together in time created under historically specific conditions, contemporaneity is also a fiction that maintains real conditions of exclusion and segregation from a given society at different moments in time. By examining the process through which the contemporary is singularized, African American novelists recover those forms of being in time that are excluded from the dominant fiction of contemporaneity. In fact, the recovery of a temporally plural understanding of contemporaneity has driven forward some of the most fascinating developments in the African American novel in recent years. I should note, however, that I am outlining but one facet of a much larger problem, which far surpasses the scope of this book and should be fully addressed in future projects: the dialectical connection between comparative racialization and comparative temporalization, which gives rise to specific narratives, forms, and genres in multiethnic American literature. In other words, to fully appreciate the important political work of American multiethnic literature in recent years, we must understand changes in literary form and genre (the turn to speculative fiction in African American, Latino/a, and Indigenous literature is one important example here) in relation to the ways differences in racialization map onto and work through differences in temporalization.

The African American time novel models new ways of understanding contemporaneity by refusing the language and logic of noncontemporaneity and developing new accounts of what it may mean to be contemporary in our moment in history. In this way, the contemporary African American time novel is crucially important to our ability to understand the intricacies of the politics of contemporaneity today. It reveals that the concept of contemporaneity is centrally involved in how we imagine both community and exclusion, and it shows that, if reduced to a singularized dominant, the idea of contemporaneity upholds and indeed participates in shaping structures of privilege and segregation, and the fiction of contemporaneity centrally determines how we imagine social and racial difference. The contemporary African American time novel provides us with a striking counternarrative of our moment in history that rejects the notion of an omnipresent long now and demonstrates that temporal crises and the struggle with contemporaneity have a long history—a history bound up with strategies of exclusion, segregation, and domination. Imagining contemporaneity beyond the limits of a purportedly universal idea of presence, the African American time novel develops new conceptions of futurity that emerge from the confrontation with the long history of assigning contemporaneity a central role in mechanisms of exclusion and domination that are aimed at a denial of presence. It is precisely by mobilizing this history—the complex relation to a past that has always been marked by crises of futurity—that the African American time novel is able to recover hope from the grasp of a present elsewhere understood as absolute and inescapable.

The novels of Whitehead and Laymon outline possibilities for freeing the concept of the contemporary from the grasp of capitalism's strategic singularization. Such novels lay bare the interconnection between temporalization and the singularization of the contemporary on one hand and the history of mechanisms of exclusion and segregation on the other. The jargon of noncontemporaneity, which is based on a universalized, homogeneous notion of contemporaneity, these novels show, has come to displace and maintain racist narratives of natural, essential difference. The act of historicizing the contemporary in the novels of Whitehead and Laymon can be understood as a project aimed at restoring to presence the plurality of temporalities that make up true contemporaneity and, ultimately, as a way to restore a sense of hope and futurity by reclaiming the contemporary as a critical, political, and aesthetic category. This complex, plural understanding of what it may mean to be together in time rearticulates the logic of time and reveals to us how our conception of the relation among past, present, and future must change significantly as soon as we examine the fact that racialization and racial exclusion have always relied on temporalization and temporal exclusion.

TEMPORAL HOMOGENIZATION

Inclusion in the contemporary, the privilege of being together in time and thus being able to partake in the dominant narrative of the future, as shown in novels like Whitehead's *Apex Hides the Hurt* (2006), comes at a cost for those who have historically been denied both presence and futurity. For the African American subject, *Apex* argues, it means forgetting about the history of racial exclusion. Whitehead's novel forwards a striking critique of multiculturalism's attempt to register the history and presence of race as a relation of noncontemporaneity while formulating a notion of futurity predicated upon erasure of the past and the historical present. The protagonist of *Apex* is a "nomenclature consultant" who possesses the skill of knowing any given object's true name. The protagonist's biggest claim to fame, which established him professionally, is the development of a "multicultural band aid," available in a wide variety of skin colors: Apex. In a memorable scene, the protagonist reflects on the logic of the band aid and its profound success, which, he realizes, is directly connected to the racial politics of his time: "The deep psychic wounds of history and the more recent gashes ripped by the present, all of these could be covered by this wonderful, unnamed multicultural adhesive bandage. It erased. Huzzah."[9] Multiculturalism, the protagonist knows, hides historical injury and obscures history's direct relation to the present.

The novel's plot revolves around the protagonist's latest assignment. He is hired to help rename a town, a project principally driven forward by software tycoon Lucky Aberdeen. Originally a settlement of former black slaves called Freedom, the town that is to be renamed yet again currently bears the name Winthrop. The protagonist learns that three groups are championing different names for the town: conservative white residents seek to preserve the name Winthrop; the black population wishes to revert to the town's original name; and Aberdeen, representing the town's business interests, champions the name New Prospera. While the name Winthrop replaces the name Freedom and thereby overwrites the town's ties to the history of slavery, the name New Prospera instead seeks to replace the town's historical lineage with a new, happily ahistorical, communal sense of futurity. The appeal to a new, friendly, welcoming togetherness in a better, homogenized future promised by commerce, Whitehead's novel argues, amounts to a version of temporal exclusion and erasure by different means. *Apex* illustrates that the price of inclusion into multiculturalism's new futures is the erasure of the past. The latter solution, *Apex* shows, forms the core of the cynical futures proffered by multiculturalism's promise of a new common project, its new sense of being together in time, which requires the erasure of all other historical timelines and forms of temporality. The time of New Prospera, advertised to residents as the time of a new, unified commonality, is ultimately nothing other than the singular temporality of a capitalist future, which rests upon a homogenized contemporary. Contemporaneity in this sense is predicated upon the abandonment of both history and alternative temporal imaginaries: being together in time according to this conception of contemporaneity means being together in the same time and erasing competing ideas of (what it means to live in) time.

J. Sutter, the protagonist of Whitehead's novel *John Henry Days* (2001), faces a similar problem with regard to the temporal politics of multiculturalism. Sutter dislikes the southern United States. The reason for his dislike is connected to a specific temporal problem that Sutter understands as arising from the functional integration of historical injury into the present of multiculturalism. In response to a friend who cannot understand Sutter's position and consequently remarks that "this isn't Mississippi in the 1950s, J.," Sutter notes: "It's always Mississippi in the 1950s."[10] Sutter identifies a particular version of temporal immobility. He finds himself confined not only to an unchanging present but also to a present that itself is coded as perpetually past by the unchanging structures of American racism. The reason for Sutter's double bind, the novel shows, is the seemingly paradoxical temporal logic of multiculturalism's efforts to integrate the African American subject into the present by virtue of noncontemporaneity. The plot of *John Henry Days* revolves around the release of a set of commemorative stamps, which honor four great American folk heroes. This set of stamps includes three traditional figures of US folklore: Mighty Casey, Pecos Bill, and Paul Bunyan. As a gesture of multicultural goodwill, the US Postal Service decides to feature John Henry on the fourth stamp in the series. John Henry achieved mythical status for reputedly beating the newly invented steam drill in a head-to-head competition, after which he dropped dead. This impressive display of strength and skilled manual labor, so the US Postal Service claims, constitutes the essence of Americanness. At the event celebrating the launch of the series, a representative of the Postal Service expresses this point in his laudation of John Henry: "John Henry was an Afro-American, born into slavery and freed by Mr. Lincoln's famous proclamation. But more importantly, he was an American. He helped build this nation into what it is today and his great competition with the steam drill is a testament to the strength of the human spirit" (66). It initially appears as though the romanticization of manual labor allows for the retroactive inclusion of the black laboring subject into the category "American," from which he was traditionally excluded. However, it is clear that this form of integration depends upon a form of temporal exclusion. The Americanness of John Henry depends upon the superseded and now romanticized form of labor and subjectivity that he signals, a form of labor already marked as obsolete in the tale of John Henry's mythical struggle against the steam drill. His victory was momentary and could not stave off the flow of history. John Henry beat the steam drill. Yet it is not his heroic act but rather his consequent death as the final confirmation of his temporally residual existence that allows for his inclusion in the category "American," since it is through his eternal pastness and noncontemporaneity that his death confirms the inevitability of white progress and dominance. In other words, John Henry is included in and stabilizes the meaning of the category "American" precisely through his temporal exclusion from it (literally via his death and figuratively by symbolizing noncontemporaneity). To Sutter, the stamp therefore lays bare multiculturalism's temporal logic, which celebrates only those aspects of the present that can be successfully confined to noncontemporaneity and to eternal, idealized pastness. And while his colleague reads Sutter's understanding of Mississippi's temporality as a refusal to acknowledge historical change, his actual argument points toward the temporal dimension of racial exclusion that not only is maintained in multiculturalism but takes on a central function in celebrations of racial diversity. The historical and political matter of racial difference is temporalized and thereby transformed from a problem of historical and political structures of racialization and racial exclusion into a matter of essentializing temporal differences between cultures and identities. Multiculturalism, Whitehead's novel proposes, seeks to integrate the black subject by virtue of consolidating the connection between blackness and noncontemporaneity. In turn, *John Henry Days* shows that temporal immobility is a central aspect of historically specific relations of racialization and exclusion and that the jargon of noncontemporaneity is crucial to how we imagine otherness in times of multiculturalism.

Insofar as it relies on either noncontemporaneity or temporal erasure, any notion of the future that emerges out of multiculturalism's singularized present, these novels show, poses a problem rather than being a site of potentiality for the black subject. The relation of temporal erasure to multiculturalism is a topic that we encounter in some of the most fascinating African American novels in recent years, including Kiese Laymon's 2013 debut novel *Long Division*. The novel's young protagonist, fourteen-year-old Citoyen "City" Coldson, experiences a version of this problem in an event that sets in motion the novel's plot. City and his classmate LaVander Peeler represent Mississippi in the national round of a contest that resembles a spelling bee but asks students instead to use a specific word in a sentence that illustrates the word's "correct, dynamic usage."[11] However, as they move through the individual rounds of the competition, the boys quickly realize that the event is fixed. It is clear that LaVander, a black model student from Mississippi, is supposed to win the contest. City is disqualified in the first round, since he cannot bring himself to use the first word he is given, *niggardly*, in a sentence (38). But when LaVander is given his final word, which can decide the competition in his favor, the boys come to understand why the contest is rigged. LaVander's final word is *chitterlings*, and both LaVander and Citoyen realize that though it is an easy word for LaVander to use, it signifies southern blackness and invokes a romanticized version of "the folk" that can easily be integrated into celebratory national multicultural narratives. The purpose of the contest, City realizes, is to develop a positive narrative about the integration of black rural Mississippi. City understands in this moment that LaVander has been put in an impossible situation, having been prepared to "win the regional contests" but not "for what it would feel like to not be given a chance to really lose":

> I didn't get it until that second. It wasn't at all that we were there just for decoration, like LaVander Peeler said. . . . [We] were there to *win the contest*. They'd already decided before the contest that one of us needed to win. The only way they could feel good about themselves was if they let us win against the Mexican kids, because they didn't really believe any of us could really compete. Yeah, we were all decoration in a way. But it was like LaVander Peeler, specifically, was being thrown a surprise birthday party by a group of white people who didn't know his real name or when his birthday really was. (38)

Tears rolling down his face, LaVander finally uses the word correctly in a sentence. He later retracts his first answer and throws the contest, but the first answer sets off a big celebration: confetti, balloons, and "that 'Harlem Shake' song." The moderator of the show excitedly screams through the sound system: "LaVander Peeler, you have done the unbelievable! Times are a-changing and you, you exceptional young Mississippian, are a symbol of the American Progress. The past is the past and today can be tomorrow" (38).

After this experience, the young protagonists of Laymon's novel cannot help but suspect that the future thus conceived may come at a high price. Since today can only be tomorrow if the past is left behind, and futurity for the children is contingent upon forgetting about the past and thereby gaining access to a present free from competing temporalities, they inevitably wonder, "What happens if we disappear in the future?" (55). The temporal problems in Whitehead's and Laymon's novels thus raise difficult questions about our present: How do we talk about contemporary forms of racism when racism itself is either located in comfortable pastness or erased to make way for a new future that requires a radical break with the past? How do we engage with persisting forms of exclusion and segregation in a climate in which instances of racism and racial discrimination are understood as untimely matters of backwardness in which the past flares up momentarily in a present that is otherwise understood as having moved past such problems? This logic, Laymon's novel shows, suggests to the children that dwelling on past injustices and preserving the memory of racism and slavery as a way to address problems of the present hinder their development and get in the way of the grand, new future of multiculturalism, which promises to bring everyone together in a common present without past. If you want to be able be able to understand yourself as contemporary, and you want a future, they are told, you must forget about the past. Strikingly, novels like those of Whitehead and Laymon reveal that the temporal logic of diversity, the present and future of multiculturalism and multicultural capitalism, is that of homogeneous time. But while it may appear paradoxical that the logic of diversity is bound up with a push toward temporal homogenization, Pratt shows that the aim to singularize and unify time emerges particularly strongly in the context of the tension between diversity and racial and national identity. The emergence of "homogeneous, empty time" assumes an important role in the historical appearance of forms of temporal thought that serve as the temporal regimes underwriting and making possible the rise of capitalism. And yet, Pratt emphasizes, we must trace the emergence of homogeneous, empty time back to the struggle over the formation of US racial and national identity. "In an exceedingly diverse nation," Pratt writes, "this collective temporality [constitutes] a crucial unifying resource." The emergence of a homogeneous, empty time "associated with progress and delivered via the medium of print culture," Pratt elaborates, "would produce a future dominated not just by America but also by Americans."[12] As I show in detail elsewhere, the recently renewed interest in appealing to broad categories like "American" or "the people" is a key strategy of the contemporary Right that seeks to undermine the efforts of progressive racial politics.[13] Reductively associating the focus on identity with fragmentation and holding out categories like "American" and "the people" as a unifying and pseudo-egalitarian force only thinly veil the underlying attempt at homogenization and singularization that, as Pratt shows, has long defined the American temporal and racial imagination. Real-time capitalism's push toward the hegemony of homogeneous time, which overwrites and erases temporal plurality, binds itself to racist and white nationalist attempts at temporal and racial homogenization, which often dovetail in profoundly troubling ways with the temporal imagination of diversity politics highlighted in the novels of Whitehead and Laymon.

The struggle against homogeneous, empty time determines the writing that refuses to conform to such a conception of time and that keeps alive competing forms of the temporal imagination of those who do not recognize themselves in the narrative of a singularized present. The contemporary African American novel makes legible the continued reliance of processes of racialization and racial exclusion upon the logic of temporalization and temporal exclusion. And while novels such as those of Ben Lerner, William Gibson, and Don DeLillo attempt to reconnect the time and temporal crises of our time to history and illustrate that we have not reached an end point or a singularity but rather are confronted with yet another stage in an ongoing historical process, the African American time novel engages with the present temporal crises decidedly differently. Since crises of futurity are an integral part of the experience of American racism and racial exclusion, the African American novel does not need to carry out the process of reconnecting time to history; it is at every moment quite clear that crises of futurity are expressions of regimes of domination and segregation and that they occur for historically and materially specific reasons. From this standpoint, the association of our present with the end of time and futurity reveals itself as a historically foreshortened diagnosis maintained by a singular focus on the experience of only one specific part of American society. As soon as we examine the notion of a universally timeless contemporary world from a standpoint that takes into account aspects of race, gender, and class, the ahistorical and demographically narrow understanding of the relation between material structures and sociopolitical life emerges quite clearly. The African American time novel addresses itself to problems of time and the temporal crises in the present in order to show that we must understand the timelessness of the present not as a temporal singularity but as the present manifestation of a strategy of domination that has a long tradition.

Novels such as Mat Johnson's *Pym* (2011) show that the universalization of a dominant time and the singularization of the contemporary are crucially bound up with the logic of whiteness. Johnson's novel is a reimagination and a critical reading of the only novel Edgar Allan Poe's completed, *The Narrative of Arthur Gordon Pym of Nantucket*. Poe's *Pym*, as Cindy Weinstein argues, "is front and center" in a tradition of American novels that show a central emphasis on time. "American literature takes on a new shape" if we trace what Weinstein describes as an entire tradition within the field that focuses on time, and it is thus not surprising that Johnson should turn to Poe's novel in his attempt to trace the relation between race and time in the American imagination.[14] Johnson's novel narrates the logical relation of time and racialization in Poe's *Pym* as an expression of the American racial imagination that continues to determine the present. The novel begins with a critique of diversity management in the context of the contemporary university that in style and logic closely resembles Whitehead's novels. The bulk of the novel is dedicated to the journey of its narrator, Chris Jaynes, to Antarctica. Chris has recently been dismissed from his position of professor of African American Literature ("the only black male professor on campus") for being unwilling to teach the African American canon and refusing to serve on the Diversity Committee.[15] After his dismissal, while Chris is searching for new projects to keep himself busy, a friend of Chris's who deals in rare and antique books introduces him to a book called *The True and Interesting Narrative of Dirk Peters, Coloured Man, As Written by Himself*. This book suggests that Poe's novel may in fact be based on a true story. According to the book, Dirk Peters was one of the crew members who embarked upon the very journey to Antarctica chronicled in Poe's text. Chris is excited about the potential implications of this discovery and assembles an all-black team to retrace the route described in Peters's manuscript:

> It meant . . . that there truly had been something living down in Antarctica. Something large and humanoid in nature. Maybe it was a lost strain of Neanderthal, or simply a variant of *Homo Sapiens* that through location had managed to avoid modernity. And more important to me, it meant that Tsalal, the great undiscovered African Diasporan homeland, might still be out there, uncorrupted by Whiteness. That there was a group of our people who did achieve victory over slavery in all its forms, escaping completely from the

> progression of Westernization and colonization to form a society outside of time and history. (39)

However, the journey to Antarctica results in the discovery of a civilization of giant white people (to whom the travelers refer as "Snow Honkies"), who live in underground ice tunnels in complete separation from the outside world—frozen in time. Much like Whitehead's multicultural band aid, which hides historical injury and thereby flattens the past into a broad multicultural present determined by a white norm, the absence of history and the resulting sense of timelessness in Johnson's novel are linked to the logic of a white norm: "I saw it all become clear to me. That is how they stay so white: by refusing to accept blemish or history. Whiteness isn't about being something, it is about being no thing, nothing, an erasure. Covering over the truth with layers of blank reality just as the snowstorm was now covering our tent, whipping away all traces of our existence from this pristine landscape" (225). With striking passion and conviction Johnson's novel reveals the connection between the erasure of history and the logic of whiteness. Timelessness itself has a time and history, one that binds the temporal logic of racialization to the persisting understanding of whiteness as the absence of race.

Pym illustrates that the contemporary is not a matter of temporal neutrality. Rather, it is the time of privilege, power, and exclusion. The fiction of contemporaneity operates in tandem with the fiction of whiteness to normalize a dominant imagination of being in time. It is precisely this logic that drives the critique of the multicultural present in the novels of Whitehead and Laymon, demonstrating the troubling degree to which the notion of a diverse present may leave the foundations of the racial-temporal imaginary unchanged. This argument, it is worth noting here, also underwrites Gary Shteyngart's *Super Sad True Love Story*, which examines the relation between contemporaneity and sociality to illustrate the degree to which the ideal of full contemporaneity is bound up with white privilege. While most characters in the novel struggle with the desire to be contemporary and the myriad of ways in which they appear to be constantly lagging behind the contemporary (which is always a matter of differences of race, gender, and class that mark characters as noncontemporary), the super-rich and the most powerful in Shteyngart's imagination of a dystopian society are able to reach the point at which the coincidence of absolute privilege and full contemporaneity allows for the escape from time itself: "dechronification." Those who lag behind the contemporary are marked by time. Those who can consider themselves fully of the moment are able to escape time entirely. From this standpoint, time without time and omnipresent contemporaneity emerge not as the defining problems of our present but instead as problems that emerge once the historical strategy of detemporalizing whiteness runs into its own logical and structural limits.

The contemporary African American novel makes legible the logic of exclusion and othering that underlies the jargon of noncontemporaneity. Authors such as Whitehead foreground the importance of tracing history's competing temporalities into the present by showing that the fiction of multicultural contemporaneity continues to rely upon historical structures of temporal homogenization and erasure. It is also for this reason that we must refuse the logic of noncontemporaneity. Noncontemporaneity, as Lauren Berlant argues, may provide us with "a history of the forces that bear on the everyday and interrupt its appearance of apparent homogeneity to reveal cracks in the local experience of life that can be mobilized toward alternative imaginaries."[16] But in the context of a history of racial exclusion that continues to operate through constructions of noncontemporaneity we must also be careful not to replicate established logical operations of exclusion via romances of the noncontemporaneous. Instead, we should try to reclaim the concept of the contemporary and free it from its truncated, singularized function in the context of capitalism and racist structures of exclusion.

The African American *Zeitroman* is therefore not a matter of exploring alternative temporalities or noncontemporaneities; rather it addresses itself to those temporalities that are constitutive contradictions of the standardization of difference, which is at its heart tied to a history of denied contemporaneity, of exclusion from the contemporary. Moreover, novels such as *Pym* suggest that the dominant form of temporality of any given moment in US history is characterized by a form of temporal and historical exclusion. As *John Henry Days* suggests, the exclusion of the black subject and black culture from the contemporary is directly related to the foundational narratives of what it means to be American, and the logic of neoliberal diversity politics, rather than moving beyond this tradition, instead maintains the temporal confinement to the past culturally as the precondition for inclusion in the present. One of the most significant functions of the contemporary African American novel is thus its ability to situate the temporal contradictions of the present in a long history of material and political relations that remain invisible as long as the neoliberal present is perceived as a singular and universal time.

HOW TO BE CONTEMPORARY

As we have seen, the African American time novel shows that the concept of the contemporary is crucially involved in the project of temporal unification and homogenization, and it foregrounds the important connections between our temporal imagination and the specific social and political function that forms of temporal thought have assumed over the course of history. Racialization, these novels emphasize, also means temporalization. This in turn means that we ought to interrogate terms like *the contemporary* and *contemporaneity* not just because they are currently fashionable in critical discourse but also because they link ongoing debates about today's presentism to the historical relation among time, race, and racism. We must ask, therefore, what exactly we mean when we speak of contemporary art and literature—and we must ask of whose art and literature we speak. What, moreover, do we mean when we speak of the contemporary African American novel? And what exactly is contemporary in the contemporary African American time novel? Finally, what exactly is the historical and temporal meaning of the term *contemporary*, and what is its aesthetic, political, and critical function and possibility today?

As we saw in the introduction, art critics like Juliane Rebentisch note the boom in contemporaneity that, seemingly paradoxically, has become one of the principal characteristics of contemporary art. But while she agrees that this may initially seem to suggest the often-described collapse of futurity into an absolute present to which contemporary art is unable to imagine alternatives, Rebentisch also adds a crucially important suggestion. "Now there is no denying that all this exists in the contemporary art world: empty eclecticism, historical amnesia, indifference, boredom," Rebentisch writes. But, she continues, "the question . . . is whether these phenomena should be taken for the whole. I find such a conclusion hasty, even wrong."[17] Such incredulity regarding the ability of the narrative of the long now to describe the totality of artistic production and sociopolitical relations is all too rare among the growing number of critiques of the crisis of contemporaneity today. Questioning the by now virtually canonical idea that our era is defined by an omnipresent sense of contemporaneity is the first important step toward a more complex and nuanced understanding of the concept and indeed the problem of contemporaneity in our time. If the well-worn narrative about our time and its art and culture does not in fact explain the whole, then we must ask: What is missing? What do we have to believe about our historical moment and the category of the contemporary in order to suggest that this narrative could in fact explain the whole, that it could describe the universal condition of art and thought in our time? What other narratives about our present and about contemporaneity itself are we not able to see if we focus too closely on this by now virtually canonical narrative? Put differently, might the way we talk about the contemporary and its connection to the temporal crisis of our era hinder more than help our efforts to confront current problems of art, thought, and politics? It is time, therefore, to talk about the contemporaneity of contemporary literature and about literature's attempt to grapple with the complexities of the concept of the contemporary in other ways than pointing toward instances in which literature may be said to confirm the impression of a general crash of futurity.

Theodore Martin describes the formation of the contemporary as "the well-nigh literary process by which time becomes 'the times'— by which a flood of fleeting moments is turned into a shared historical moment."[18] In *Anywhere or Not at All: Philosophy of Contemporary Art*, Peter Osborne adds a further dimension to such an understanding of the term by proposing that we ought to understand contemporaneity as a "global or a planetary fiction."[19] Surveying the emergence and usages of the term, Osborne shows that its twofold construction—as an "*idea, problem, fiction*" on one hand and as "*the time of the globally transnational*" on the other—means that, "in its strongest sense, the term 'contemporary art' identifies the artistic construction and expression of contemporaneity."[20] Understanding the term *contemporary literature* precisely in the manner indicated by Osborne's examination of contemporary art allows us to commit fully to the literary dimension that Martin indicates. That is, understanding how the novel participates in constructing the fiction of contemporaneity allows us to make legible the ends of this fiction—in every sense of the expression. The African American novel's engagement with the contemporary reveals whose fiction it is, how it operates, at which outcomes it is aimed, and ultimately, what its limits are. If contemporaneity is the result of shaping many ways of being in time into a general sense of relating to a present that is subsequently understood as shared and common, then we must not only ask to what end this happens but also which ways of being in time and which ideas of what it means to be contemporary are not included in a given fiction of contemporaneity. If we examine the contemporary novel's treatment of this problem, then we can see that the issue is not the transformation of time into "the times." Rather, the problem lies in the transformation of a multitude of ways of understanding one's temporal relation to the world into one dominant, singularized sense of inhabiting the present that is then understood as contemporaneity. The African American time novel reveals the fiction of contemporaneity as a crucial aspect of historical processes of racialization and racial exclusion and an integral part of ongoing real-time capitalism's attempts at unification and homogenization.

"Not all people exist in the same Now," writes Ernst Bloch. "They do so only externally, by virtue of the fact that they may all be seen today," he elaborates, "but that does not mean that they are living at the same time with others."[21] Throughout his work, Bloch stresses the importance of understanding the Now as comprising a variety of competing and "non-synchronous" forms of temporality. The Now is plural, and it is also influenced by what Bloch calls the "untimely"—those "times older than the present" that shape the present and may harbor great danger. The most pressing example of the latter is for Bloch the relation between the Right and the desire to renew romanticized and idealized aspects of the past that Bloch observed in the rise of German Fascism.[22] But if the Now is rife with a plurality of competing temporalities, then what does it mean to be contemporary? How does the concept emerge, and how do we develop a sense of the contemporary and our relation to it? And how is it possible that a concept as complex and internally multiple as the Now should become so unified in our time that it appears to us repressively homogeneous and omnipresent? Martin argues that while "the historical category of the contemporary," the version of the concept that denotes the unified time of capitalism, is a "recent invention," the "temporal phenomenon of 'contemporaneity'—the relational fact of being 'together in time'—is surely as old as time."[23] But the two understandings of the term cannot be separated quite that easily without losing sight of how the creation of a sense of contemporaneity is bound up with and indeed makes possible the development of modern sociability. The emergence of contemporaneity is the temporal basis of the modern social imagination, which in turn constitutes a crucially necessary component of the rise not only of the modern nation-state but also of capitalism and the logic of modern colonialism and imperialism. The notion of being contemporary, of being together in time, itself has a time and history. It emerges under specific historical conditions, its logic changes depending on historical context, and it serves at every moment particular economic and sociopolitical interests.

Brendan Dooley argues that contemporaneity emerges as "the perception, shared by a number of human beings, of experiencing a particular event at more or less the same time." Contemporaneity, he adds, "is not simply a crowd phenomenon, since the observers in question may be out of sight or earshot of one another and still imagine themselves as a group." What matters, in other words, is the perception and imagination of the common relation to an event—not the actual degree of commonality of the experience. Contemporaneity emerges as a new way of imagining the relationship between self and world that is based on the sense of "participating in a shared present, or existing in a length of time called 'now.'" Contemporaneity therefore also contributes "to individuals' sense of community, or their identification with another," Dooley writes, adding that, "with good reason, anthropologists and historians have identified it as a hallmark of modernity." The origin of contemporaneity lies in early modern times, according to Dooley, since it was during this time that "the first world-wide communications networks emerged; and in spite of the frequent delays, shifting borders, linguistic barriers, unreliable carriers and differences in the reckoning of time, Europeans began to share a knowledge of one another and of events in the world taking place in the present."[24] Dooley shows that the rise of contemporaneity relies on the rise of modern communication media that make possible a common relation to the present as the unfolding of history. Joel Burges and Amy J. Elias echo Dooley in stating that the rise of a simultaneous relationship to time and the present emerges "as a result of technological, economic, and cultural developments that expand and extend our sense of the now." And like Dooley, Burges and Elias argue that contemporaneity emerges under specific historical conditions and serves a particular purpose. "The experience of contemporaneity," they write, "can be traced to three events: the creation of the mechanical clock, the advent of capitalist modernity, and the development of the modern nation-state."[25] If, as Burges and Elias suggest, the emergence of simultaneity brings with it a gradual expansion of the Now, then we can see that it is possible to understand the temporal crises of our moment as connected to the logic of contemporaneity itself: full contemporaneity, the notion of a globally shared relation to the present and its events, collapses the logic of time into an expanded, omnipresent now. And yet this process is not inevitable. If contemporaneity is indeed more accurately understood as fiction and not as fact, as a matter of the narrative construction of present reality and not as empirical reality, then we ought to analyze the temporal crises of our moment not as a sociopolitical or epistemological given but as a crisis of narrative and a particular moment in the historical development of the fiction of contemporaneity. One way to pursue this line of inquiry is to examine the relation between material and historical changes and their connected cultural and narratological forms, which together made possible the rise of contemporaneity and shaped its historical development as a fiction of being together in time.

Contemporaneity is an important building block of modernity and its social, political, and material structures. We are able to see this point more clearly when we connect it to Benedict Anderson's examination of the emergence of national consciousness. Anderson locates the origin of national consciousness at the intersection of the rise of capitalism, the emergence of print culture, and the reduction of linguistic diversity.[26] Both the rise of national consciousness and the emergence of capitalism require linguistic standardization and the reduction of linguistic multiplicity, which was in part achieved through the rise of print culture. This in turn resulted in the creation of languages of power (such as administrative languages).[27] And yet this process would not have been possible without a fourth element: the creation of a unified sense of relating to the present. Contemporaneity emerges as an imagined temporal community that is dialectically connected to the rise of the material and sociopolitical structures of modernity. In other words, the rise of contemporaneity is made possible by and in turn assists the rise and expansion of capitalist modernity. Capitalism depends upon temporal unification and standardization. But just as important as the standardization of a global form of understanding time—capitalist clock time and Greenwich mean time, for instance—is the creation of a common, unified relation to time: contemporaneity. Capitalism's dependence upon synchronism, as Burges and Elias note, results in the reduction of temporal diversity, just as the linguistic standardization that accompanies the age of print resulted in the marginalization and ultimately the erasure of linguistic complexity, of local and regional languages, vocabularies, and vernaculars: "Within capitalism, if all things become, really, one thing (the commodity), then all times become, really, only one time: the present."[28] And while it is no doubt important to highlight and examine time's ever-greater homogeneity as a result of the global expansion of capitalism, and while the expansion of the contemporary and the attendant crisis of futurity provide an important index of capitalism's central contradictions today, we must nevertheless not forget that contemporaneity does not exist only as capitalism's narrative about the present. For if, as Dooley suggests, contemporaneity is "the sense of people moving as a group simultaneously through time,"[29] if contemporaneity is bound up with group formation, then it is as important to ask who is included in the group that together moves through as it is to ask who is not permitted membership and thereby denied a sense of contemporaneity. If the ability to participate in a shared sense of time is one of the fundamental markers of integration into a society, then exclusion from the contemporary is one of the most profound denials of social presence. On a basic level, our understanding of the degree of our own contemporaneity is a measure of our integration into or exclusion from our society. What a privilege it is to be able to consider oneself truly contemporary. And since contemporaneity is always a matter of privilege as well as exclusion and the strategic reduction of temporal complexity, the question of what it means to be contemporary should therefore be posed differently: In whose version of the contemporary do we live?

Judy Wajcman offers us a point of entry here. In *Pressed for Time*, she argues that it is imperative for us to understand time as "the result of our collective entanglements with the material world." This suggests, moreover, Wajcman continues, that time "is infused with power relations, such as those of gender, race, and class."[30] As a result of its connection to precisely these power relations, Jacques Rancière argues in "In What Time Do We Live?," time is never singular but always rife with multiple temporalities, which means that we must "call into question the thesis of the homogeneity of time." He writes,

> There is no global process subjecting all the rhythms of individual and collective time to its rule. There are several times in one time. There is a dominant form of temporality, for sure, a "normal" time that is the time of domination. Domination gives it its divisions and its rhythms, its agendas and its schedules. . . . It tends to homogenize all forms of temporality under its control, defining thereby what the present of our world consists of, which futures are possible, and which definitely belong to the past—thereby indicating the impossible.[31]

Likewise, Burges and Elias stress that "while simultaneity is often understood as a reduction of [temporal] multiplicity, creating a singular time beholden to capital, the present is actually animated by a tension between the simultaneous and the multiple, variously contracting and protracting a sense of contemporaneity in which times conjoin."[32] The seeming omnipresence of the contemporary under current capitalism does not, therefore, mark a definitive end point of time nor the actual erasure of competing temporalities from our present, but it should be understood as the ongoing attempt at temporal homogenization of a dominant system that aims to overwrite competing forms of temporality. The idea of the timelessness of the present emerges as a result of focusing solely on those instances in which real-time capitalism imposes its temporal logic upon our time. And yet capitalist contemporaneity is not able to define our present entirely. To assume it does is to disregard those temporalities of our present that either remain incompatible with the time of global capitalism or are directly connected to a historical awareness of the logic of temporal domination. It is important, therefore, not to lose sight of the fact that, as Burges and Elias stress, "time is multiply measured both within a society or culture and between cultures."[33] After all, if the rise of contemporaneity is directly bound up with the rise of the Western nation-state and capitalism, then it must also be understood as a specifically Western way of imagining temporality, as the creation of a historically and materially specific form of relating to and making sense of the shared Now that was subsequently exported across the globe and strategically deployed in a variety of regions, overwriting a wide range of competing notions of temporality and contemporaneity. Commentators such as Ziauddin Sardar have pointed out that the techno-managerial idea of the future that dominates global discourse is a version of the future defined in the West's image, one that leaves little room for, say, Islamic notions of futurity.[34] The global standardization of a sense of contemporaneity is part and parcel of this overarching project of temporal colonization that aims to standardize both our way of understanding our relation to the Now and our imagination of future possibility by establishing a singularized contemporary as the temporal dominant of a world remade in the image of the West and global capital.

Osborne argues that the sense of a homogeneous global present is constructed via the planetary fiction of contemporaneity, a fiction created to maintain and support the structures of global capital. The contemporary, Osborne maintains, should be understood as "the fictional relational unity of the historical present."[35] Instead of suggesting that global capitalism creates a unified sense of the present to which we cannot imagine an alternative, therefore, Osborne foregrounds the importance of a historicized understanding of contemporaneity: global capital requires the construction of contemporaneity as the fiction of global temporal unity. Capitalism aims to construct a singularized version of contemporaneity in its own image in order to create a unified relation to the present that supports existing material and sociopolitical structures. An era's particular fiction of contemporaneity, just like an era's dominant ideas, is an index of its material and sociopolitical logic and its power structures. But capitalism's ability to maintain a given fiction of contemporaneity relies on the more or less successful attempt to erase and overwrite competing forms of temporality and being together in time. Describing the purported omnipresence of the contemporary today as an index of the ever-expanding present of capitalist realism may in one sense be aimed at a critique of the universalizing impulses of contemporary capitalism, which seeks to subsume all aspects of life under the logic of the market. However, this line of argumentation ultimately reveals itself as complicit in the erasure of competing temporalities in the present and, in spite of its very commitment, participates in the construction of a singularized sense of contemporaneity as the planetary fiction of capital.

Capitalism has to work hard to erase competing forms of being in time. We ought not make it easier. The attempt to create standardized temporality has always been a most difficult task, Bliss Cua Lim argues. Lim is particularly fascinated by the spectacle of chaotic local times that made the rise of homogenous time so difficult. "The decades before the adoption of standard time," Lim argues, "afford a fascinating look at the way in which homogeneous and heterogeneous public temporalities brushed against each other. It was a period in which the discovery of simultaneity failed to correspond to synchronicity; instead, the new technologically enabled experience of simultaneity was forced to contend with plural, competing, noncoinciding 'presents.'"[36] This struggle to create a homogeneous relation to the present was never fully successful, and as a result, critics like Terry Smith argue, the concept of the contemporary inevitably rose as an always multiple idea. As long as we use the concept of the contemporary as nothing but "a holding term" whose task is to "tempor[al]ize, while letting the institutions around one . . . do the defining," it becomes what Smith describes as "unthink": we "confine it to a service, rather than a substantive role." How, then, may we use the term more substantively? The answer, Smith suggests, lies in our ability to explore the concept's lost complexity and recover contemporaneity's "multiplicitous character."[37] Contemporaneity, as Smith argues, cannot be thought helpfully at the level of ideal universality. Doing so removes all specificity and critical usefulness from the term. For Smith, this problem acquires increased urgency in our moment. "In the aftermath of modernity, and the passing of the postmodern," Smith wonders, "how are we to know and show what it is to live in the conditions of contemporaneity?"[38] Contemporaneity, according to Smith, "consists precisely in the acceleration, ubiquity, and constancy of radical disjunctures of perception, of mismatching ways of seeing and valuing the same world, in the actual coincidence of asynchronous temporalities, in the jostling contingency of various cultural and social multiplicities, all thrown together in ways that highlight the fast growing inequalities within and between them."[39]

"The word *contemporary*," Smith concludes, "has always meant more than just the plain and passing present. . . . [T]he term *contemporary* calibrates a number of distinct but related ways of being *in* or *with* time, even of being *in* and *out* of time at the same time."[40] If the term has any meaning at all for contemporary criticism, in particular if we seek to bestow upon it a positive, political meaning, then we must free the concept from its singularization and return to it its critical potential. Salvaging the contemporary begins with the effort to recover the plural, heterogeneous character of the contemporary.

WHOSE TIME IS IT ANYWAY? THE SINGULARIZATION OF THE CONTEMPORARY

By focusing our attention on what Osborne describes as the "*will* to contemporaneity," which he defines as "the will to force the multiplicity of coeval social times together,"[41] we can examine how the fiction of contemporaneity erases and overwrites other temporal narratives and forms of temporal understanding. We can, in this way, restore to presence those ways of being in time and of being contemporary that global capitalism seeks to overwrite, thereby revealing homogeneous contemporaneity as a strategic fiction of capital. Contemporaneity, Smith argues, certainly describes a way of being in time, and it also describes "a way of so existing with others . . . who may share something of our own temporality."[42] But contemporaneity is also a way of being together in time with those who "live, contemporaneously, in distinct temporalities of their own." Contemporaneity is thus not only a matter of being together in time; it also means to "share a sense of the strangeness of being in time, now."[43] This strangeness of being in time and the disjunctive senses of temporality that cannot be subsumed under capital or that run counter to the productive ways of relating to the present that the capitalist contemporary aims to standardize offer a way to reclaim contemporaneity as a fundamentally social category. Being contemporary today does not just describe the individualized struggle to be "current" or to keep up with the times. Rather, the desire to be contemporary is a struggle for presence, and understanding this struggle for contemporaneity in the era of the long now plurally is to politically activate the concept of the contemporary.

As soon as we ask by whom and to what end the fiction of contemporaneity is constructed, we see that such questions begin to unearth that which is overwritten by the dominant narrative of the contemporary. After all, if there are ways of understanding time and contemporaneity that are excluded from the process of constructing a dominant sense of contemporaneity, then surely anxiety-laden proclamations of the problem of inescapable, repressive contemporaneity must ring hollow and indeed appear profoundly cynical to those whose temporal imagination was denied integration into the contemporary. Temporalization is central to how we imagine social and racial difference. Moreover, temporalization is crucial to maintaining the logic of social and racial difference. Proclamations of the beauty and simplicity of the relation between North American Indigenous peoples and nature, for instance—a relation that is coded as eternally past and thus timeless, in contradistinction to the technologized now of colonial culture, which professes to mourn the loss of its connection to nature and the environment—allow us to maintain long-standing notions of difference between Indigenous culture and the culture of contemporary North America (the colonial contemporary). By perpetuating narratives of the beauty of the Indigenous subject's essential connection to nature that the contemporary dominant lacks, and by ascribing to the Indigenous subject a constitutive, romanticized, eternally past connection to the land, we maintain the exclusion of indigeneity from the contemporary.

Contemporaneity is a matter of privilege. And while the formation of the contemporary creates a common way of being in time, it also functions as an important broker of power and a mechanism of exclusion and segregation insofar as it provides a narrative framework within which we construct our imagination of difference. The jargon of noncontemporaneity allows us to naturalize difference and police the boundaries of segregation. By trading in an overtly racist language of difference for the celebration of idealized temporal differences between ethnic groups and racialized subjects, we sneak the logic of essentializing distinctions between races in the back door. Racialization is temporalization, and the temporalization of race maintains the notion of contemporaneity as temporal neutrality or timelessness, which in turn works in concert with the understanding of whiteness as the absence of race. Racialization relies on an imagination of race stabilized by a complex architecture of comparative temporalization, which excludes differently racialized subjects via the construction of various versions of noncontemporaneity. How luxurious a problem must excessive contemporaneity therefore seem to those who have historically been denied inclusion in the contemporary? How banal must the struggle with the current crisis of futurity seem to those whose history consists of instance after instance of denials of futurity and a lack of hope for a different, better world?

What I wish to advance here, then, is an argument for the importance of understanding the concept of the contemporary not simply as the benign placeholder for a more concrete effort at periodization or a more precise description of a temporal relation that we cannot quite be bothered to work out. The concept does a lot more work than this, and it is crucial that we understand it. Instead of continuing to lament the repressive ubiquity of the contemporary, we must explore how the singularized, homogeneous idea of contemporaneity serves as a building block for our imagination of what it means to belong not only to a moment but also to the social, political, and cultural structures that define a moment. Contemporaneity is a measure of integration into or exclusion from the dominant structures of a given historical moment in a given sociocultural context. Contemporaneity defines what kind of subject we should ideally be, how we should ideally act, and what values and beliefs we should ideally hold to be recognized as a functional subject at a specific moment in history. Contemporaneity is a tool of normalization whose measure of success is expressed in degrees of presence. The degree of our contemporaneity, that is, registers how close we are to being a given moment's ideal, functional subject. Contemporaneity does not mark temporal neutrality. Instead, it consists of a complex set of expectations and sociopolitical and cultural imperatives. The closer we are to becoming the ideal subject of contemporary capitalism, the more contemporary we feel. Defined in this way, full contemporaneity, truly living in the moment, is a mark of privilege and expresses the norm against which all subjects are measured, which means that exclusion from the contemporary is also a measure of the degree of exclusion from the dominant of a society. Contemporaneity is a one of the highest prizes of a society built upon persistent mechanisms of exclusion, inequality, and segregation, mechanisms that the logic of a singularized sense of contemporaneity helps keep intact. Contemporaneity is an indicator of privilege and power, and it is at every point bound up with the logic of race, gender, and class. Full contemporaneity is the zero point of a scale that registers deviations from the norm as degrees of noncontemporaneity, and the desire to aspire to this universalized sense of contemporaneity is a measure of our conformism to the rules and structures of a social and material dominant.

The African American novel thus assumes a particularly crucial role in our moment precisely due to the centrality of engagements with time in African American literature across history. As Daylanne K. English illustrates in *Each Hour Redeem* (2013), "Authors throughout the African American literary tradition have always understood, juxtaposed, and exploited the different temporalities inherent in print culture's various forms in various eras." And yet, English shows, the "clear centrality of time in the African American literary tradition" has also "remained relatively neglected as a category of analysis."[44] English's magisterial overview of engagements with time in early African American literature, nineteenth-century African American literature, the Harlem Renaissance, and the Black Arts Movement lays the groundwork for necessary studies of time in contemporary African American literature. This chapter attempts to make its own, modest contribution to this larger project by interrogating the status of the time novel in contemporary African American writing. African American literature's engagement with time, English argues, registers "what we might term the 'temporal damage' rendered by racialized injustice across centuries." The plays of Suzan-Lori Parks, for instance, English proposes, suggest that there is cause for hopefulness, for they indicate that "some African American writers may be starting to imagine ways to heal that damage."[45] The novels of Laymon and Whitehead in turn show that hope for our time lies in a more complex understanding of what it can mean to be contemporary, one that returns us to the temporality of hope itself. Hope emerges in these novels as a complex, nonlinear, and discontinuous relation to the past. Hope and futurity are born out of a plural contemporary that carries both the weight and the possibilities of the past's unfulfilled promises and dreams. The African American time novel gives us an understanding of contemporaneity and futurity, therefore, that recalls Honoré de Balzac's famous definition of hope in *A Prince of Bohemia*: "Hope is a memory that desires."[46]

As we saw above, *Long Division*'s protagonist City struggles to make sense of the problematic relation between race and time. Literature, as City discovers over the course of the novel, provides the children with a solution to the temporal foreclosures that result from the history of racism and multiculturalism's jargon of contemporaneity. Still reeling from the effects of the fixed competition, City travels to rural Mississippi for the summer to spend time with his grandmother. There he finds a mysterious book called *Long Division*. This book is narrated by the second protagonist of Laymon's novel, also called City, who lives in the year 1985. The 1985 City, as 2013 City learns in reading the book, spends his summer in Mississippi trying to impress his first true love, Shalaya Crump. Laymon's novel subsequently shuttles back and forth between the two versions of City and their respective times, narrating their struggles with the history and presence of racism. Moreover, 1985 City and his love interest, Shalaya, travel through time from 1985 to 2013 and back to 1964, to the era of the civil rights movement and the struggles for change and liberation in the context of which their grandfathers lost their lives. *Long Division* is a time travel novel. What the children encounter on their travels, however, is not the temporal alienation we ordinarily associate with time travel novels but rather something akin to affinity and indeed contemporaneity across time. As they travel through time, the children encounter racism, violence, and hatred, as well as continuing structures of segregation and violence that join them across temporal periods to those who have suffered from racism. *Long Division* is also a love story: it is the story of the budding romance between City and Shalaya and the loving bonds that emerge across time between children who discover what it means to live with the history and presence of US racism. The different strands of these loving relationships in Laymon's novel converge in a temporal problem that City struggles to work out. Shalaya suggests that she could love City, but her love is predicated on City helping her, as she puts it, to "change the future in, I don't know dot dot dot a special way" (25). Over the course of the novel, City and the other children learn what this might mean. As a result of their travels through time, they understand toward the end of the novel, they have "changed the future by changing the past" (245). But they also know that changing the past, revisiting and confronting history and thereby creating new possibilities for tomorrow, is a deeply painful act. And yet the children read this pain as a sign of hope. It is "how we know that we're changing the future in a special way," they note, realizing that the "special change, the kind that lasts, hurts" (246).

After having traveled through time via a small hole in the ground in a way that has profoundly reshaped his understanding of his relation to history and temporality, 1985 City reflects on what he learned about the future. "I . . . knew that 'tomorrow' was a word now like the thousands of other words in that hole," he remarks (262). The way to overcome foreclosures of the future, City learns, is to treat is as a problem of our imagination: "I closed my mouth, pulled down the top of the hole, and imagined more words in the dark" (262). But City discovers he is not alone in the hole that allows him to travel between different historical moments. In the dark, he recognizes LaVander Peeler and 2013 City, and together they begin to imagine new words and new tomorrows: "Slowly, we opened our red eyes in the dark and taught each other how to love. Hand in hand, deep in the underground of Mississippi, we all ran away to tomorrow because we finally could" (263). Running away to tomorrow through the power of words and the imagination is made possible by an alinear form of temporality that establishes continuity and contemporaneity across timelines and constantly folds back on itself. Laymon's novel mediates this particular version of temporality on the level of both form and content through the logic of rereading and rewriting. Running away to tomorrow, the children finally understand, is accomplished through rereading and by way of the temporal imagination to which the act of rereading gives rise: "We started rereading *Long Division* from the beginning, knowing that all we needed to know about how to survive, how to live, and how to love in Mississippi was in our hands. The sentences had always been there" (267). These lines with which Laymon's novel concludes defy the linear understanding of an ending and instead gesture toward a new beginning by locating possibility, the new, and futurity in the act of rereading. *Long Division* concretely models the kind of utopian thought that philosophers like Bloch describe as "impeded futures."[47] Rereading, the children learn, allows us to see what remained hidden or what could not be understood during previous readings, and rereading the past from a different standpoint allows us to trace possibilities for rewriting the present and thus imagine a different tomorrow. Laymon's novel traces a futurity that is immanent in the word and in our imagination, an alinear conception of both time and futurity made legible through rereading that recovers from the past those avenues for change which were initially foreclosed and demands the fulfillment of those demands for justice, liberation, and love that were initially silenced.

The logic of the children's time travel thus does not simply give rise to the experience of anachronism or parachrony that is a trademark element of time travel stories but rather provides a different conception of historical time that emerges through the constant conversation between past and present, as a constant process of rereading and rewriting that is as alinear and discontinuous as the process of writing itself. And it is the alinear temporality that lies at the heart of writing and reading novels, the temporality that gives rise to the anticipatory futurity the children are able to imagine at the end of the novel, that *Long Division* mediates in its own form and structure. No doubt, the suggestion that we may be able to conceive of time, history, and futurity in a way that is alinear and crucially involves instances of time folding back on itself to create new imaginaries by revisiting the never completed past may initially appear overly abstract. But Laymon's novel accomplishes something profound: it models this suggestion concretely by reminding us that this logical point describes something with which we are already intimately familiar. It is precisely how novels are written and read. Laymon's novel thus contains a firm, genuine belief in the importance of the social and political function of the novelistic imagination. "Some books can completely change how we see ourselves and everything else in the world," City's principal tells him early on in the novel. *Long Division* engages in a constant process of self-examination that asks how the contemporary African American novel may be able to generate new ways of relating to a present that seems devoid of futurity. Literature, the children learn, teaches us to read, reread, and thereby rewrite, and it affords us new ways of imagining ourselves in the world, thus accomplishing what English senses as a crucial aspect of the African American novel today: making legible the temporal damage that results from the history of racism. *Long Division*—Laymon's novel and the book in Laymon's novel—for us and for the children, outlines a different relation to history and the historical present. In this way, it embraces the work of literature as a method for exploring paths that may lead us to new, better tomorrows. City learns that people "use words to make folks disappear," but he also ultimately understands, as his grandmother puts it, that it is therefore "in his hands" to use words to make people "reappear" (259–60). Revising and rewriting a brief note he first composed after an earlier experience with time travel, City reflects in the novel's closing passages on the acts of writing and reading and their power in the world:

> I reread it. And I wondered. And I wandered. And I write. And I reread that. And I wrote more. And I erased some lies. And I wrote more. And I erased some truth. And I thought about Honors English teachers and librarians. And I forgot about them. And I thought about what people like Shalaya, Baize, Evan and me needed to read in school to prepare to fight, love, and disappear. And I forgot about that. And I wrote more. And the more I wrote and erased, the more I felt Baize and other characters slowly—word by word, maybe even sense by sense—coming back. (261)

Long Division begins and ends with an ellipsis. Additionally, like the first and last page of the novel, each shift in time and narration is indicated by a white page with three dots. *Long Division* is a novel about omissions, about things that are absent or have been left out. But it is also a novel that seeks what is still forthcoming, possibilities and openings. It finds such openings in the present and future as well as in the past, and in their discontinuous, nonlinear interrelation. *Long Division* is also the story of the search for a lost girl, Baize Shephard, a classmate of 2013 City. Baize, the lost girl whose notoriety lies in the fact that she is a little "extra," personifies crucial aspects of the novel's logic. If she could be any punctuation mark, Baize tells City toward the end of the novel, after City has discovered her in a different time, she'd be an ellipsis, because "the ellipsis always knows something more came before it and something more is coming after it" (245). What is missing, the little bit of extra, is what must be recovered, for it is the extraness of what is missing—of those possibilities that were denied and silenced, and carried over into the present from the past—that contains hope and the possibility of what is yet to come. *Long Division* argues that love and the desire to change the future dot dot dot in a special way are intricately linked, and this link can break the limits of singular time and make it possible to gain access to different temporalities. Laymon's novel emphatically and passionately foregrounds what Russell West-Pavlov describes as one of the fundamental ways of understanding time and the present beyond their homogenization: as the "dynamism and rhythm" of transformative processes, the "complex overlappings and interactions" that "make up the plural temporalities that . . . [are] the constantly present alternative to a singular and abstract time.'"[48] If she had her own book, Baize concludes, she would "have a front cover with the words 'Long Division' across the top and below 'Long Division' would be a blue-black ellipsis" (245). The historical present, always plural because it is constantly shaped by what preceded it and by what may yet succeed it, becomes the site of hope for the children. "We'd all be inside the book, too," Baize explains, "with those other characters already in the book and we'd all fall in love with each other" (245).

The alternative to the singularized contemporary and the jargon of noncontemporaneity modeled by novels like *Long Division* may be understood as an example of what Rancière describes as heterochronies: "Other forms of temporality, dissentious forms of temporality that create distensions and breaks" in the time of the present.[49] The discontinuous and alinear form of temporality and indeed of contemporaneity in Laymon's novel aims to highlight and politically activate the competing forms of temporality in our present. In this way, the novel launches its attack on the repressive temporal logic of multiculturalism and neoliberal diversity politics, which it reveals as a new stage of segregation and repression. It is important to stress, however, that heterochronies should not simply be understood as romanticized alternative temporalities bestowed with mythical transformative or political potential. As Madhu Dubey emphasizes, we must be wary of critical models that remain attached to the idea of margins as the locus for progressive, liberatory, or transgressive politics, since this attachment tends to emerge out of an "overly totalized notion of the 'dominant'" that "almost always entails as its corollary a romanticized notion of the 'residual.'"[50] Such logic would replicate precisely the set of problems that the novels of writers like Whitehead and Laymon seek to transcend. Heterochronies are positioned against such totalized notions of the contemporary. Heterochronies are not a matter of a politics of the temporal margin nor a politics that idealizes noncontemporaneity. Instead, heterochronies designate the multitude of timelines that exist within and, importantly, structure our present and that must be understood as the true complexity of the contemporary. Heterochronies allow us to imagine contemporaneity beyond a singular, dominant sense of being in time. They restore the contemporary as a substantive, critical category that describes a plurality of being in time. Heterochronies, Rancière argues, are moments "of suspension of the usual plots that absorb every situation into the global process, on the way dispossessing those who live in 'our time' of the ability to understand it." "A heterochrony," he argues consequently, can thus be understood as "a redistribution of times that invents new capacities for framing the present."[51] In novels like Laymon's, heterochronies describe instances in which the relation between time and racialization becomes visible, instances that make legible the homogenization of time as expressions of the will to contemporaneity of the dominant. A heterogeneous understanding of contemporaneity that traces new social and political capacities in the present is therefore not a matter of reducing plurality and multiplicity to sameness, nor is it a matter of championing pure pluralism. Instead we may understand true contemporaneity dialectically, as a negative totality, as a sense of commonality and a collective relation to our time that takes form precisely through the tensions among its myriad poles, allowing for a common relation to the present as history precisely by way of maintaining the visibility of the plurality of times of the present. Contemporaneity thus conceived is not a matter of aspiration or consent to the temporal dominant but rather a critical relation to the present.

SPECULATIVE CONTEMPORANEITY: PREILLUMINATIONS OF A BETTER WORLD

One of the biggest problems with which City struggles is the relation among memory, the present, and the future. "They always expecting us to forget," City's grandmother notes at one point in the novel, adding, "I'm tired of forgetting." But this confuses City, since his grandmother also frequently points out to him that forgetting can be an important, helpful act, since it ensures that one is not limited or held back by the past. Memory, City begins to sense, is a complicated operation, one that can aid as much as it can hinder his ability to deal with the past and work toward a different, changed tomorrow. But how, City wonders, can he tell the difference between good and bad versions of both memory and forgetting? "I couldn't completely understand how Grandma could go from telling me that grown folks forget what they need, to saying she was tired of forgetting," he remarks (109). The complicated status of memory and forgetting is a prominent topic in the African American novel's engagement with time. Memory, of course, is a crucially important mechanism that ensures historical injuries and injustices are never forgotten. In turn, it is also clear, as we saw in the novels of Whitehead and Laymon, that forgetting serves as one of the main tools of historical erasure and thus becomes a mechanism for continued segregation and exclusion (even or especially if it masks itself as the precondition for unification and homogenization). And yet, as novels like Toni Morrison's *Beloved* (1987) show, under certain conditions forgetting also becomes an important operation that establishes a different way of relating to the past and may indeed be centrally involved in the struggle for futurity. *Beloved* interrogates the complicated relation among past, present, and future in part in relation to the different functions of forgetting.[52]

Beloved begins with a dedication: "Sixty million and more." The dedication introduces one of the central problems with which the novel grapples. The "sixty million and more" must be remembered. But memory also brings with it temporal impasses for the present, pitting memory against history and also against the present and future. This ultimately complicates what otherwise seems a simple and utterly self-evident point: we must never forget the history of the global slave trade, we must always remember the sixty million and more. Only a couple of pages after the novel asks us to remember the sixty million and more, one of its central characters, Sethe, begins a series of reflections on the logic of the relation among past, present, and future that unfolds the complexity of what initially seemed a straightforward project of remembering the past. Remembering the past is an important aspect of relating to the present insofar as it ensures that we do not repeat the horrific actions of our past. But the past in *Beloved* is from the outset more complicated than this. The novel's characters struggle with the absence of temporal and historical development. "Her past had been like her present," Sethe observes when reflecting upon her mother's life, "intolerable."[53] Remembering, Sethe realizes, stands in the way of change and progress by creating a relationship to the past and time that seems to make impossible any sense of futurity. And since memory stands in the way of creating change in the present and therefore a (better) future, Sethe reasons, "the future" appears to be "a matter of keeping the past at bay" (48). Frustrated with memory, Sethe struggles with her brain's seeming inability to make use of the past to construct an image of the future, trapping her in a present altogether determined by the past: "Loaded with the past and hungry for more, it left her no room to imagine, let along plan for, the next day" (49). *Beloved* asks under which conditions remembering the past may reify rather than oppose temporal segregation and temporal immobility. The consequence of the events she experiences, the constant grip that the past (and in turn Beloved) has on Sethe and her present, is described as an erasure of temporality, a collapse of the future into a time from which there is no escape and in which there is no development or mobility: Sethe finds herself "wrapped in a timeless present" (217). Those who help Sethe and Denver do so in part because they understand the problem that plagues them. For the character Ella, helping also contains "something very personal": "Ella didn't like the idea of past errors taking possession of the present. . . . The future was sunset; the past something to leave behind. And if it didn't stay behind, well, you might have to stomp it out" (302).

Critics who have examined the novel's engagement with time and history tend to struggle to connect *Beloved*'s internal time to the novel's place in external history. Kimberly Chabot Davis, for instance, examines Morrison's novel in relation to postmodernism's exhaustion of history and suggests that while *Beloved* should be understood as a postmodern novel inasmuch as it "exhibits a postmodern skepticism of sweeping historical narratives, or 'Truth,' and of Marxist teleological notions of time," the novel also "retains [a] . . . commitment to the crucial importance of deep cultural memory, of keeping the past alive in order to construct a better future."[54] Given the novel's virtually immediate commitment to undercutting memory, however, such readings of *Beloved* do not fully capture the novel's relationship to time, memory, and history. One cause of this limitation is Davis's attempt to situate the novel within postmodernism, which falsifies the novel's historical context as well as its logic and political project. *Beloved* expresses a moment in literary history characterized by the departure from postmodernism and the turn to different engagements with time. Connecting *Beloved* to the analysis presented in previous chapters, we can see that Morrison's novel is an early example of what has become a dominant gesture in the contemporary American novel: indicating the limitations of a subjective relation to time (in this case memory), which stands in direct contrast to historical time, since the latter is able to produce ways of relating to the present that generate the futurity erased from the present by memory. *Beloved* should therefore be read not as a historical novel that stresses the importance of cultural memory but as a time novel that examines crises of the present and futurity in relation to memory and by doing so highlights the limitations of the historical novel for contemporary African American literature. In fact, the departure from the historical novel in African American literature, which is bound up with the emergence of speculative fiction and Afrofuturism in black writing, may be understood as connected to a general project of examining how the black subject and the African American novel remain excluded from the contemporary. The historical novel is without doubt still an important aspect of the African American novel. But by tracing the logic of temporal segregation from the present and a crisis of futurity particular to African American culture, Morrison also illustrates the problematic status (even complicity) of the historical novel in the context of these crises. Instead of defending cultural memory against postmodern attacks on historical time, *Beloved* gives us an account of the relation between memory and history that is aimed at retemporalizing the present.

The traditional (thus ordinarily white and male) time traveler's biggest fear is getting stuck in a time that is not his own. Out of (his) time, the traveler feels temporally alienated, untimely. The horror of such a scenario of course presupposes that the normal condition of the traveler is contemporaneity—fitting into and being of his own time. Stuck in another time, however, the traveler not only feels alienated but also understands he must not change anything in a time that is not his own for fear that too much change may result from his actions. The simple solution to the time traveler's fear is to avoid temporal homelessness by remaining in (his own) present. But what if the present is the time in which one is stuck and that is not one's own? What if the time one perceives as profoundly alienating is one's own now? And what if the problem in this situation is not the fear of changing too much but the inability to change anything? The experience of being trapped in a timeless present, which serves as the conceit of a range of contemporary novels by white male writers, is not new for African Americans. It describes, as we see in *Beloved*, the African American experience of both history and the present. Not only is the black subject stuck in a *perpetual* present, but she is stuck in a time that is not her own. This simultaneity of captivity and exclusion, of being confronted with an erasure of futurity while also being denied inclusion in the contemporary, becomes a driving political and aesthetic problem of the African American time novel. By exploring the link between the notion of a perpetual present and the historical connection between racial exclusion and temporal exclusion, novelists like Morrison turn to what Peter Boxall describes as one of the novel's foundational aspects: its inquiry into the troubled and complex relation between past and present. This aspect of the novel, Boxall argues, is captured in the famous line from William Faulkner's *Requiem for a Nun*, a text that directly engages with the racial logic of this problem: "The past is never dead. It's not even past."[55] In recent years, African American novelists have variously deployed the problem of the undead past and the specter of repetition to grapple with temporal crises in relation to the logic of race today. Tananarive Due's African Immortals series and Octavia E. Butler's *Parable* novels, as well as African American time-travel novels such as Butler's *Kindred* or John A. Williams's *Captain Blackman* are examples of the variety of genres that authors have mobilized to reimagine the past's influence on our understanding of time. The novels of Colson Whitehead, however, arguably contain one of the most significant and complex archives of temporal reimagination in contemporary literature.

As the novels of Laymon and Whitehead show, the possibilities for inclusion in the present are limited to two repressive choices: to join in a historyless contemporary or be marked as constitutively noncontemporary. Neither option leaves room for futurity for the black subject: the future is either erased by making noncontemporaneity the precondition for integration into the present or it is made available as a deformed semblance of futurity, as a future that depends on total assimilation into a singularized multicultural contemporary in which all temporalities, severed from substantive connections to history, collapse into a long now. The rhetoric of diversity, as we encounter it in the novels of Whitehead and Laymon, is a strategy for integration into the present that maintains the denial of plural contemporaneity. Faced with the problem of repressive contemporaneity, the children in Laymon's novel ultimately learn to navigate the complex relationship between memory and forgetting. Forgetting is a long-standing strategy of domination, and as the children know, it is also one of the most problematic ways of dealing with the memory of racial violence. And yet forgetting, if strategically deployed, also provides them with a way to free themselves from the weight and repressive influence of the past and instead develop a different, active relation to the past that opens the path to another future. These other relations to the past in Laymon's novel map onto the difference between rereading and repetition: only by rereading the past can the children develop the new words and imaginaries that offer them a way to run away to tomorrow. It is in this relation to memory and forgetting, by understanding futurity as emerging from a specific relation to the past, that *Long Division* locates the importance of tomorrows—and this indicates an important aspect of the contemporary African American novel's engagement with time and futurity more widely conceived.

In his 1984 essay "The Necessity of Tomorrows," Samuel Delany laments the dearth of black science fiction writing. In addition to himself, Delany is only able to identify three other writers of black science fiction: Octavia Butler, who published her first novel four years before the publication of Delany's essay, Steve Barnes, and Charles R. Saunders. The absence of black science fiction, Delany argues, is a profound problem, for African Americans must demand the future: "We need images of tomorrow; and our people need them more than most." "Without an image of tomorrow," Delany elaborates, "one is trapped by blind history, economics, and politics beyond our control. One is tied up in a web, in a net, with no way to struggle free. Only by having clear and vital images of the *many* alternatives, good and bad, of where one *can* go, will we have any control over the way we may actually get there in a reality tomorrow will bring all too quickly."[56] But science fiction, if it is to serve as a tool for keeping alive hope and bringing about a different, better world, is not just a matter of constructing dream worlds and fantastic accounts of future societies. Rather, Delany argues, science fiction creates the preconditions for the emergence of the future by engaging with the contradictions of a present that continues to be influenced by the past, which indicates latent possibilities for change. "If science fiction has any use at all," Delany writes, "it is that . . . it gives us images *for* our futures."[57] Exploring the possibilities and alternatives inherent in a present that is understood as temporally plural by way of speculative fiction can be understood as exploiting one of the most significant sites of contradiction of the system of maintaining deeply entrenched systems of social exclusion and normalization described above. The concept of the contemporary, Osborne argues, projects upon an always plural and fractured present a "temporal unity that is actually, in principle, futural or anticipatory." The fiction of contemporaneity, in other words, is a narrative about the present that is strategic and aimed at a particular future. "The concept of the contemporary," Osborne adds, is "inherently speculative."[58] And precisely since this is so, the project of laying bare how the fiction of contemporaneity singularizes the time of the present to bring about a particular kind of future is able to create the preconditions for the creation of different futures by exploring the full temporal heterogeneity of the contemporary.

Not surprisingly, speculative fiction plays a central role in this effort. To restore the concept of the contemporary to its substantive definition, therefore, is also an exercise in identifying in the present those images and imaginaries that may give rise to different futures. To reclaim the plural contemporary is to reclaim futurity. Whitehead's *The Intuitionist* is one of the most striking examples of an author's experimentation with the limits and possibilities of both speculative fiction and the contemporary. The plot of *The Intuitionist* revolves around elevator inspectors, the conflict between two very different schools and methods of elevator inspection, and the hunt for the work of the famous experimental elevator theoretician James Fulton, who may have left behind the plans and blueprints for the "black box"—the perfect elevator. Whitehead's novel is a work of speculative fiction that is set in an alternate version of the mid-twentieth century, in a rereading and rewriting of the history of the modern metropolis and American modernity that is at once strange and utterly familiar. The novel is set in a period in which "the times are changing."[59] Old, entrenched structures of social and spatial segregation are beginning to crumble. The novel's protagonist, Lila Mae Watson, is not only part of an alternative school of elevator inspectors (Intuitionists, who are opposed and frequently disparaged by adherents to the traditional way of inspecting elevators, the Empiricists) but also one of the first black elevator inspectors in the industry. Whitehead gives us a story about one of modernity's key inventions, the elevator, which made possible the modern skyscraper and with it the modern city. At its heart, *The Intuitionist* is a novel about the particular imagination of the future that is bound up with the rise of modernity and about those futures that are excluded from modernity's rise. *The Intuitionist* is about verticality as a particular way of understanding the future and the logic of time this presupposes. It is about modernity's architects, who "understand that the future is up" and that "the future is in how high you can go," as well as about Lila Mae, who seeks to find her future in a world that sees the times are changing but nevertheless finds it "difficult to shake old habits" (16). *The Intuitionist* formally and generically mediates the blended temporality of modernity and affords us a speculative glimpse into the plurality of modernity's temporal trajectories; it lays bare the temporalities of modernity that could have been, were not, but may yet be. It masterfully points toward the fissures in the modern fiction of the contemporary and the futures that rest on it, and it shows how firmly a singularized logic of modern progress is anchored in the past and how viciously it is defended against alternative temporalities.

When Lila Mae Watson discusses Fulton's revolutionary work with Natchez, her friend and colleague, he impresses upon her the importance of understanding the significance of the black box in terms of the intersection of the future and race, of racial uplift in a different, better future: "When I hear them talk about his invention, they always saying it's the future. It's the future of cities. But it's our future, not theirs. It's ours. And we need to take it back. What he made, this elevator, colored people made that. It's ours" (139–40). Fulton's perfect elevator denotes the possibility of change, of a different way of imagining the future and radical social change: "Just think of it—Fulton's black box. Do you know what it means? The second elevation is coming. Everything around us, all that out there, will come down" (182). And while the possibility of change indeed hinges upon one particular character, Lila Mae, who is described as "flux itself" (20), the novel undercuts such messianic proclamations of change and possibility by locating the source of change in a particular relation to the present. Indeed, it is in this way of understanding the relationship between present and future, in the speculative engagement with plural contemporaneity, that we can locate a project that characterizes much of Whitehead's work. *The Intuitionist* puts in place the building blocks and the basic set of problems to which Whitehead returns in more recent novels such as *Zone One* (2011).

Zone One is a postapocalyptic zombie novel that examines the crisis of futurity in relation to the temptation to respond to the crises of the present by turning our gaze backward in an effort to revive an idealized version of the past. *Zone One* shows that this backward orientation appears as particularly problematic and bound up with its own history of power relations when examined from the perspective of the black subject's confinement to pastness. The novel's protagonist, Mark Spitz, who remains, like all characters, not racialized for most of the novel and whose nickname is the only indicator of race (a nickname given to him because of "the black-people-can't-swim thing"), is a survivor of the zombie apocalypse.[60] Spitz works for an agency, Project Phoenix, which is assembled of parts of what remains of the US government and is part of a general reconstruction effort. The slogan of the project—"We make the future!"—continues to collide with and ultimately collapses into the influence of the past, which grows ever stronger. Indeed, the most common ailment of survivors is an often-crippling condition called Postapocalyptic Stress Disorder, or PASD, whose episodes periodically erase the distinction between the afflicted humans and zombies. The zombies themselves are split into two groups, the skels and a group of undead that the surviving humans not only prefer but also frequently humanize: the stragglers. Stragglers are spatially and temporally static zombies who do not roam the streets in search for human flesh but instead inhabit feedback loops of the past, perpetually remaining in the same place. The survivors surmise that these places must carry pleasant memories for the stragglers, which explains their unwillingness to move on. As Mark Spitz notes, encountering a straggler is like encountering a tableau or diorama of a moment frozen in time, a motif formally utilized throughout the novel. In particular, since Mark Spitz cannot help but observe that the apocalypse has a strong tendency to generate narrative closure—after all, the perceived epistemological end of time is not kind to the time of narrative—we could describe the formal structure of Whitehead's *Zone One*, which attempts to unmask the dangers of temporal stasis and the lure of the past, as a tableau vivant with zombies. What stands in the way of actually "making the future" and leads to the ultimate failure of the American Phoenix project is summarized by Mark Spitz in a notable comment: "One always gets killed when one stands with one leg in the past" (93).

But what may initially seem like a return to the problem confronted by J. Sutter as well as Morrison's Sethe (if the past can make the present dangerous and the future impossible, then should one avoid any attachment to the past?) gives way to a complex engagement with the connection between pastness and futurity that we may read as an attempt to bring together the various facets of the problem laid out in Whitehead's previous novels. Whitehead's novel foregrounds the problem of the nostalgic response to a present in crisis, but it also seeks to recover a sense of futurity from such a present without entirely severing the connection to the past. But what is the solution to the problem of getting killed when one stands with one leg in the past if not to avoid connections to the past altogether? In the conclusion to *Zone One*, a character "writes her way into the future" (232). Yet, as Mark Spitz learns, futurity must be understood not as fully formed cultural futures and images of difference but as action in the present. "Normal meant 'the past,'" Spitz knows, and since this is the case, futurity must be formulated in opposition to the normal, and the future itself is best understood, he realizes early on in the novel, as "the clay in their hands" (65). Consequently, the novel concludes with Spitz embracing the effects of the end times, since he is able to see their utopian aspects and the openings they make possible. "The world wasn't ending," Spitz says of his situation in the final lines of the novel. "It had ended, and now they were in the new place. They could not recognize it because they had not seen it before" (257–58). The unrecognizability of the new place replaces the common narrative of the eternal present after the end of time with an account of this present as a time of possibility. This present is able to bring about a version of the new and of futurity that is conceived as a radical break with the normalized relation to the past that makes way for a more complex understanding of the interrelation of past, present, and future.

The logic of Whitehead's novel may be articulated via the distinction between two forms of nostalgia described by Svetlana Boym: restorative nostalgia and reflective nostalgia. The former is characterized by backward orientation and is the kind of nostalgia with which we are most often familiar and which we see at work, for instance, in Project Phoenix. Reflective nostalgia, by contrast, is connected to a utopian project. S. D. Chrostowska succinctly lays out Boym's distinction: as opposed to restorative nostalgia, which "spatializes time" and "repristinates" a "transhistorical reconstruction of the lost 'home,'" reflective nostalgia "dwells in longing as such and does not seek restoration qua 'homecoming.'"[61] Restorative nostalgia responds to crises of futurity by turning toward a nostalgically idealized past that, in the absence of the ability to imagine substantive, positive change, it seems to make great again. Reflective nostalgia, by contradistinction, describes the longing for the fulfillment of past wishes and addresses the present that this nostalgia regards as a time marked by absence, broken promises, and the denial of past dreams and possibility. The utopian core of such an engagement with the past, not as pure pastness but as the basis for utopian longing in the present, returns us to Balzac's definition of hope as "a memory that desires." Restorative nostalgia generates stasis and repetition and is, as *Zone One* as well as Octavia Butler's *Parable* novels or more recently N. K. Jemisin's *Broken Earth* series show, one of the most dangerous responses to a crisis of futurity. Instead, Whitehead, Butler, and Jemison argue for an understanding of the present as time in flux in which change becomes the only constant.

The possibility of futurity in *Zone One* lies in recognizing what Ernst Bloch describes as the utopian possibility that lies in the present's "latent potential," which, as Peter Thompson explains, can be better understood as "preilluminations, of a better world" or "messages of hope sent to us from a not yet possible future reality but already known to us from our own need for the fulfillment of past desires and memories as 'anticipatory consciousness.'"[62] The "historical surplus," as Bloch would have it, of these unfulfilled historical desires and precedents refuses to be silenced, and its demands on our present are a cornerstone of what Bloch calls the "not yet," the latent potential in the always multitemporal present that is the source of change and transformation.[63] Vincent Geoghegan suggests that such an account of time also means that "paradoxically, talking about the future may be one way to come to terms with the past."[64] Reframing the tension between past and present in a way that becomes a source of futurity means that "memory traces are reactivated in the present," which "helps shape the new.[65] Novels such as Colson Whitehead's *Zone One* historicize the purported foreclosure of narratives of the future and remain deeply suspicious of restoratively nostalgic attachments to the past, thus serving an invaluable epistemological function in the context of the temporal crises brought about by real-time capitalism. Much like Bloch, who, as David Kaufmann notes, aims to "create a science of the future from the materials . . . at hand," novelists like Whitehead ask us to imagine futurity as the unformed ball of clay that rests in our hands and contains the possibility for the creation of an infinite variety of shapes.[66]

Instances in which the competing temporalities that the dominant system seeks to erase or homogenize become visible constitute what Rancière calls "interruptions": "Moments when one of the social machines that structures the time of domination breaks down and stops." Such interruptions in turn make possible a politics of futurity that, in Rancière's words, attempts to trace "another possible world within the existing world."[67] The African American time novel provides us with an aesthetic source of the political impulse Rancière understands as central to our ability to engage with the contradictions of our present. The African American time novel has over the course of the past two decades or so answered Rancière's recent call to oppose "the constraint of normal time" by "constructing alternative possibilities for addressing the present."[68] The formal and generic exploration of the heterochronies of the present is one of the most urgent political projects of the African American *Zeitroman*, one that can be described with Rancière as aimed at "the potentialities of art forms that work at the crossroads of temporalities."[69] In addressing itself to the seeds of futurity in the present, to the latent potential contained in the fissures of dominant temporality, the African American time novel reminds us that its ability to trace future possibility in the present is one of art's most significant functions.

In the final pages of *The Intuitionist*, the novel's narrative switches back and forth between past and present, Fulton and Lila Mae. Fulton is completing his work on the perfect elevator, the black box, and in these final moments of his work Fulton permits himself to imagine the future and the possible effect that his black box may have. He knows his invention is out of place and indeed out of time in the present. His invention requires a different time to make its impact. He knows that those who surround him in the present, especially the white majority, are not "ready for it"—not ready for the city of the future and the new society the black box can bring about. After all, he notes, "they can barely make sense of the cities they have now" (251). Still, he wishes that he could "be there now, in the places they will build when they have the perfect elevator" (251). But just like the characters in Egan's novel, Fulton realizes that the future does not lie in his imagination of a perfect world, nor is he pursuing the future as a way to improve his own life. Instead, he understands that the future is a gift, one that he can only give to others. The future, he knows, requires "timing." The time needs to be right in order to put to work the mechanisms and ideas he is developing in the present. All he can do, he knows, is to create the preconditions for bringing about a different, better future, but it will be up to those to whom he has given the tools to put them to use in creating a different future. What is required, he notes, is that those who pick up and make use of what he has given them must "have a good sense of timing"—they must make use of his ideas when the time is right. Fulton knows that "it is late," and he is running out of time. But he must finish his work, and so, in the closing paragraph of the novel, he gets to work and "he writes the elevator" (252).

Like Fulton's elevator, Whitehead's novel creates the future as possibility by opening up the present, the past, and their interrelation. "His handwriting has gotten worse since he started," the novel's narrator says of Fulton. "It worsens the closer he gets, as if his words are being pinched and pulled by the elevator on the other side of his writing. Like they were being pulled into the future" (253). This, *The Intuitionist*'s final pages stress, is what it means to write the future: to make legible the present's latent possibility, which pulls the act of writing toward the future. The future is not a lofty dream, nor is it the detailed account of a perfect society. The way to reclaim the future lies in our ability to reread the past and rewrite the present. To be able to change the future "dot dot dot in a special way" depends on the hard and at times painful work of continuing the work of rereading and rewriting past and present. This is, in the end, what binds Fulton to Lila Mae, whom he notices as the only one on his university campus who is "awake at this hour of the night," the only person who, like Fulton, works in the present to create the possibility of the future: "Hers is the only light in the whole building. Just like his light" (253). And so, without being aware that he has done so and without ever having gotten to know her, Fulton writes the words "*Lila Mae Watson is the one*" in the margins of his writings. The future is Fulton's gift to Lila Mae, a gift of possibility and work that can be continued when the time is right, a gift to an unknown person to realize an unknowable future.

In the novel's final moments, Lila Mae does what Fulton hoped she would do: "She returns to her work." "It didn't have to be her," Lila Mae knows, "but it was" (255). Being the one, she knows, is not a matter of being chosen or of predestination. It is merely a matter of being the right person at the right time to continue to do the work that someone else has begun. Lila Mae understands that continuing Fulton's work is not a matter of blindly following what has been written but of making changes. "Fulton left instructions," she notes, but she also "knows that she is permitted to alter them according to circumstances," for "there was no way that Fulton could foresee how the world would change" (255). The future is made possible by a mechanism set in place in the past that opens up the plurality of the present. Futurity thus understood, echoing the logic we also encounter in the work of Egan and Lerner, is a gift we are able to give to those who may use it to create true change and a better world. It is the gift the children in *Long Division* receive in the form of the book they discover, and it is the gift the novels of Laymon and Whitehead give to us. And yet this gift also depends on the hard work through which we transform words, imagination, and possibility into reality. Words and our imagination provide us with the possibility for change. But, as City ultimately realizes in *Long Division*, true change takes work: "People always say change takes time. It's true, but really it's people who change people" (219). Lila Mae understands this, too, and she also understands that the future depends on hard work in the present. And so Whitehead's novel concludes not with overly grandiose predictions of future changes but instead with a modest though all the more passionate understanding of what it means to reclaim the future: Lila Mae "returns to the work. She will make the necessary adjustments. It will come" (255).

. . .

CHAPTER 4

Periodizing the Contemporary

Literary History after Postmodernism

An era can be said to end when its basic illusions are exhausted.
—Arthur Miller, "The Year It Came Apart"

Upon the publication of William Gibson's 2003 novel *Pattern Recognition*, critics could not help but voice their confusion at Gibson apparently abandoning cyberpunk, the very genre with whose invention he is often credited. To the surprise of many, Gibson had published a novel set not in a highly technologized future but rather in the globalized present. In a brief critical essay on Gibson's novel, Fredric Jameson suggests that what appears to be a difference in genre may in fact be better understood as a historical change: the imaginary future of cyberpunk fiction has become our present reality. Rather than seeing Gibson's latest novel as evidence of the abandonment of a genre, Jameson interprets Gibson's turn to realism with *Pattern Recognition* as a closing of the gap between genre and social reality, locating Gibson even "closer to that 'cyberpunk' with which he is often associated."[1] If this is so, then we may understand *Pattern Recognition* as confirming the impression that the future has crashed into the present. The current crisis of temporality, that is, gives form to the novel insofar as it underwrites the absorption of the futuristic imagination of cyberpunk into contemporary realism. Already in 2000, in a brief article published in *Time* titled "Will We Have Computer Chips in Our Heads?," Gibson suggested that cyberpunk's future might be waning in the new millennium: "The cyberpunk hard guys of science fiction, with their sharp black suits and their surgically implanted silicon chips," Gibson writes, "already have a certain nostalgic romance about them. Information highwaymen, cousins of the 'steam bandits' of Victorian techno-fiction: so heroically attuned to the new technology that they have laid themselves open to its very cutting edge. They have become it; they have taken it within themselves. Meanwhile, in case you somehow haven't noticed, we are all of us becoming it."[2] Gibson's turn to realism and the commentary on cyberpunk's change in temporality implied by this turn (no doubt confirmed by the nostalgic return to cyberpunk in Ernest Cline's 2011 novel *Ready Player One* and certainly in Steven Spielberg's 2018 movie adaptation of Cline's novel) contain a logical proposition of central importance for the understanding of recent literary history that this chapter explores in some detail: the exhaustion of the future is a matter not of its disappearance but of its structural, functional realization in the present.

Phillip Wegner notes that cyberpunk should be understood in relation to a moment when traditional narratives of the future could no longer be maintained.[3] Some of Gibson's earliest stories, including "The Gernsback Continuum" (1981), confirm Wegner's suggestion. In "The Gernsback Continuum," Gibson lays the groundwork for the development of cyberpunk by exploring the ruins of futures past. Cyberpunk emerges as a way to develop a new imagination of the future as established narratives of futurity are exhausted by the flow of history, in a time when "the rockets on the covers of the Gernsback pulps" no longer invoke the new but instead conjure up the memory of the rockets that "had fallen on London in the dead of night, screaming."[4] *Pattern Recognition*'s turn to realism, however, seems to stand in a different relation to history and time than Gibson's initial development of a cyberpunk aesthetic. Pattern Recognition is not about futures beginning to look old and outdated. It points to a more complicated problem. Cyberpunk's future has not disappeared. It has become the very logic of our present; it has transitioned from speculative fiction to realism. The problem to which *Pattern Recognition* draws our attention, therefore, is that the new has collapsed into our now.

This historical transition complicates our understanding of the relation between the concept of the new and recent literary history. In fact, already in 1995, Jim, the protagonist of Kim Stanley Robinson's novel *The Gold Coast*, notes that "you have to do something new, but there's nothing new left to do." "Serious trouble that," he concludes.[5] Jim senses that the problem of the end of the new may be a matter of postmodernism's exhaustion, which generates a formal impasse: "Jim solves this problem by writing postmodern poems that he hopes to make post-postmodern by scrambling them with some random program. The problem with this solution is that postmodern poetry already reads as if the lines have been scrambled by a random program, so the effects of Jim's ultraradical experimentation are difficult to notice" (68). Robinson's protagonist presents us with a problem that connects the crisis of futurity to the historicity of literary form after postmodernism. Together, the novels of Gibson and Robinson indicate that the crisis of temporality and futurity brings problems for our understanding of literary history: How do we talk about and how may we periodize that which succeeds postmodernism?

In her essay "On the Period Formerly Known as the Contemporary," Amy Hungerford questions the usefulness of periodization in our time. Maybe, she suggests, we should abandon the project of periodization altogether. After all, she wonders, "how interesting are the arguments about how to choose beginnings and ends?" Instead of worrying about "the hieroglyphics we have nominated for the header of this period," Hungerford proposes, we should simply produce scholarship on contemporary literature.[6] Of course, the latter suggestion sounds far easier than it is in our moment. For the contemporary itself constitutes one of the most pressing aesthetic, philosophical, and political problems for the contemporary novel. And since the novel locates the current struggle with contemporaneity in the specific historical conditions of our moment, to examine contemporary literature—lest we simply ignore this important facet of literature's account of its relation to the conditions of the contemporary—inevitably means that we will have to make historicizing and periodizing arguments. Consequently, the idea of simply producing scholarship on contemporary literature ultimately is not opposed to periodization. Literature's engagement with the current crises of temporality of the sort we find in the time novel indicates that to examine contemporary literature historically is to periodize it.

But Hungerford's essay also contains a second important line of inquiry that is important for our purposes here: she wonders if the dominant way we talk about recent literary history limits the things we can say about literature. Hungerford appears to believe it does—and I share this conviction. Ultimately, therefore, I do not take Hungerford's argument to be a matter of simple opposition to the project of periodization. Rather, I understand it as a provocation that challenges critics to develop fully historicized accounts of the methodological bases underlying periodizing projects, which is particularly important in our moment, when the temporal foundation of literary history as a critical practice seems to be eroded by a pervasive crisis of our temporal imaginary. Like Hungerford, I do not believe that what is required in this situation is a new universal periodizing marker to establish new ends and beginnings. After all, while there is no doubt a current rush to claim the next big periodizing term and its associated critical prestige, this race runs the risk of replicating the problem examined in this chapter: the creation of ideas of periods that lack internal historical mobility and obscure those important differences within the designated period that might offer us more concrete insights into the complex relation of literature to external history than the periodizing term itself is able to express.

How, then, do we talk about the relation between postmodernism's exhaustion and potential aftermath and the future's crash into the present in the novels of Gibson and Robinson? Moreover, if the problem of periodization is in fact related to a larger historical transformation that creates a crisis for time, thought, and indeed for our critical vocabulary, then might we circle back to the same problem and realize that periodization itself may have become impossible? Hans Ulrich Gumbrecht's discussion of the crisis of literary history today suggests that this is the case, that the current crisis of temporality marks the end of our ability to write histories of literature. "The formal possibilities of literary history," Gumbrecht argues, emerged under very specific historical conditions "in the mid-nineteenth century alongside nineteenth-century historicism." What emerged specifically was "a complex structure of imagining time and, through it, of experiencing change" that "was so universally accepted that people soon tended to confuse it with 'historical consciousness' in the sense of a metahistorical condition." "Its most basic feature," Gumbrecht claims, "was the asymmetry between an open future lived as the horizon of expectations and a past that the ongoing time, at each moment, seemed to leave behind as a closed space of experience."[7] In the present moment, however, Gumbrecht argues, this notion of the open future has given way to an increasingly broadening present. Today, Terry Smith similarly argues, the relation between the present and the notion of contemporaneity seems profoundly troubled. While the modern can be understood as "inclined above all to define itself as a period," he argues, the temporal crisis that defines our time means that "in contemporaneity periodization is impossible.[8] It seems, then, that we should abandon the attempt to periodize literature, since the idea of periodization no longer has meaning in a present without time, in a moment when all we have is now.

But the conclusion that periodization today seems impossible hinges upon two erroneous assumptions. First, it is predicated upon the idea that the present is indeed defined by a singular, unified, and universal sense of contemporaneity, an idea whose illogic is laid bare by the contemporary novel. Second, it is a conclusion that results from insufficient attention to the forms of temporality that underlie the ways the novel continues to imagine historical time. Even if the idea of time on which our established conception of literary history rests is exhausted by the new temporal logic of our era, we can declare the end of time and literary history only if we assume that the time of the present is indeed uniform and homogeneous (that there is no other time than that of real-time capitalism, in other words) and that literary history may operate only on one form of temporal knowledge. The conception of historical time established in the nineteenth century, however, as Massimiliano Tomba shows in great detail, hinges upon the singularization of the concept of history and the logic of temporality upon which historicist thought is based. This conception of time overwrites all forms of temporal knowledge that are incompatible with the temporal regime stabilizing the ascendance of modern capitalism, whose idea of progress and innovation requires the reduction of time's plurality to a singular, linear form of time. The modern temporality of progress, Tomba argues, is one of "homogeneous and empty time,"[9] and insofar as the temporal episteme that binds itself both to nineteenth-century historicism and to the bases of literary history not only experiences a crisis but is in fact surpassed by the structural logic of real-time capitalism, the success or failure of our attempts at periodizing the present depends on our ability to historicize the multiple temporalities that truly make up the time of our present. And while Gumbrecht argues that "a new start for literary history would presuppose a series of discussions, answers, and solutions that cannot be produced by literary studies alone,"[10] I show in this chapter that the American novel has committed itself over the course of the past three decades to just this project of historicizing both time and literature after the future's crash.

In what follows, I examine the theory of literary history proposed by the contemporary American novel, and based on this, I argue for the value of an alternative understanding of recent American literary history. After all, the history of the time novel can hardly be traced through linear chronology, for it is a history of discontinuity, of starts and stops, of abandoned trajectories and revisited projects. This history suggests that periodization should not be understood as a simple matter of beginnings and ends, of naming periods defined by false dominants that obscure more than they make legible and are only mildly tempered by the attention to residual or emergent forces that still commit us to chronolinearity. The time novel shows that periodization is first and foremost a matter of attention to the relation between form and history, of examinations of the temporality of literary forms that allow us to recognize individual patterns of the overall varied and temporally complex historical development of literature. This chapter attempts to provide one answer to the question that critics like Gordon Hutner have placed at the forefront of current attempts to rethink American literary history after postmodernism: How might we historicize the contemporary?[11] One answer, I suggest, lies in the novel's engagement with the category of the contemporary, which rises to the defining aesthetic problem of our moment and commits us to a reexamination of postmodernism's temporality. In the context of the present crisis of temporality, the category of the contemporary is transformed from temporal neutrality to a periodizing term insofar as terms such as *the contemporary novel*, possibly for the first time in history, express a historical relation—the moment when the novel addresses itself directly to a present in which we seem unable to imagine ourselves as anything but contemporary. The contemporary novel allows us to see why in the context of a present defined by the inability to imagine an "after," the answer to our struggle to periodize postmodernism's exhaustion cannot lie in the addition of another *post-*.

THE (NONSYNCHRONOUS) TIME OF POSTMODERNISM AND POSTMODERNITY

Postmodernism. What a dull term it has become. "The term no longer outlines the urgent horizon of the contemporary," argues Ursula K. Heise, adding that "it now tends to refer to a period or style just past, mildly dated in the way flip-top cell phones are."[12] Arguments such as Heise's are by no means rare in contemporary literary criticism. In fact, Andrew Hoberek suggests that, while there exists no fully developed theory of what precisely distinguishes contemporary literature from postmodern literature, "declarations of postmodernism's demise have become critical commonplace."[13] There should therefore no longer be anything surprising about the suggestion that postmodernism is a thing of the past. After all, Fredric Jameson's seminal essays "Periodizing the 60s" and "Postmodernism; or, the Cultural Logic of Late Capitalism" are now over thirty years old, and more generally the works that form the cornerstones of our understanding of postmodernism and its periodization, including seminal works by Linda Hutcheon, Ihab Hassan, David Harvey, Andreas Huyssen, John Barth, and Jean-François Lyotard, are now on average thirty to forty years old. Already in 1990, John Frow asked, "What was postmodernism?," and Raymond Federman proclaimed its end in his book *Critifiction* in 1993, suggesting that "postmodernism changed tense when Samuel Beckett changed tense."[14] And since the cultural artifacts on which these works base their insights largely date back to the 1960s and 1970s, we are inevitably confronted with the question of whether the established models of postmodernism help or hinder our efforts at studying the literature of the past two to three decades.

But the matter of postmodernism's end is not as simple as it may seem. Though they mainly speak to the culture of the 1960s and 1970s, the macrotheoretical models of postmodernism continue to influence contemporary literary scholarship and are still frequently utilized to generate analyses of recent literature. This is no doubt in part a result of the simple fact that many of the works forming our canon of postmodern criticism were published in the late 1980s and 1990s, which was followed by a wave of critical activity that extended the application of these models to the study of the culture of the 1980s and beyond. Studying postmodernism meant studying the present, but it seems clear that the temporal relation among culture, history, and critical method has changed since then. Yet Jameson, for instance, continues to use the terms *postmodernism* and *postmodernity* in his recent work to describe cultural and material aspects of our present. In his introduction to the 2008 collection of essays *Antinomies of Art and Culture*, which constitutes one of the earliest collections of essays attempting to develop a rigorous distinction between postmodern and contemporary art, Terry Smith suggests that the persistence of postmodernism is not merely a matter of lacking attention to the flow of history, intellectual laziness, or unwillingness to augment the theoretical model with which we have worked for a long time. Rather, Smith argues, "while few defenders of Postmodernism as a style in art or architecture remain, many still take postmodernity as the best available critical theory of global capital and its cultures in the contemporary world."[15] According to Smith, then, the term *postmodernism* should be regarded as historically outmoded, as Heise and Hoberek suggest. And yet, because we have not developed a new vocabulary through which we can articulate the present, the term *postmodernism* also appears to maintain a certain presence.

Postmodernism's continued presence is exemplified by works of Americanist literary criticism such as *The Covert Sphere* (2012), in which

Timothy Melley forwards a passionate argument for the continued relevance of the term *postmodernism*. Melley suggests that the system of the national security state characterizing US state policy since the beginning of the Cold War "has had major political and cultural consequences. It has inspired a large body of visual culture; generated cynicism about government; fostered skepticism about historical narrative; and contributed significantly to the rise of postmodernism."[16] The latter claim is particularly striking, since Melley proposes a new periodization of postmodernism and suggests that its rise was bound up with and should thus be understood in direct relation to the rise of the national security state. The covert sphere required and can only continue to operate effectively via "a transformation of the discursive means through which the public 'knows,' or imagines, the work of the state," Melley argues, a change that "provided a heightened . . . stimulus for the production of postmodernism."[17] The covert sphere is postmodern inasmuch as it requires the logic of postmodern culture and theory to accomplish its work and insofar as it in turn played an instrumental role in the rise of postmodernism. And since the covert sphere is still very much with us—or rather, as Melley shows, since it assumes an even more important function in the context of the war on terror—postmodernism is as well.

In spite of the initial difference in temporality suggested by its title, Jeffrey Nealon's 2012 book *Post-Postmodernism, or The Cultural Logic of Just-in-Time Capitalism* argues for an understanding of postmodernism that is remarkably similar to Melley's. Nealon proposes that the addition of a second *post-* should be understood as marking the distinction between contemporary culture and that of the '60s and '70s, the decades we traditionally associate with high postmodernism. Nealon's reasoning is utterly convincing: if we compare today's cultural forms to those of the '60s and '70s, there is little doubt that things have changed significantly and we need to develop an adequate account of the historical change expressed in this formal difference. Yet, while Nealon insists upon the significant differences between postmodernism and today's culture, throughout the book he also stresses that the second *post-* carries a substantial conceptual and temporal awkwardness connected to postmodernism's apparent simultaneous exhaustion and persistence in a different implementation. Nealon ascribes this to the fact that postmodernism has not actually fully disappeared. Instead, he argues, it is now expressed in the structures of our neoliberal present, and since the 1980s, we have been witnessing an intensification of postmodernism. At the same time, Nealon argues, this intensification is also the reason we must no longer hold on to postmodernism, because "the ethos of liberation that surrounds cultural postmodernism (the transgressions of hybridity, the individual ethics of self-fashioning, Dionysiac celebrations of multiplicity, endlessly making it new) can't simply be walled off from the substantially more sinister work that these very same notions index within the economic realm—they're the watchwords of neoliberal capitalism as well."[18]

The site of overlap between Melley's and Nealon's books, the notion of a long postmodernism or of postmodernism's contemporary presence, indicates something important about the origin of the awkwardness that seems to introduce itself virtually inevitably into both periodizing models: this awkwardness emerges from a constitutive problem bound up less with the historical process Nealon and Melley wish to trace than with the relation between the terms postmodernism and postmodernity. For Nealon, the current crisis of futurity is directly related to the ascendance of post-Fordism and neoliberal finance capitalism since the '80s: "If in the US 'the 60s' functioned politically as a kind of shorthand for resistance and revolution of all kinds, 'the 80s' most immediately signifies the increasing power and ubiquity of markets and privatized corporatization in everyday life."[19] In the current moment, Nealon argues, "the future of capitalism . . . rests not on the extraction of profit from commodities or services but on the production of money directly from money—making profit by wagering on an anticipated future outcome. And the future, it seems, is now."[20] From the beginning, however, Nealon notes that his periodizing distinction may carry more force on the level of economics and theoretical debates (the book is largely concerned with the latter) than for cultural analysis. Nealon deploys the term *post-postmodernism* to describe an economic relation. The underlying rationale of his argument is the same as that expressed by Smith above, who suggests that while postmodernism has most certainly disappeared at the level of culture, the term *postmodernity* is still helpful insofar as it designates a period in material history. This slippage among concept, temporality, and reference lays bare a problem, one that is centrally involved in our struggle to come to terms with postmodernism's exhaustion and continued presence—an end that is seemingly without aftermath.

The terms *postmodernism* and *postmodernity* are set up as periodizing terms in ways that assume a temporally parallel, dialectical connection between an economic period (postmodernity) and its cultural mediation (postmodernism). Nealon collapses this relation into a single term, thus heightening the conceptual and temporal problems contained in the relation between postmodernism and postmodernity. Smith, on the other hand, suggests that one of the two terms (*postmodernism*) no longer describes the present, while the other one (*postmodernity*) does. But what exactly is the temporal relation between the two terms? After all, the economic and material structures we associate with postmodernity, as Nealon shows so convincingly, did not actually begin to rise to structural dominance until, at the very earliest, the mid-1980s. And if we assume that postmodernism as a cultural and epistemological form mediates a specific stage in the development of postmodernity, then we must also note that postmodernity was far from dominant during the '60s and '70s, the decades we generally consider to be the height of postmodernism. The term *postmodernity* is, of course, also notoriously imprecise. Macrotheoretical models of postmodernity often define it in relation to a set of other terms, many of which add little conceptual and historical precision. The term *late capitalism*, for instance, is still frequently used to designate the current stage of capitalism. However, the term originated in 1902 and has since been deployed to designate moments in capitalism that include the crises of the 1930s and 1940s and seemingly all of capitalism's history since the end of World War II. Other models of postmodernity associate the term with consumer capitalism, globalization, postindustrial capitalism, the media or the digital age, or, as in the work of Jean-François Lyotard, the age of computerization. But even if we overlook the imprecision of this range of terms and focus very broadly on the most commonly identified aspects associated with postmodernity, then we must note that postmodernity was at best an incipient structure during the period that we commonly associate with high postmodernism and with which the macrotheoretical models engage—the 1960s, 1970s, and 1980s. The World Wide Web did not become widely accessible until the mid-1990s (Netscape, the first publicly available web browser, was released in 1994), free-market capitalism was a far from hegemonic global force during the '60s, '70s, and '80s, national economies were only beginning to transition to a globalized system of floating currencies, and postindustrial, immaterial, digital capitalism slowly began to emerge in the effort to manage the crises of Fordism. Yet by the time these structures reach dominance, in the 1990s and the new millennium, literature and culture are characterized by notably different forms and narratives than during the time of high postmodernism. In fact, as we saw above, in the mid-1990s, novels like *The Gold Coast* begin to declare the death of postmodernism and show signs of the struggle to imagine its aftermath that we encounter so frequently in the contemporary American novel. We are faced, then, with a situation suggesting that *postmodernism* and *postmodernity* may be better understood as terms that express an asynchronous relationship. Postmodernism corresponds to postmodernity in its incipient stage. Once the material structures we associate with postmodernity rise to dominance, literature begins to depart from the forms we ordinarily associate with postmodernism. Dominant postmodernity marks the exhaustion of postmodernism.

We are beginning to see a crucial aspect of the problem that informs our current inability to develop a vocabulary and idea of temporality that allow us to make sense of postmodernism's exhaustion and aftermath. And we see, moreover, that there is a connection between our inability to speak to postmodernism's exhaustion without aftermath on one hand and the current crisis of temporality, which seems to be marked by a similar absorption of the new into the now, of the future into the present, on the other. *Postmodernism* and *postmodernity* are terms that should function as periodizing markers, but they are remarkably bad at doing what they are supposed to do. In fact, the terms tend to hide more than they reveal. Jim's struggle with the relation between postmodernism and the new is therefore not surprising, and it is less a struggle with the exhaustion of literature than with the limitations imposed by our periodizing vocabulary on our ability to describe how literature may change over the course of history and how it may relate to the present. The category of the new plays a central role in our established understanding of the relation between modernism and postmodernism, and it seems that it is also significant for accounts of the exhaustion of postmodernism. But *the new* has always been a prickly term in the context of periodization. In *Decline of the New*, one of the earliest works of criticism to interrogate the exhaustion of modernism and speculatively advance the idea of a potential post-modernism, Irving Howe foregrounds modernism's characteristic relationship to time and the new. Howe writes, "In its multiplicity and brilliant confusion, its commitment to an aesthetic of endless renewal—in its composition of the 'tradition of the new,' a paradox envisaging the limit of *limitlessness*—modernism is endlessly open to portraiture and analysis. For just as some of its greatest works strain toward a form freed from beginning or end, so modernism strains toward a life without fixity or conclusion."[21] Yet what marks modernism's trademark engagement with the new and resistance to fixity and closure, Howe realizes, becomes problematic once modernism is confronted with its own end. And thus, a few pages later, Howe's examination of modernism's time and its relation to the new acquires a moving self-reflexivity:

> How, come to think of it, do great cultural movements reach their end? It is a problem our literary historians have not sufficiently examined, perhaps because they find beginnings more glamorous, and a problem that is now especially difficult because there has never been, I think, a cultural period in Western history quite like the one we call modern. But signs of a denouement begin to appear. . . . How enviable death must be to those who no longer have reason to live yet are unable to make themselves die! Modernism will not come to an end; its war chants will be repeated through the decades. For what seems to await it is a more painful and certainly less dignified conclusion than that of earlier cultural movements: what awaits it is publicity and sensation, the kind of savage parody which may indeed be the only fate worse than death.[22]

The striking aspect of Howe's analysis for our examination of literature in the present is that the logical and historical failure of expressing the relationship between modernism and its aftermath with not one *post-* but two poignantly obscures a fundamental temporal commonality. The recognition that modernism may no longer be new and yet continues to have a presence, or, put differently, the tragic simultaneity of exhaustion and continued life, also characterizes the contemporary American novel. This tension in turn troubles our attempts to periodize the contemporary in relation to the postmodern.

Jameson describes the disappearance of the new as a fundamental aspect of the distinction between modernity and postmodernity. This suggestion underlies one of the best-known accounts of the transition from modernism to postmodernism as a matter of the disappearance of uneven development, which was a defining characteristic of modernism. Jameson locates the beginning of the postmodern at the point when this situation of uneven development is resolved and the new is, for better or worse, widely included and accepted into the social fabric. In fact, Jameson concludes, postmodernism appears entirely uninterested in upholding the category of the new as something spectacular.[23] "The way we feel today, in full postmodernism," Jameson writes in *Postmod-*

ernism or, The Cultural Logic of Late Capitalism, is that "we ourselves are somehow new, that a new age is beginning, that everything is possible and nothing can ever be the same." Yet Jameson also insists that "now everything is new; but by the same token, the very category of the new loses its meaning and becomes itself something of a modernist survival."[24] The category of the new plays a central role in literature's attempt to make sense of its (and our) place in history. But this is not just a matter of creating new things or ideas, as Jim realizes. Rather, we must ask what exactly is referenced by the new. How, that is, may we understand the new as a category that does not simply name innovation or novelty but establishes a relationship between literature and the present as history at a given moment? How, in other words, does the new function as a way to engage with historical transitions as an aesthetic problem, as a question of the relation between art and changes in our material reality? After all, even the canonical texts of high postmodernism display a keen interest in the category of the new and contain a sense of futurity that emerges out of and mediates a particular historical development. By tracing the relation between the novel and material history that the engagement with the new tries to establish, we are able to get a better understanding of the novel's historical development, one that troubles the understanding of literary history that is bound up with the terms *postmodernism* and *postmodernity*.

The anti-Oedipalism of novels like Donald Barthelme's *The Dead Father* (1975), for example, mediates the crumbling of Fordist modernity in connection to the as yet undefined new to which this historical opening might lead. A story of the journey of a group of young people toward the burial site of the Dead Father, who is not yet entirely dead, the novel directly conjures up the waning of Fordist modernity and the exciting possibilities opened up by this prospect. Reduced to a tragically comic figure, Barthelme's gigantic father (one leg consisting of a Fordist factory) struggles with the gradual loss of all those elements of traditional life that he fathered. Yet his death opens up the possibility of future liberation (albeit in characteristically disavowed form as futurity without a distinct future) and is a cause of great exhilaration among the group of young people as well as one of the mechanisms that drives the novel's plot. Similarly, the periodic breakdown of language and narration in the novel is at every point bound up with its anti-Oedipal project, which attaches linguistic and narrative conventions to paternalistic thought and those structures that also formed the foundation of the paternalistic logic of Fordism. The aim that drives the novel's plot is the journey toward the Dead Father's final death. The novel's form and content fuse at the intersection of temporality and paternalism, at the moment when future possibility concretizes itself in the act of wresting meaning and representation from its paternalistic pastness. Memorably, the novel's introductory passage closes with a formulation of the temporal unevenness out of which its form emerges, emphasizing the sense that postmodernism mediates the emergence of postmodernity while still awaiting the death and disappearance of Fordist modernity: "*We want the Dead Father to be dead. We sit with tears in our eyes wanting the Dead Father to be dead—meanwhile doing amazing things with our hands.*"[25]

Postmodernism's engagement with death and endings is directly wedded to its futurity: it is the set of amazing things that the characters in Barthelme's novel are doing with their hands while awaiting the Dead Father's ultimate death. This historical link between the crisis of Fordism and postmodernism's movement toward the new is also expressed in Federman's account of the rise of postmodernism: "It was in this climate, this funerary climate, surrounded by such negative conditions, confronting all these apocalyptic predictions that the fiction writer, in the mid-sixties, considered his task and began writing the new novel."[26] The death of paternalism, as is also the case in novels such as Kurt Vonnegut's *Breakfast of Champions* (1973) and Thomas Pynchon's *The Crying of Lot 49* (1966), determines the novels' relation to death and endings but also, just as importantly, to their sense of futurity, difference, and change. In postmodernism, that is, the range of ends is connected to the end of Fordist modernity and paternalism. This end may not (or should not) signal a fully formed future. Instead, it betokens joyful anticipation and potentiality. The tension between the rejection of modernism's engagement with the new and postmodernism's momentum generated by the opening up of a different, disavowed form of the new indexes a distinct sense of uneven development at the heart of postmodernism. This uneven temporal development finds expression in the excited anticipation arising from the contemplation of the future possibilities brought about by the beginning end of Fordist modernity. The contradiction between apocalypse and jouissance that marks the culture of the '60s and '70s indicates not the absence of uneven development but a new version thereof. Postmodernism is the cultural mediation anticipatory of a new world whose possibility emerges from the collapse of Fordist modernity.

What begins to trouble the novel beginning in the mid-1980s and particularly since the 1990s, however, is that the crisis of Fordism, which spelled great potentiality for high postmodernism, gave way to a new world that did not exactly correspond to postmodernism's utopian wishes. The anticipation that gave rise to postmodern experimentation collides with the emergence of a new stage of capitalism. Instead of a new, liberated world for humanity, we witnessed the rise of a form of capitalism that had been liberated from and managed the crisis of the collapse of Fordist modernity. Beginning in the mid-1980s, novelists engage with the idea of the exhaustion of the future as a way to register disillusionment as the postmodern new begins to reveal itself as nothing other than the now of postmodernity, the present of a new stage of capitalism that brings about not liberation but new forms of domination and exploitation. A great number of novels that we ordinarily include in our postmodern canon may therefore be understood as novels that indicate the beginning of the exhaustion of postmodernism. Two years in particular stand out in this regard and offer an extraordinarily rich and significant archive of novels: 1984 and 1985. These two years witnessed a burst in novelistic output and the publication of a great number of novels that anticipate the death of postmodernism in the novel of the '90s and the crash of the future into the present. When the Smiths ask in 1984, "How Soon Is Now?," the novel begins to answer: quite soon indeed.[27]

To be sure, we should certainly not understand the cultural mediation of capitalism's complex and varied historical transition away from Fordist modernity as giving rise to a unified, linear sense of periodization. After all, capitalism does not express itself uniformly across different geographical areas (even within a single national context), nor can the formal relation between the novel and the different facets of contemporary capitalism that are identified by analytical terms as varied as *post-Fordism*, *neoliberalism*, *dominant finance capitalism*, *immaterial* or *affective capitalism*, *digital capitalism*, or *real-time capitalism* be temporally and logically illustrated via a singular periodizing term. What I seek to indicate, therefore, is not the need for a new set of periodizing terms but rather the advantage of a more varied and differentiated notion of periodization. Periodization is not a matter of naming the totality, for such an attempt will inevitably fail and ultimately hinder our attempts at making sense of the novel's historical development in relation to external history. If we examine the years 1984 and 1985, for instance, we see that these years saw the publication of a range of novels that are not helpfully described by labeling them as postmodern. In fact, our understanding of the idea of postmodernism remains unhelpfully monadic as long as our logic of periodization overwrites rather than makes legible how different facets of the novel develop as a result of the constant attempt to make sense of changes in material history. Likewise, by examining the immanent temporality and historical development of the work of individual authors, we can see that labeling an author as postmodern hides some of the most salient aspects of an author's development of a variety of forms in order to make legible the logic of historical change. One of the central characteristics of Gibson's novels, for example, is their close attention to the shelf lives of futures, forms, and genres. And as we began to see at the beginning of this chapter, the formal changes in Gibson's work and their relation to changes in our temporal imagination and material history yield invaluable insights into our current struggle with temporality and the attempt to periodize the contemporary. Describing Gibson as a postmodern author overwrites the immanent formal and historical development of his work. Gibson's novels develop important accounts of the changed relation between novelistic form and genre on one hand and material history, time, and the category of the new on the other, however. And this immanent historical development of Gibson's work indicates a crucial facet of the novel's recent history and in turn foregrounds the value of periodizing not by naming beginnings and ends but by tracing the relation between external, material history and the history of the novel's formal development.

A comparison of *Pattern Recognition* and Gibson's 1984 novel *Neuromancer*, for instance, indicates that the transition from future to present, from cyberpunk to realism, mediates a historical transition. Case, the protagonist of *Neuromancer*, is a "cyberspace cowboy," a freelance laborer in a capitalist world largely based on immaterial trade and knowledge exchange. Case plugs himself into cyberspace (the "matrix") to complete assignments. At the beginning of the novel, Case is reeling from the severe punishment he received for stealing from one of his employers: Case's ability to plug into cyberspace has been taken away from him by damaging his nervous system. Case is trapped in what he perceives as the "prison of his own flesh."[28] Spiraling toward self-destruction, Case dreams of cyberspace, yet his hope to be able to reconnect "fad[es] nightly" (4). Case's world is defined by a sense of historical inbetweenness. While much of the new world is determined by decentralized virtual networks of trade, exchange, and communication, traditional, paternalistically organized family empires like the Tessier-Ashpool clan continue to wield considerable power and recall the particular combination of quasi-aristocratic lineage and capitalism that is a central aspect of US modernity. Since the "abstraction" and "unrepresentable complexity" of cyberspace is a source of great enjoyment for Case and allows him to leave behind the old, being confined to the a life of traditional physicality excludes Case from the new. His first entry into cyberspace after repairing his neural damage is for Case an intensely liberating experience: "Somewhere he was laughing, in a white-painted loft, distant finger caressing the deck, tears of release streaking his face" (51–52). But while the rise to dominance of digital capitalism at least initially brings a sense of liberation for Case, Cayce Pollard, the female protagonist of *Pattern Recognition*, relates to global, digital capitalism decidedly differently. The present in *Pattern Recognition* is defined by the rise to dominance of those aspects of life that were still new and exciting to Case but now index a world that Cayce understands as uniform and devoid of futurity. *Neuromancer*'s new has become *Pattern Recognition*'s now.

Like Gibson's *Neuromancer*, various American novels turn to the topic of time to grapple with the rise to dominance of a stage of capitalism that appears to functionally integrate postmodernism's liberatory dreams into the present. Samuel R. Delany's *Stars in My Pocket Like Grains of Sand* deals with the catastrophic effects of "Cultural Fugue," a temporal and epistemological singularity. E. L. Doctorow's 1984 novel *World's Fair* deploys a version of the bildungsroman in the attempt to represent a moment in time when a previous idea of the future begins to decay. The young protagonist of Doctorow's novel grows up in the shadows of the abandoned structures of the 1939 World of Tomorrow world's fair, and his struggle to develop a vision for his future is juxtaposed with the rust and flaking paint of the monuments to a prior era's idea of tomorrow. Similarly, the struggle of the female protagonist of David R. Palmer's *Emergence* (1984) to come to terms with being a Homo post hominem expresses the same moment of transition that Paul Auster's *City of Glass* (1985) narrates through an engagement with paternalism that is as much marked by quintessential tropes of deconstruction and the linguistic turn as by its nostalgia for lost forms of paternalism. We find the same critical engagement with the emergence of nostalgia in relation to matters of historical temporality in William Gaddis's *Carpenter's Gothic* (1985) and Cormac McCarthy's *Blood Meridian* (1985). Through the tension between the time of the novel's setting and the proleptic narration of the novel's own time in the chapter openings, for instance, McCarthy's novel mediates the historical transition that defines the mid-1980s. The profound significance of these two years for our understanding of a key moment of transition in literary history no doubt warrants a longer project. Such a project would centrally examine the formal mediation of historical change and its consequences for temporal knowledge that we find in the novels indicated above and in a range of connected novels, including Kathy Acker's *Blood and Guts in High School* (1984), Kim Stanley Robinson's *The Wild Shore* (1984), Jay McInerney's *Bright Lights, Big City* (1984), Richard Powers's *Three Farmers on Their Way to a Dance* (1985), and David Brin's *The Postman* (1985).[29] In the space available to me here, however, I instead turn to a novel that examines the year 1984 as a moment of historical transition, a novel that directly provides us with a shorthand of sorts for the role played by the mid-1980s in the exhaustion of the dreams of postmodernism: Thomas Pynchon's *Vineland* (1990).

Set in 1984, *Vineland* represents the 1980s as a period defined by the death of the sociopolitical and cultural energy and momentum of countercultural movements of the 1960s and 1970s. *Vineland* is one of several novels that examine the 1980s as a time of exhaustion and the emergence of a new sociopolitical reality that brings with it new forms of alienation. We encounter similar discussions in novels of the early 1990s such as Michael Cunningham's *A Home at the End of the World* (1990) and Bret Easton Ellis's *American Psycho* (1991), as well as in more recent novels such as Colson Whitehead's *Sag Harbor* (2009) and Kiese Laymon's *Long Division* (2013). The latter novels are also significant insofar as they revisit the significance of the mid-1980s for contemporary racial politics. From its position of slight temporal remove, *Vineland* provides us with an account of 1984 that illustrates the end of the optimism and energy of the '60s and '70s—and the rise of conservative delight in their exhaustion. One character in the novel, a policeman named Hector, finds great enjoyment in the idea that old hippies like the novel's protagonist Zoyd Wheeler, "after all them years of nonconformist shit," are "gonna end up just like everybody else."[30] The tense of the statement indicates that the exhausted energy of the countercultural movements of the 1960s is at this point still an ongoing ending, which is, however, already clearly recognizable in its trajectory. The mid-1980s are therefore marked by a sense of temporal unevenness particular to this moment. In fact, Hector suggests, Zoyd himself is marked by noncontemporaneity, lagging behind the general historical development: "Still simmerin away with those same old feelings, I see—

figured you'd be mellower by now, maybe some reconciliation with reality, I dunno. . . . [Y]ou sixties people, it's amazing! . . . I know you still believe in all that shit. All o' you are still children inside, livin' your real life back then. Still waitin for that magic payoff" (28). In 1984, Zoyd's commitments register as tragically antiquated, naive, and immature in a world that, Hector argues, has grown up and entered a new phase defined by the politics and reality of the Reagan era. Hector is pleased that Zoyd himself is becoming disillusioned, which Hector understands as an indication of his willingness to embrace the new reality of the present: "I used to worry about you, Zoyd, but I see I can rest easy now the Vaseline of youth has been cleared from your life's lens by the mild detergent solution of time, in its passing" (31). Even in Zoyd's memory, the most urgent issues that defined the '60s seem far away: "War in Vietnam, murder as an instrument of American politics, black neighborhoods torched to ashes and death, all must have been off on some other planet" (38).

To describe both historical moments, the 1960s and the 1980s, with the same periodizing term, Pynchon's novel indicates, would be to overwrite the difference between two moments in history that Zoyd perceives as amounting to the difference between two different planets. Furthermore, Pynchon's novel indicates an understanding of the present that corresponds to the representation of the present in novels like *Pattern Recognition*. The relation between the 1960s and the 1980s is more than a matter of mere exhaustion. It is a matter of a time and culture that, like Zoyd, has been claimed by the present: "The years had kept rolling, like the surf he used to ride, high, calm, wild, windless. But increasingly the day, the necessary day, presenting its demands, had claimed him" (39). Zoyd recognizes the inevitability of the exhaustion of the 1960s and concludes that he must face "the deep autumnal wind of what was coming" (71). To Zoyd's great disappointment, his former wife and fellow hippie, Frenesi, takes this new world as an opportunity to radically alter her previous commitments, join the police force, and abandon all interest in future change and transformation:

> Come into her own at last, street-legal, full-auto qualified, she understood her particular servitude as the freedom, granted to a few, to act outside warrants and charters, to ignore history and the dead, to imagine no future, no yet-to-be-born, to be able simply to go on defining moments only,

> purely, by the action that filled them. Here was a world of simplicity and certainty no acidhead, no revolutionary anarchist would ever find, a world based on the zero of life and death. (72)

Pynchon's novel is an important work that traces the historical emergence of the sense of omnipresence and the crisis of futurity that have come to define our present moment in the turn against postmodernism beginning in the 1980s. The mid-1980s, which DeLillo's *White Noise* (1985) understands to be a "kind of settling-in-period . . . [m]iddle age,"[31] witness the emergence of various novels indicating that we cannot continue to hold those beliefs and attitudes that defined the '60s and '70s without appearing out of time, a sentiment that also marks the earliest accounts of the historical impossibility of postmodernism that the novels of the 1990s address more explicitly. One might suggest, therefore, that it is possible to read the switch to present-tense narration midway through the final chapter of *White Noise* as an expression of the emergence of the sense of temporality that defines our moment, the contraction of time into presence.

Moreover, the temporal logic and historical argument of *Vineland* indicate the importance of examining the immanent temporality of Pynchon's work. *Vineland* dialogues with Pynchon's work of the 1960s, a conversation that is continued in his 2009 novel *Inherent Vice*. *Inherent Vice* returns nostalgically to the naive futurism of the 1960s. It is a far less effective political novel than is *Vineland*, but it illustrates Pynchon's engagement with the consequences of the completion of the historical change that *Inherent Vice* still narrates as ongoing: *Inherent Vice* examines the 1960s from the position of the new dominant anticipated by *Vineland*. In *Inherent Vice*, Pynchon examines the 1960s as defined by the exhaustion of staples of modernist culture itself, first and foremost replacing Raymond Chandler's and Dashiell Hammett's hard-boiled detectives with Doc Sportello, the hard-baked detective of the nostalgically reconstructed surfin' '60s. *Inherent Vice* returns our gaze to Pynchon's own 1960s (anti)detective novel and illustrates why it is no longer possible to write a novel like *The Crying of Lot 49* in 2009. Through its nostalgic return to the commitment to possibility and change in the 1960s, *Inherent Vice* advances an argument about the impossibility of the postmodern novel in our time, illustrating the historical chasm between the two moments and the radically different sociocultural and political projects with which they are bound up.

ACTUALLY EXISTING POSTMODERNISM

Our examination of the American novel's engagement with time and futurity indicates that a more precise account of the temporality of postmodernism and postmodernity would have to trace the temporality that emerges from the tension between these two terms, since they describe different periods and different dominant structural and cultural forms. However, recent debates surrounding postmodernism's potential aftermath that have begun to challenge the significant influence the established models of postmodernism continue to exert upon present criticism by and large continue to maintain the assumption that the terms *postmodernism* and *postmodernity* express a synchronous relation. But neither the history of literary form nor material history actually supports this assumption, and as the American novel itself indicates, the attempt to periodize the contemporary would benefit not from an expansion of the concept into a long postmodernism but from a shorter, more precise, and internally varied definition of *postmodernism* as the period of incipient postmodernity. Moreover, such a temporally more modest account of postmodernism allows us to increase the visibility of its massive historical function as the cultural and theoretical plane that facilitated the transition into a new capitalist structure. Understanding postmodernism as a brief historical phenomenon and interrogating the conditions of its exhaustion in the mid-1980s in turn highlights postmodernism's central role in the structural transition into the present of real-time capitalism. And such an understanding of postmodernism ultimately allows us to trace the origins of our era's aesthetic and temporal crises.

And yet the contemporary novel's departure from and opposition to the postmodern novel beginning at the moment when the term *postmodernity* names the dominant material logic of the present is difficult to describe through our established temporal and periodizing vocabulary. Terms such as *postmodern economy*, for example, become difficult to locate historically, because they describe a situation in which postmodernity has become dominant—which, however, is also the point at which many novels begin to grapple with the problem of postmodernism's exhaustion. And while critics such as Rachel Adams have proposed new periodizing markers such as "American literary globalism," designed to distinguish between postmodernism and the contemporary,[32] the fact that postmodernity as postmodernism's dialectical counterpart is generally associated with terms such as *late capitalism*, *postindustrialism*, or *globalization* ultimately means that speaking of literary "globalism" does not exactly communicate the substantive historical distinction that Adams and other critics rightly consider necessary. This has a reason. Nealon points to the fact that the vocabulary and logic of postmodernism have become those of neoliberalism—and this is crucially important. "When one dialectically overcodes the liberated cultural effects of postmodernism with the substantially more dire economic realities that rely on the same concepts," Nealon suggests, "one can no longer assess the cultural effects in quite the same way."[33] But while this is no doubt the case, this insight indicates more than postmodernism's exhaustion. It raises the question of the degree of the structural relation between postmodernism and postmodernity, or what Nealon calls neoliberalism. Gérard Duménil and Dominique Lévy argue in *The Crisis of Neoliberalism* that neoliberalism distinguishes itself from previous modes of capitalism by the fact that it is not a socioeconomic or political given, but is better understood as a strategy.[34] Pierre Bourdieu forwards a similar argument in a little-discussed essay, suggesting that neoliberalism might in fact best be understood as a utopian program that speaks itself into existence. "What is neoliberalism?," asks Bourdieu at the beginning of his essay "The Essence of Neoliberalism." In the essay's subtitle, he provides a clear, direct answer: "A programme for destroying collective structures which may impede the pure market logic."[35] But Bourdieu immediately undercuts his initial suggestion and wonders if we can really consider this program and the new economic order it brings our new material and social reality: "What if, in reality, this economic order were no more than the implementation of a utopia—the utopia of neoliberalism—thus converted into a *political problem*? One that, with the aid of the economic theory that it proclaims, succeeds in conceiving of itself as the scientific description of reality?" Neoliberalism can thus be understood as a matter of "*making itself true* and empirically verifiable" in a manner that literary scholars would readily associate with the transformation of a utopian wish into realism.

But what if we understood the phenomenon Nealon highlights as logically and indeed historically bound up with Bourdieu's account of neoliberalism? Are we not in fact confronted with precisely the kind of transition that Bourdieu describes: the transition of a fiction to the status of realism? If neoliberalism is a matter of the structural implementation of a utopia, of speculative theory, ought we not commit fully to the historical connection between neoliberalism and postmodernism and suggest that postmodernism does not simply coincide with neoliberalism in the present, but rather postmodernism was in fact instrumental in the process of resolving the capitalist crises of the 1960s and 1970s? After all, postmodernism gave rise to those cultural and theoretical forms that were necessary for the development of the (ideo)logical and sociopolitical basis of the new capitalist system. If we understand neoliberalism in this way, as the historical development of a strategy that is driven forward by the dialectical relationship between fiction and reality, then it becomes clear that literary criticism has a clear disciplinary stake in the general effort to study the history of neoliberalism and the particular sets of conceptual and temporal problems that its move from fiction to reality creates in our present. Furthermore, if we examine the rise to dominance of neoliberalism in the United States as a transition from theoretical fiction to reality in a process that gathered momentum in the general effort to manage the structural crises of capitalism of the 1960s and 1970s and began to transition into an economic order that since the 1980s and 1990s can be described as dominant neoliberalism and our new economic reality, then it becomes clear that it is possible to locate important elements of the recent history of the novel in relation to this context. This includes, as we have seen, the transition away from the experimental forms of high postmodernism and toward the forms of realism that have come to define our moment in literary history. Postmodernism does not simply lose its original edge or become co-opted and structurally intensified by neoliberalism. Rather, postmodernism emerges as a central part of precisely the set of fictions that gave rise to neoliberalism and began to be structurally implemented as the new dominant system in the late 1980s and early 1990s, the point at which we witness the novel's departure from postmodernism's characteristic forms. Neoliberalism's transition from fiction to reality also binds itself to the gradual erosion of the future and its contraction into a timeless present, thereby undercutting those forms of temporality that define literary history as we know it. The turn to realism in times of neoliberalism is thus not just as an expression of dominant neoliberalism but a way of formally registering the transformation of both neoliberalism itself and postmodernism's quintessential forms from experimental fiction into realism.

Postmodernism disappears from literature once it becomes the new structural reality of our present. The logic of chronology that underlies the predominant models of periodization, however, is wedded to a temporality that measures life cycles. It traces births, lives, and deaths. But postmodernism did not exactly die. It transitioned from a fictional life to a real existence. Likewise, postmodernism did not really end. And we are not in a period that has moved beyond postmodernism. More accurately, the fictions of postmodernism of the '60s and '70s have become the reality of the capitalist present, and what becomes visible in this process is not postmodernism's end but its ends. This is also to say that the conceptual awkwardness which tends to arise from attempts to speak about this transition can be understood as a result of the fact that literature turns away from postmodernism once it realizes postmodernism's actual function and ontology. It is no longer possible to write postmodern literature, but not because history has moved past postmodernism and rendered it unable to speak to the present. Postmodernism is no longer a vehicle for current literature, especially literature that seeks to politically engage with the present, because postmodernism's fictions have become the dominant language of contemporary capitalism. From this standpoint, postmodernism can be understood as not just the cultural logic but indeed an integral, active component of the management of the crisis of Fordist modernity and the beginning of the transition into capitalism's current stage. Once we can speak of a situation in which neoliberalism begins to reach a relation of dominance as the new system of capitalism, beginning in the 1980s, we see the disappearance of the forms characteristic of the postmodern novel and the emergence of a series of new forms that are well aware of postmodernism's disappearance into the new dominant and that directly engage with the new sociopolitical and epistemological forms required by neoliberalism. Far from describing a solely negative development for the novel and an increasingly cynical artistic and critical climate, to speak of the neoliberal novel may thus provide us with a way of describing the novel's engagement with precisely those contradictions that the transition into neoliberalism has laid bare, creating one timeline of the recent history of the American novel as that of the novel's turn back to matters of time and temporality in order to free thought and literature from the grasp of neoliberalism's omnipresence.

Consequently, it appears that we should orient ourselves terminologically in relation to other systems that imagine their existence speculatively, as a process, and as the temporality arising from the transition from utopia to realism. The term *Realsozialismus* (actually existing socialism) famously seeks to highlight the differences between socialism as a utopian project and socialism as a matter of real or actual politics and material structures in the present. Might we not likewise benefit from expressing the difference between postmodernism and its exhaustion by way of its structural implementation in our present neoliberal reality as the difference between postmodernism and *Realpostmodernismus*, actually existing postmodernism? The move of neoliberalism from fiction to reality is, after all, congruent with the transformation of postmodernism into actually existing postmodernism. The intensification Nealon seeks to make legible may therefore be better captured by a more precise understanding of the nonsynchronous relation between postmodernism and postmodernity. After all, to reiterate, we are faced with an intensification not of postmodernism but instead of postmodernity. What intensifies in Nealon's view is the economic side of the relation, postmodernity, which begins to emerge in the '60s but does not rise to dominance until the '90s. Postmodernism, in turn, does not intensify; instead it wanes at that moment, and we see the emergence of new literary forms and narratives driven by an inward turn of sorts motivated by literature's inquiry into its own possibility in the era of the omnipresent now, in the age of actually existing postmodernism. This terminological and conceptual change appears particularly necessary since the novel itself is well aware of this historical development, seeing as the turn to realism in the contemporary novel is a matter not only of the inescapability of neoliberalism but also of the formal commitment to registering the temporality and logic of neoliberalism's presence.

One might suspect, therefore, that this is the source of the unease Nealon senses when he points to the complicity between neoliberalism and postmodernism while also noting that the second *post-* rubs uncomfortably against the temporal logic of this relation. Put differently, one way of explaining criticism's current struggle to come to terms with what may succeed postmodernism is to understand it as a temporal consequence of the fact that postmodernism did not disappear but instead actualized itself in neoliberalism, which, in its structural implementation of a broad present of instantaneous exchange and communication, is in turn connected to a cultural and social logic defined by the very impossibility of generating another *post-*. The contemporary novel registers this transition from fiction to reality by turning to realism and matters of time and temporality. One of the central and most belabored aspects of postmodernism is the effacement of time by space. To be sure, one must read the literature of the 1960s and 1970s somewhat selectively to maintain the validity of this by now almost stereotypical description of postmodernism. What may hold for some aspects of white American literature, for example, is not quite as true for African American literature of the period, which relates quite differently to the pressures on temporality that characterized aspects of material and cultural life in those decades. Still, the aspects of postmodernism that have since been standardized in neoliberalism are in many ways the most stereotypical aspects of postmodernism, such as the focus on a politics of identity and difference and the central tenets of the linguistic turn. In fact, as Nealon does not directly state but indicates throughout his book, Jameson's account of postmodernism (and to a similar degree that of Jean-François Lyotard, irrespective of the profound political differences between the versions of postmodernism Jameson and Lyotard forward) can serve as a guidebook for tracing some of neoliberalism's fundamental aspects. The reappearance of realism and the centrality of time in the contemporary novel mediates a present that is the time of actually existing postmodernism.

This is, ultimately, why we struggle to talk about what may succeed postmodernism, as well as its potential afterlives. The additional *post-* does not help us make sense of this development because we are confronted with a transition not from life to death but from fiction to reality. The impression that the end of postmodernism is somehow related to its ubiquity in fact underwrites some of the earliest accounts of postmodernism's exhaustion, which begin to emerge in the early 1990s, at the moment in which neoliberalism reaches dominance. Federman comments, "Now that the entire world, the entire universe for that matter has become Postmodern, . . . [postmodern] writers can now stand back and watch, with some degree of amusement, the consequences of what they set in motion some years ago."[36] Postmodernism did not fail because of its immanent contradictions or because it was an avant-garde movement that became too popular and spread across the globe. It brought about and was actualized in the current stage of capitalism. This is what is at stake, then, in understanding the relation between postmodernism and postmodernity as a matter not of contemporaneity but of noncontemporaneity, whose formal qualities are bound up with the temporal unevenness of the two terms. Once the gap between the postmodern avant-garde and neoliberalism's everyday life closes, along with the gap between future and present—once, in other words, we are confronted with actually existing postmodernism, and postmodernism's true ontology and function reveal themselves—we witness the emergence of new literary engagements with the present, including the emergence of the contemporary time novel. The exhaustion of postmodernism is a matter not of caducity but of full implementation and instrumentalization—of a speculative fiction becoming reality. This is what Gibson has in mind when he suggests that cyberpunk has not disappeared but instead has become our present, and that in turn "we are all of us becoming it." It is therefore possible at this point to provide one answer to the question Federman posed over twenty-five years ago: "Does Postmodernism have any future?"[37] The answer is no—because postmodernism has a presence that is centrally bound up with the crisis of futurity which marks our time. In turn, the recent history of the novel is marked by developments such as the emergence of the contemporary time novel, which engages directly with our struggle to imagine an "after." The second *post-* Nealon introduces to mark this literary shift therefore remains unable to speak to those facets of the contemporary novel that attempt to address the sources of and possible solutions to the pervasive crisis of futurity that emerges once postmodernism's new rises to the status of contemporary capitalism's now.

ENDINGS AND THEIR ENDS

Amir Eshel's 2013 book *Futurity: Contemporary Literature and the Quest for the Past* reiterates the general sense of a pervasive crisis of futurity that marks recent Western culture and examines its consequences for our understanding of contemporary literature. Eshel argues that "the modern era created a sense of new time, filled with immeasurable promise," a sense of futurity that has now disappeared.[38] In recent years, the excited anticipation of a different future has given way to the belief that "there may be no future at all for the human race, whose only choice lies between different kinds of endings."[39] Eshel's book shows that contemporary critical and theoretical discourse is fundamentally and pervasively shaped by the understanding of "our era as lacking a sense of human agency and as deprived of futurity altogether."[40] Yet, Eshel argues, it is precisely here that literature can intervene, as it is a crucial site for developing a new vocabulary allowing us to engage with a world that elsewhere "closes in like a trap" and "a language that diminishes" as a result of "the sense of a world deprived of a future."[41] Over the course of this book, I have tried to trace the emergence of such a new temporal imaginary in the contemporary American time novel. Eshel's suggestion that our imagination of the future may now be confined to the choice between different kinds of endings, I would argue, draws our attention to another aspect of the novel's ability to provide us with a way to examine the relation between our temporal vocabulary and material history. In fact, the term *neoliberalism*, frequently disparaged for its nebulousness and lack of precision, in particular when deployed in the context of literary analysis, becomes helpful here. In a classic essay on the time of the novel, John Henry Raleigh demonstrates that the time underlying the form of the novel emerges in part in connection to a specific form of temporal thought that arose in the context of eighteenth-century liberalism. In fact, Raleigh argues, it was not until modern liberalism was well established and had reached a dominant historical status that the novel addressed itself to this new situation by way of a formal transition. The novel did so, Raleigh argues, by addressing itself to the temporal logic of liberalism itself, in much the same way that the contemporary novel's turn to time and realism constitutes an effort to work through the temporal logic of neoliberal omnipresence. While the famous turn of the nineteenth-century (realist) novel toward time and history clearly sets it apart from the novel of the eighteenth century, Raleigh suggests that the nineteenth-century novel inherits its form of thinking time from eighteenth-century liberalism. "Dickens and Trollope," for example, Raleigh writes, "were committed . . . to historical time, or time as a straight line, from the past into the future. In their case the idea of time was tied up with the idea of progress . . . with the result that one looked forward to a pleasant but indefinite future and shunned a definite but unpleasant past. This attitude—rationalistic, progressive, secular— . . . is known as liberalism." "But what is noteworthy about the liberal attitude toward time-history," Raleigh adds, "is that, while it is generally confident about the future, it is vague about the concrete content of the future." Liberalism's imagination of time and futurity, Raleigh suggests, is crystallized in the time of the novel and in particular in its endings. The ending of a novel, Raleigh argues, "is a specific and concrete manifestation of the general sense of time-history underlying the novel as a whole."[42] From this standpoint, the changing valences of liberalism throughout history register in different ways of conceiving the future in the novel's endings. Raleigh further argues that while Victorian society is still marked by a more direct relation to the heritage of liberalism that is bound up with the Victorian novel's trademark happy endings, liberalism takes on a more complicated function for "the moderns," who, beginning with Thomas Hardy and culminating in William Faulkner, are "the rationalists, the dependents on a liberalist future" for whom "there is only tragedy, or misery, waiting in the future."[43]

Insofar as liberalism is bound up with a particular form of thinking time, which then expresses itself in the novel in general, and in the novel's endings and their relation to the future in particular, one might wonder how the contemporary novel's endings express the temporal logic of neoliberalism, which is marked by the collapse of capitalism's trademark notion of time, progress, and futurity at the moment when it pushes this logic of time to its full implementation and thus its immanent boundaries. Once neoliberalism's omnipresent contemporaneity and absorption of the future into the present not only become the structural logic of capitalism but are also woven into the sociocultural fabric, how do novels' endings engage with the problem of the end of time? The coinciding of end and new, of apocalypse and hope in the postmodern novel is anticipatory inasmuch as it is formulated in relation to the refusal of a damaging and damaged past as well as the refusal of the predetermined futures of modernity's emancipatory narratives. The disavowal of teleological futures is not, therefore, a matter of the utter absence of futurity, which would fail to account for both the frenzied forms of futurism that determined the 1960s and 1970s and the anticipatory openness of the postmodern novel's endings. This is the temporal logic of the ending of Kurt Vonnegut's *Slaughterhouse Five* (1969), which oscillates between the departure from the past ("Poo-tee-weet?," whose interrogative mood itself is a gesture toward openings) and the desire for a new form of thinking temporality, a future without old futures and linearities, that Billy Pilgrim finds in the Trafalmadorians's idea of time—and of course, the place of the ending of the novel itself, as both an ending and a middle, complicates the association of the refusal of modernity's futurity with the absolute end of time.[44] Similarly, while Kilgore Trout cries out, "*Make me young*!" to the narrator of *Breakfast of Champions* (1973)—notably in the narrator's father's voice—this refusal of the renewal of modernity's paternalism and its time is balanced against the novel's final word (or rather, two words): "ETC."[45] And just as the moment of suspended waiting for the calling of lot 49 is bound up with both anticipation and the departure from modernity's time of Oedipalism in Thomas Pynchon's *The Crying of Lot 49* (1966), Donald Barthelme's *The Dead Father* (1975) ends with the Dead Father's desperate plea for more time, for just one more moment, which the group of young people who have accompanied him to his grave deny him to make way for their own post-Oedipal future. Barthelme's novel ends with one word: "Bulldozers" (177). But just because one may have chosen to depart from the temporal logic of modernism's architecture and spatial configurations does not mean, of course, that the act of bulldozing cannot also be understood as another way of clearing the present to make room for possibility.

In novels such as Bret Easton Ellis's *American Psycho* (1991), which mediate the emergence of a historical situation that we can begin to associate with full neoliberalism in the late 1980s and early 1990s (as opposed to neoliberalism as an incipient structural logic in the 1970s that takes on a particular function in relation to the crisis of the previous stage of capitalism), the relation to the present changes decidedly. Instead of postmodernism's celebration of a present defined by the anticipation of the large-scale move beyond modernity's old limiting futures, the logic of the present in *American Psycho* is one of confinement and the exhaustion of difference into ultimate sameness. In a neoliberal world in which all aspects of life are routed through the logic of the market, finance, and consumerism, the novel's protagonist, Patrick Bateman, struggles with the inability to register as an individual precisely at the moment when neoliberalism dissolves all former forms of social relationships and community into the universal commitment to individualism and identity. Trapped between his desire to "fit in," which he reiterates throughout the novel, and his quest to set himself apart as an individual, Bateman ultimately cannot accomplish either and is constantly mistaken for someone else in a society in which now, "*everybody's* rich, . . . *everybody's* good looking, . . . *everybody* has a good body."[46] The terrifying murders committed by Bateman can be understood as desperate attempts to wrest individual recognition from a society defined by the functional standardization of difference, culminating in the horror of ultimate sameness. But Bateman is never able to escape the condition anticipated by the novel's second epigraph, borrowed from the Talking Heads: "And as things fell apart / Nobody paid much attention." The true horror of the novel therefore lies not in Patrick's actual murders but in his inability to get the people around him to care about the murders.

However, it is precisely in the attempt to understand the end of difference in relation to the new neoliberal dominant that emerges in the late 1980s, which Ellis's 1991 novel is able to retrospectively historicize, that we can locate both an index of the novel's move beyond postmodernism and the recent novel's aim to interrogate neoliberalism's logical limits. The novel's constant play with the tension between fiction and reality—does Bateman actually commit the murders or does he only imagine them?—mediates the transition from fiction to reality of a range of neoliberalism's enabling narratives. Bateman is confined to a situation in which various wishes, such as the liberal narrative of individualism and postmodernism's politics of difference, which assign such great value to the subject, are structurally fulfilled. However, since neoliberalism fulfills them on capitalism's terms and assigns them a central function in the new dominant, these wishes, Bateman finds, have been robbed of their satisfying content. Reeling from his inability to register as an individual because he can signal his identity only via the same channels used by all those around him—the reservation lists of restaurants and clubs, business cards, expensively modified bodies, clothing, and so on—Bateman seeks to turn the new reality, which robbed the dream of individuality of its gratifying core through its complete structural implementation, back into fiction. The climax occurs in a memorable scene toward the end of the novel in which Bateman finds himself in a police chase. However, at the beginning of the scene, first-person narration gives way to a third-person point of view accompanied by overuse of his first name, Patrick. Bateman imagines himself in the car chase as seen and narrated through the lens of a camera eye, the protagonist of an action movie whose actions and dialogue in the chase scene are the sole motor of plot and the sole, exaggerated focus of the audience's attention. Yet, as becomes clear, such turns back to fiction constitute nothing more than forms of escapism from the reality of the present, and the novel's final words seemingly solidify the foreclosure of all future possibility: "THIS IS NOT AN EXIT" (399).

While Nealon accepts this absence of futurity as a dominant given and proclaims the virtually complete exhaustion of the literary in its context, Eshel presents in some ways the inverse of such a conclusion and suggests that, whereas mainstream culture is defined by the reproduction of this notion of an absence of futurity, literature is defined as an artistic medium today partly by its ability to work through this purported impasse. And while there certainly are numerous examples of the ways literature remains complicit with the general crisis of futurity, Eshel advocates a more nuanced approach, arguing that "the charge that Western culture of recent decades lacks 'any thinking of time,' as Alain Badiou puts it . . . flies in the face of numerous works of contemporary fiction."[47] In this context, Eshel defines futurity in direct relation to the literary, whose ontology today consequently is for Eshel at its heart a matter of temporality and futurity: "Futurity marks the potential of literature to widen the language and to expand the pool of idioms we employ in making sense of what has occurred while imagining who we may become."[48] Eshel's engagement with American fiction is largely limited to his reading of Paul Auster's *Oracle Night* (2003) and Cormac McCarthy's *The Road* (2006), but the novels with which I engage in this chapter confirm that Eshel's basic suggestion is correct. However, as we have seen, we have to trace the beginnings of this development in the novel back to the 1980s, the decade to which Nealon rightly ascribes such great importance for our understanding of contemporary American literature. Eshel's point is echoed by Mark McGurl, who argues that, especially in the context of what he calls "the waste land of the present," we must pay particular attention to literature's "interest in the complexities of temporality" and understand it as an aspect of the specific strengths of literature.[49]

It is then possible to read Ellis's novel not merely as a confirmation of the suspicion that neoliberalism marks an ultimate limit and horizon of time and thought but rather as a novel that places itself in relation to a history of novels that address precisely such moments of perceived stasis and timelessness. Moreover, we can read *American Psycho* as an argument for the importance of locating critical engagement with the neoliberal present in the realm of reality and realism, since it is precisely Bateman's escape into a variety of established forms of fiction that leaves him unable to come to terms with the experience of the limits of his time. In fact, it is possible to argue that novels such as *American Psycho* do for us in the time of neoliberalism what Marcel Proust did for the temporal crises that plagued the modernist imagination, suggesting at the same time that the notion of the end of time is, of course, not new and ought to be historicized in itself. Erich Auerbach's reading of Proust's *In Search of Lost Time* may help illustrate this point. "Even the souls of the damned know that there is a life other than theirs," writes Auerbach. But in Proust, he continues, "there is nothing of this sort": "Permanently and hermetically sealed off in a rotten social structure (that is nevertheless the prevailing one) and in the domain of hypersensitive powers of observation that are so logical as to drive one both mad and into atrociously digressive trivialities, the gargantuan novel paces back and forth, as if in a cage, between a very small number of motifs and events."[50] Life and the experience of time in Proust's novel, Auerbach argues, are trivialized to the degree that they become a matter of confinement and are severed from history itself and, ultimately, rendered timeless, a situation that, even more than the above sketch of Proust's novel, describes Bateman's experience of his own world. But it is precisely through the novel's own foreclosures, limits, and confinement, Auerbach argues, that Proust is able to make legible the logical foundations of the temporal problem and its connection to thought and social form that the novel examines. Here, Proust succeeds in fully committing himself to the limit, making it visible as precisely that, a limit, based on which he is able to make it visible not as a categorical limit but rather as a historically specific end. It is in this way, Auerbach argues, that "Proust's narrator can achieve what the entire generation of his author could not."[51] And it is also in this way, therefore, that we can understand the ways in which *American Psycho* importantly addresses itself to neoliberalism. In other words, it is precisely through Bateman's tragic failures that Ellis's novel uncovers the logic of that which imposes upon the contemporary the semblance of impossibility and at the same time historicizes the end of time and the neoliberal contemporary. *American Psycho* allows us to understand the departure from postmodernism in relation to the rise to dominance of neoliberalism and exemplifies the time novel's commitment to the project of developing forms of reading the seemingly empty time of neoliberalism's omnipresence as history, with its own historically specific aporias. A focus on this aspect of the recent American novel outlines the contours of a rich archive of novels that follow in Ellis's path, including works such as Jonathan Lethem's *Amnesia Moon* (1995), in which the tension between speculative fiction and realism mediates the structural congruency between postmodernism and neoliberalism; Percival Everett's *Glyph* (1999), which asks how we may write novels about the standardization of poststructuralism and postmodernism, about which it seems to be impossible to speak; or Jess Walters's *The Financial Lives of Poets* (2009) and Jennifer Egan's *The Keep* (2006), which explore how fictions and reality, old and new crash into each other and transform the way these concepts relate to our present.

PATTERN RECOGNITION: ON PERIODIZATION

A great number of the new periodizing terms that have been introduced since the midaughts, including *digimodernism* and *altermodern*, are set up to operate in a way that resembles branding, not historical analysis.[52] And branding, as we know, is not about communicating detailed or precise information. It is about something else entirely. Terms that function in such a way may be valuable for those who coin them, but they are ultimately of little value to literary criticism. But we can avoid this problem by replacing attempts at large-scale periodization with the more modest aim of recognizing and interpreting the formal patterns that emerge when we examine how a particular facet of literature, such as the novel, confronts a set of historically specific structural, sociopolitical, or philosophical crises or transitions as aesthetic problems. Historical analysis and periodization begin when we ask how a particular form or genre may relate to the historical, material conditions with which it is bound up. Such an analysis aims to understand the possibilities and limitations of different forms and genres to engage with a historically specific set of material relations, social problems, political challenges, or philosophical crises. We explore the possibilities and limitations of the novel, in contradistinction to poetry, drama, or short fiction, in the context of a historical situation that presents a specific set of problems for thought and for aesthetics. As we can see in our time, the novel develops a range of strategies for confronting a new historical situation, and it is helpful for our understanding of how the novel changes over time to analyze these strategies. As I hope to have shown in the previous chapters, such patterns do not express themselves uniformly across the American novel. Instead, they register on the level of particular novelistic forms like the time novel. And of course, the time novel comes to us in a range of configurations and with varied commitments. In recent years, we have seen the rise of a new range of novelistic realisms and autofiction, for example, and we have witnessed the growing importance of genre fiction, in particular in the multiethnic American novel. Paying close attention to such individual aspects of an overall varied and at times contradictory historical development allows us to develop concrete insights into the important work that particular forms and genres may do under specific historical conditions. Without periodization thus conceived, we struggle to make sense of literature's complex and fascinating journey through time and the multitude of ways in which individual facets of literature assume significant relationships to the real world and carry out important work for thought and politics. To be sure, such an understanding of periodization, one that finds less value in the attempt to identify large-scale cultural dominants than in examinations of the significance of individual formal and generic changes, may strike some as disappointingly microscopic. I would argue, however, that the payoff of understanding periodization as a more modest project is immense. While we abandon the ability to forward seemingly more spectacular claims about the rise and fall of this or that period or to pass judgment on the continued life and death of art forms like the novel, paying close attention to a particular form like the time novel not only allows us more complex and ultimately more precise insights, but in fact permits us to make stronger periodizing claims. That is, while I limit my discussions in this book to the time novel, doing so allows me to foreground the significant value of the time novel today, which in turn indicates the general value of the novel as a form of knowledge and of world making. While it is only one facet of a much larger and more complex novelistic presence, periodizing the time novel nevertheless indicates the importance of reading novels today.

Such a narrowed focus on smaller patterns of an overall varied and temporally plural periodizing project also foregrounds some larger commitments. Especially since we are confronted with a crisis of temporality that originates in part from the limitations of our temporal vocabulary, periodization constitutes an important, necessary opportunity to identify or even transcend those limits of our vocabulary that determine how we talk about the novel now. Rather than naming beginnings and ends or identifying dominant forces, we can understand periodization, with Kojin Karatani, as an ongoing process that is necessarily self-reflexive. Periodization, that is, always also means reperiodization. Periodization is a way of making sense of our place in history, of trying to discern meaningful patterns that allow us to understand the complex dynamic of historical change—in the past as well as in our present. Periodizing literature is pattern recognition squared. That is, by periodizing literature we ask in part how different facets of literature have devised new ways of making sense of and formally mediating historical change. And since periodization is therefore not an objective, external process but part of the very attempt to understand our relation to external history and map history's flow, it also requires us to historicize periodization itself. This suggestion no doubt sounds awkward. But it indicates nothing other than the need to understand periodization as historical knowledge, as a form of making meaning that emerges under specific historical conditions and in connection to particular forms of knowledge and politics. Historicizing periodization means examining the advantages and limitations of periodizing models, subjecting our efforts to make history thinkable to historical scrutiny, because asking how we attempt to know history affords us crucially important insights into our struggle to know the present. To study periodization historically is an important aspect of our larger effort to study historical thought. And since, as Gumbrecht shows, our time is characterized by the exhaustion of the form of historical thought that has determined how we understand and make sense of history since the nineteenth century, periodizing the contemporary is one of the most pressing projects for both temporal thought and art today. Understood in this way, as a series of contestations of established notions of periods that change our understanding of the very significance of the historical events themselves, periodization constitutes the basis of historical study.[53] History, Peter Osborne stresses, "is 'temporalized.' It becomes possible for an event to change its identity according to its shifting status in the advance of history as a whole."[54] In the case of our attempt to historicize the contemporary, as we have seen, we can find important insights in our present by reperiodizing postmodernism—not to locate its beginning and end more or less correctly but instead as a way of understanding postmodernism itself differently. Such a reperiodization then allows us to examine the logic and formal constitution of the novels that begin to be written once postmodernism itself disappears into its own structural implementation as the new capitalist dominant.

One of the most helpful accounts of periodization and reperiodization can be found in David James and Urmila Seshagiri's discussion of the history and presence of modernism in the context of the rise of the new modernist studies. James and Seshagiri ask what the current return to literary forms reminiscent of modernism should mean for our understanding of contemporary literature and the history of modernism. I engage with the contemporaneity of modernism in more detail elsewhere.[55] What I wish to focus on here is the value of James and Seshagiri's discussion of periodization itself, which stresses that continuing to periodize modernism's history is crucial to our ability to understand both modernism and the contemporary. They argue that we must not simply understand the work that forms traditionally associated with modernism may do in the present as a simple matter of repetition or of a long modernism that never waned. Instead, the return of modernist forms in our moment should encourage us to think of periodization in a more complicated way, and it indicates that we ought to reperiodize modernism itself, for the new conditions of the present may afford us a better understanding of what modernism was.[56] But while critics like Susan Stanford Friedman and Eric Hayot have recently argued against conceptions of periodization that focus on linear progress, on beginnings and ends, reinforcing a "presentist and dissociative form of historical thinking," James and Seshagiri show that these critics also ultimately return to traditional notions of chronology and deeply entrenched periodizing distinctions.[57] James and Seshagiri, however, defend a more complex understanding of periodization as a "valuable and self-reflexive strategy that endows literary history with clarity even as it encourages ongoing debate about when modernism waxed and waned." What may initially seem like a contradiction—the return to the idea of beginnings and ends—becomes for James and Seshagiri a different project. "We need to retain periodicity not to shore up a canonical sense of when modernism began," they argue, "but to establish a literary-cultural basis for charting the myriad ways that much twenty-first century fiction consciously engages modernism."[58] As we have seen in the case of the time novel, such an understanding of periodization offers us an important way to make sense of important aspects of contemporary literature and retroactively allows us to better understand the history of the time novel itself. The time novel, a quintessential modernist form, comes to us today under specific historical conditions to do work altogether particular to our time. Periodizing the time novel means tracing the internal multiplicity of the form beyond linear timelines and accounts of repetition. The history of the time novel is not linear, and the time novel is not singular. Its variations emerged under and responded to particular historical conditions in different geographical regions. The time novel's multiple forms were changed and abandoned, exported and reinterpreted, and for some time in a range of national contexts, the time novel seems to have disappeared altogether. Its return today in American literature, therefore, cannot be understood as a matter of repetition, as a sign of retro-modernism, or as an index of the fact that modernism itself never truly ended. Such arguments do not reflect the complex history and plurality of the time novel, and they tell us little about the time novel, modernism, or our contemporary moment. Thus, while *How to Read a Moment* does not forward any claims about the time novel, the novel itself, or literary periods that may be recognizable as traditional periodizing claims, this book is nevertheless deeply committed to periodization. Yet it periodizes in a way that is indicated to us by the complex, discontinuous history of the time novel itself, which cannot be meaningfully described through a vocabulary and logic that seek to name dominants, origins, and ends.

To be sure, it is not difficult to disparage periodization if we reduce it to a fascination with beginnings and ends. But while periodization is a much more complex operation than this, I also suggest, however briefly, that the continued attraction to beginnings and ends is not as simple a matter as it may seem. We are undoubtedly fascinated by beginnings and ends, and this fascination itself has a history and is bound up with a specific way of imagining and making sense of time and history, one that in turn expresses itself on the level of social and political reality. To overlook the importance of and reasons for our fascination with beginnings and ends is as problematic as failing to understand the limitations of such an approach for periodization. Peter Boxall argues that the reason for the appeal of beginnings and ends lies not in their simplicity but rather in their inconceivability. "It is perhaps the greatest existential difficulty faced by every sensate being," Boxall writes, "that both the beginning of things and the end seem inconceivable."[59] Novels like *Pattern Recognition* and a wide range of novels published in the mid-1980s examine the relation between historical change and the development of literary forms and genres in relation to the tension between the sense of an ending and the end's inconceivability. Consequently, insofar as beginnings and ends always stand in an imprecise, problematic relation to history, and inasmuch as they express inconceivable ideas, they may be best understood as fictions. But of course, to suggest that they are fictions is not to say that they are inconsequential and should not be studied. On the contrary, we should study them as fictions, as fictions of history and as historical fictions, as narratives about our relation to history that express our desire to make meaning of our place and time in the world. And like all fictions, beginnings and ends are productive.

Particularly in our moment, in a time when political dialogue and social conflicts are directly shaped by the widespread perception of a range of ends, it is of crucial importance to highlight and examine the importance of the fiction of ends. Ends make strong periodizing claims over moments in history, and our present sociopolitical reality is shaped significantly by right-wing declarations of the end of a range of fictions: the idea of traditional masculinity, the idea of uniform national cultures and racial identity, and so on. Ends and beginnings provide fertile soil for the cultivation of cultural, political, and historical fictions. Some of the most dangerous and threatening developments of our time, such as the rise of a new extreme Right, indicate that we must not only historicize beginnings and ends in themselves, but we must also pay close attention to the ways beginnings and ends serve as a popular mechanism for periodizing the contemporary, for the construction of fictions of the present that create very real social and political problems. The rise of the new Right relies on a series of fictions and ends that generate a reactionary pseudo-periodization of the present. Fictions of ends and pseudo-periodizations are powerful. The idea that the current moment in US history is defined by the end of American's former greatness, which requires a return to an idealized, lost past (in order to create a copy of American culture whose original never existed), for example, has shaped US and global politics as significantly as few other contemporary fictions. Our failure to produce alternative, competing ways of periodizing the contemporary and the departure from periodization itself leave us unable to speak to the myriad ways in which the contemporary is being implicitly periodized in academic scholarship, political debate, and popular commentary.

We are called upon, then, to always periodize and always historicize the modes of periodization that define a moment in time. If we understand periodization as a form of narrative and interpretation, as a historically specific way of telling time and making sense of our relation to history, then we see that periodization itself demands to be historicized. Gumbrecht's discussion of literary history, for instance, highlights the importance of examining the historical origins of the form of temporal knowledge upon which our traditional understanding of literary history rests. Tracing the temporal models that stabilize established methods of periodization and our understanding of literary history in relation to nineteenth-century historicism allows us to historically contextualize the continued influence exerted by linear chronology and the beginnings and ends that chart periods on a timeline upon our approach to periodization. But instead of abandoning periodization due to its connection to linearity and to beginnings and ends, instead of declaring the end of literary history due to the exhaustion of the form of temporal knowledge in relation to which it emerged, we should explore alternative conceptions of literary history and periodization that are suitable for our moment in time. Doing so also means that we follow the example of the novel, which urges us to devise a new temporal vocabulary and new forms of temporal knowledge that allow us to tell the time of the present. A new direction for literary history and periodization may lie in the pluralized understanding of time for which I have argued in this book, since such an understanding of time also opens up previously foreclosed trajectories of historical thought.

Massimiliano Tomba shows that the sources of our established forms of historicism and historical thought indeed lie in nineteenth-century Germany, but we must also understand the emergence of this form of temporal knowledge in relation to "the singularization of the concept of history, which occurred in the German vocabulary between the end of the eighteenth and beginning of the nineteenth century." This singularization occurred in the context of the rise of capitalism, which necessitated the creation of an abstract, homogenized, and standardized form of temporality. Capitalism's temporal episteme thus "constituted . . . the condition of possibility for the processualization of history in the direction of the theories of history in the nineteenth century." The temporal regime of capitalism is in turn bound up with the history of empire, since, as Tomba shows in some detail, "notions of world history or large-scale unilinear historical progress . . . allowed the measuring of the level of (Western) civilization attained by populations."[60] We would do well, therefore, to take the crisis of the temporal regime of capitalism and empire and its associated understanding of literary history as an occasion to explore a different temporal logic for periodization and for our attempt to historicize the development of literature. Periodization beyond the time of capitalism and empire means making legible those temporalities, those aspects of a period, that are overwritten by capitalism's attempts to standardize our sense of temporality. Periodization thus conceived allows us to tell historical time by reading against the grain of capitalism's homogenization of temporal knowledge. Such a project is particularly pressing for literary history, since, as Marshall Brown argues, "literature is the writing that refuses to conform. And literary history is the understanding that regards literature's refusal as a temporal gesture."[61]

Jameson's work on postmodernism is often invoked in discussions about the limitations of periodization. It is important to remember, however, that Jameson's earlier work stresses the danger of understanding periodization as a matter of identifying cultural dominants or beginnings and ends that lead to overly homogeneous accounts of historical periods. In *The Political Unconscious* (1982), Jameson argues that periods must always be understood as internally complex and multiple if we are to avoid the reductive idea of individual periods "in which everything becomes so seamlessly interrelated that we confront either a total system or an idealistic 'concept' of a period."[62] This suggestion is of the utmost importance for examinations of literary history, and it is possibly more helpful for our present context than the better-known account of periodization upon which Jameson's writings on postmodernism rely. That is, in the effort to avoid constructing an "idealistic 'concept'" of postmodernism, Jameson relies on Raymond Williams's distinction between the dominant, residual, and emergent forces that characterize a given moment in time. This tripartite distinction allows for a slightly more complex account of a period, but it ultimately still relies on a linear account of time that inadvertently extends our fascination with cultural dominants, which is deeply involved in the desire for large-scale periodization and the pursuit of prominent periodizing markers. Time itself is best understood as a negative totality, the sum total of all temporal imaginaries that exist at a given moment and stand in at times directly contradictory relation to capitalism's dominant temporal regime. Focusing on the currently dominant regime and its associated cultural and epistemological modes does little else than confirm the crisis of temporality, which is what we see all too frequently in critical and theoretical commentary today. And limiting the alternatives to this dominant regime to residual and emergent forces further constricts our analytical choices to the study of the succession of dominants. But the idea of a linear cultural and temporal dominant that stabilizes capitalism's rise is only possible because capitalism erases the time's plurality. Rather than tracing the residual and emergent, therefore, the time novel indicates a more complicated relation to history that seeks to trace those ways of understanding and being in time that do not map onto and are not recognized by the dominant temporal regime that capitalism struggles to maintain. The time novel shows that time itself is never monadic, but rather an always plural, discontinuous, and at times contradictory totality of forms of temporal knowledge. Periodization inevitably becomes reductive and less meaningful when it overwrites time's very complexity in the effort to make history understandable. An alternative form of periodization, periodization as pattern recognition, uncovers the plurality of time and of a given moment in history by reading the particular in an attempt to continuously map the universal—not to arrive at a singular or large-scale, settled meaning but in a way that seeks to contribute to the understanding of a complex system by tracing its individual facets.

Periodization provides us with interpretations of moments in time that aim to trace meaningful relations and thus seek to make sense of historical change or specific historical conditions. Of course, since history does not lend itself well to simplification, periodization yields unsatisfactory results when it is deployed as a matter of making history more easily digestible by carving it up into bite-size portions. And as Gibson's novel shows, pattern recognition can also give way to apophenia, faulty pattern recognition, defined as the perception of meaningful relations between utterly unrelated things. Faulty periodization, that is, can be understood as a mechanism for the falsified narrative construction of a moment in time or of the present, and as we are witnessing in our time, the strategic deployment of apophenia and faulty periodization is one of the most effective tools of populism. But precisely because this is so, we must also understand the importance of periodization as a way of grappling with the problem of contemporaneity. Brown emphasizes the importance of following Hayden White's understanding of history: not as "a mode of being" but as "a situatedness understood as a dialectical response to one's cultural environment."[63] Periodization is directly involved in the construction of this sense of situatedness. Periodizing the contemporary is the formulation of a historical sense of the present. Periodization is the always multiple narrative construction of the present based on a process of pattern recognition that we must understand with White and Brown as a crucial part of history itself. The multiple attempts to periodize the contemporary behave like narratives insofar as they have the power to elucidate and to obscure, to shed light on the structural relations of a moment in time, and to construct strategic fictions about a moment that have to be treated with great caution and may harbor great danger. The historically examined moment in the present is the smallest unit of periodization. The time novel shows us that this is a unit of time that is not to be experienced in its passing nor to be understood in its totality. Instead, it is to be interpreted—one meaningful pattern at a time. Periodization is a matter of reading form in time, in art, and in material reality. As a historical narrative, periodizing the present affords us a sense of contemporaneity. It is, for good or ill, a way of coming together in time. For these reasons, periodization should be understood not simply as critical practice but as an integral part of our common relation to history and the present, which in turn means that periodization is also an object of critical inquiry and historical analysis. Periodization is not a method to be embraced or rejected but a crucial way of reading in common, one that contains potential for strategic falsification as much as it offers crucial opportunities for critical inquiry and illumination. Recognizing meaningful patterns in the present, periodizing the contemporary, the time novel shows, allows us to read the present and its limits and foreclosures historically. In this way, periodizing the contemporary enables us to wrest hope and possibility from the grip of a purportedly timeless present.

Notes

INTRODUCTION

1. Don DeLillo, *Cosmopolis* (New York: Scribner, 2003), 43.

2. Don DeLillo, *The Body Artist* (New York: Simon and Schuster, 2001), 92.

3. Don DeLillo, "In the Ruins of the Future," *Guardian*, September 22, 2001, http://www.theguardian.com/books/2001/dec/22/fiction.dondelillo.

4. William Gibson, *Pattern Recognition* (New York: Berkley, 2003), 57.

5. Fredric Jameson, *A Singular Modernity* (New York: Verso, 2013), 19.

6. Gibson, *Pattern Recognition*, 180. I should note here that this quote has a poignant history: the quote is generally attributed to either Dwight D. Eisenhower or Gerald Ford, though there is no evidence that either ever uttered these words.

7. Hans Ulrich Gumbrecht, "Shall We Continue to Write Histories of Literature?," *New Literary History* 39 (2008): 528.

8. Terry Smith, "Introduction: The Contemporaneity Question," in *Antinomies of Art and Culture: Modernity, Postmodernity, Contemporaneity*, ed. Terry Smith, Okwui Enwezor, and Nancy Condee (Durham, NC: Duke University Press, 2008), 8–9.

9. Peter Thiel, "The End of the Future," *National Review*, October 3, 2011, https://www.nationalreview.com/2011/10/end-future-peter-thiel/.

10. Noah Berlatsky. "When Science Fiction Stopped Caring about the Future," *The Atlantic*, December 5, 2014, https://www.theatlantic.com/entertainment/archive/2014/12/the-new-star-wars-isnt-really-new/383426/.

11. Will Ferrell, "Where's the Future? Will Ferrell's Tour of Tech That Never Took," *Wired*, August 3, 2010, https://www.wired.com/2010/08/ff_future_ferrell/.

12. Ed Finn, "The Inspiration Drought," *Future Tense*, September 16, 2014, http://www.publetariat.com/2014/09/16/the-inspiration-drought/.

13. Nathan Silverman, "Future Fail," *The Baffler* 36 (September 2017), https://thebaffler.com/outbursts/future-fail-silverman.

14. CO.EXIST staff, "The End of the Future and the Rise of the Present," *Fast Company*, May 16, 2013, https://www.fastcompany.com/2682076/the-end-of-the-future-and-the-rise-of-the-present.

15. Douglas Rushkoff, *Present Shock: When Everything Happens Now* (London: Current, 2013).

16. David Armitage and Jo Guldi, "Bonfire of the Humanities," *Aeon*, October 2, 2014, https://aeon.co/essays/the-role-of-history-in-a-society-afflicted-by-short-termism.

17. Cuauhtémoc Medina, "Contemp(t)orary: Eleven Theses," *e-flux* 12 (2010), http://www.e-flux.com/journal/12/61335/contemp-t-orary-eleven-theses/.

18. Hal Foster et al., "Questionnaire on 'The Contemporary,'" *October* 130 (2009): 3.

19. Juliane Rebentisch, "The Contemporaneity of Contemporary Art," *New German Critique* 42, no. 1 (2015): 225.

20. AYR, "Famili: Proxy Paranoia or Technological Camaraderie," *Harvard Design Magazine* 41 (2015), http://www.harvarddesignmagazine.org/issues/41/famili-proxy-paranoia-or-technological-camaraderie.

21. Eric Cazdyn and Imre Szeman, *After Globalization* (Hoboken, NJ: Wiley-Blackwell, 2012).

22. James Bridle, *New Dark Age: Technology and the End of the Future* (New York: Verso, 2018).

23. Thiel, "The End of the Future."

24. Mike Doherty, "William Gibson on the End of the Future," *National Post*, November 27, 2014, https://nationalpost.com/entertainment/books/william-gibson-on-the-end-of-the-future.

25. Timothy Bewes, "Introduction: Temporalizing the Present" *Novel: A Forum on Fiction* 45, no. 2 (2012): 160.

26. Milan Kundera, *The Art of the Novel* (New York: Harper Perennial, 1993), 19.

27. Annette Van, "Novel Futures," *Novel: A Forum on Fiction* 41, no. 1 (2010): 161.

28. Van, "Novel Futures," 162.

29. Charles Yu, *How to Live Safely in a Science Fictional Universe* (New York: Vintage: 2010), 3.

30. See also Slavoj Žižek, *Living in the End Times* (New York: Verso, 2010).

31. Fredric Jameson, *The Seeds of Time* (New York: Columbia University Press, 1994), xii. See also Francis Fukuyama, *The End of History and the Last Man* (New York: Free Press, 2006).

32. Peter Boxall, *The Value of the Novel* (Cambridge: Cambridge University Press, 2015), 100.

33. Boxall, *The Value of the Novel*, 98.

34. Silke Müller and Susanne Weiss, *Studienbuch neuere deutsche Literaturwissenschaft, 1720–1848* (Würzburg: Königshausen und Neumann, 1999), 97.

35. I am blending my own translation with that provided by the Yale Modernism Lab (https://campuspress.yale.edu/modernismlab/the-magic-mountain/). I am basing my own translation on the version published in his collected works: "Einführung in den *Zeuberberg*," in *Gesammelte Werke in Zwölf Bänden*, vol. 11 (Oldenburg: Fischer, 1960), 602–17.

36. See Paul Ricoeur, *Time and Narrative*, vol. 2 (Chicago: University of Chicago Press, 1985), 112–30.

37. Mann, "Einführung," 612.

38. Mann, "Einführung," 612.

39. Roger Hillman, *Zeitroman: The Novel and Society in Germany, 1830–1900* (New York: Peter Lang, 1983), 13.

40. Jeffrey Insko, "Prospects for the Present," *American Literary History* 26, no. 4 (2014): 836.

41. Tobias Boes, *Formative Fictions: Nationalism, Cosmopolitanism, and the* Bildungsroman (Ithaca, NY: Cornell University Press, 2012), 34.

42. Boes, *Formative Fictions*, 27.

43. Cathy Caruth, "Afterword: Turning Back to Literature" *PMLA* 125, no. 4 (2010): 1087.

44. Caruth, "Afterword," 1088.

45. Lauren Berlant, *Cruel Optimism* (Durham, NC: Duke University Press, 2011), 6.

46. José Esteban Muñoz, *Cruising Utopia: The Then and There of Queer Futurity* (New York: New York University Press, 2009), 12.

47. Muñoz, *Cruising Utopia*, 27.

48. Catherine Gallagher, "Formalism and Time," *Modern Language Quarterly* 61, no. 1 (2000): 232.

49. Theodor W. Adorno, *Aesthetic Theory* (Minneapolis: University of Minnesota Press, 1998), 7.

50. J. M. Bernstein, *The Philosophy of the Novel: Lukács, Marxism, and the Dialectics of Form* (Minneapolis: University of Minnesota Press, 1984), 126.

51. Bernstein, *The Philosophy of the Novel*, 138.

52. Bernstein, *The Philosophy of the Novel*, 127.

53. Adorno, *Aesthetic Theory*, 143.

CHAPTER 1

1. Jacques Rancière, "In What Time Do We Live?," *Politica Comun* 4 (2013): n.p., https://quod.lib.umich.edu/p/pc/12322227.0004.001?view=text;rgn=main.

2. Cormac McCarthy, *No Country for Old Men* (New York: Vintage, 2005), 307–8.

3. Cormac McCarthy, *The Road* (New York: Vintage, 2007), 241.

4. Fredric Jameson, *A Singular Modernity* (New York: Verso, 2002), 16.

5. Ben Kunkel, *Indecision* (New York: Random House, 2006), 18.

6. George Kubler, *The Shape of Time* (New Haven, CT: Yale University Press, 1970), 29.

7. Marshall Brown, "Literature in Time," *MLQ* 65, no. 1 (2004): 5.

8. Nathaniel Rich, *Odds against Tomorrow* (New York: Farrar, Straus, and Giroux, 2013), 236.

9. Fredric Jameson, "The End of Temporality," *Critical Inquiry* 29 (2003): 695.

10. Fredric Jameson, "On the Power of the Negative," *Mediations* 28, no. 1 (2014): 71.

11. See Rita Felski, "The Invention of Everyday Life," in *Doing Time: Feminist Theory and Postmodern Culture* (New York: New York University Press, 2000), 77–98.

12. Andrew Hoberek, "Cormac McCarthy and the Aesthetics of Exhaustion," *American Literary History* 23, no. 3 (2011): 497.

13. Boxall, *The Value of the Novel*, 102.

14. Robert Rauschenberg, *White Painting* (1951), https://www.sfmoma.org/artwork/98.308.A-C.

15. See "When John Cage Met Robert Rauschenberg," Phaidon, March 2, 2015, http://ca.phaidon.com/agenda/art/articles/2015/march/02/when-john-cage-met-robert-rauschenberg/.

16. Jonathan Arac, "What Kind of History Does a Theory of the Novel Require?," *Novel: A Forum on Fiction* 42, no. 2 (2009): 193.

17. Arac, "What Kind of History," 194.

18. John Neubauer, "Bakhtin versus Lukács: Inscriptions of Homelessness in Theories of the Novel," *Poetics Today* 17, no. 4 (1996): 531.

19. Georg Lukács, *Theory of the Novel: A Historico-Philosophical Essay on the Forms of Great Epic Literature*, trans. Anna Bostock (Cambridge, MA: MIT Press, 1972), 121.

20. Neubauer, "Bakhtin versus Lukács," 531.

21. Fredric Jameson, "The Experiments of Time: Providence and Realism," in Franco Moretti, ed., *The Novel*, vol. 2, *Forms and Themes* (Princeton, NJ: Princeton University Press, 2006), 109.

22. Neubauer, "Bakhtin versus Lukács," 533.

23. Quoted in Neubauer, "Bakhtin versus Lukács," 540.

24. Quoted in Neubauer, "Bakhtin versus Lukács," 541.

25. Neubauer, "Bakhtin versus Lukács," 534.

26. Timothy Bewes, "The Novel as Absence: Lukacs and the Event of Postmodern Fiction," *NOVEL: A Forum on Fiction* 38, no. 1 (2004): 14.

27. Lukács, *The Theory of the Novel*, 122.

28. Bakhtin quoted in Neubauer, "Bakhtin versus Lukács," 543.

29. Bernstein, *The Philosophy of the Novel*, 140.

30. Bewes, "The Novel as Absence," 14.

31. Caroline Levine, *Forms: Whole, Rhythm, Hierarchy, Network* (Princeton, NJ: Princeton University Press, 2015), 51.

32. Theodor W. Adorno, *Negative Dialectics* (New York: Bloomsbury, 1981), 333.

33. Kubler, *The Shape of Time*, 29.

34. Mark C. Taylor, *Speed Limits: Where Time Went and Why We Have So Little Left* (New Haven, CT: Yale University Press, 2014), 71.

35. Jimena Canales, "Clock/Lived," in *Time: A Vocabulary of the Present*, ed. Joel Burges and Amy J. Elias (New York: New York University Press, 2016), Kindle location 2636–37.

36. Russell West-Pavlov, *Temporalities* (New York: Routledge, 2012), 120.

37. West-Pavlov, *Temporalities*, 122.

38. Norbert Trenkle, "Value and Crisis: Basic Questions," in *Marxism and the Critique of Value*, ed. Josh Robinson et al. (Chicago: MCM Prime, 2014), 12.

39. Trenkle, "Value and Crisis," 12–13.

40. Barbara Adam, *Time* (New York: Wiley, 2004), 38–39.

41. Bliss Cua Lim, *Translating Time: Cinema, the Fantastic, and Temporal Critique* (Durham, NC: Duke University Press, 2009), 73.

42. Trenkle, "Value and Crisis," 5.

43. Lim, *Translating Time*, 73.

44. Karl Marx, *The Poverty of Philosophy* (Moscow: Foreign Languages Publishing House, n.d.), 58.

45. Boxall, *The Value of the Novel*, 95.

46. Christian Marazzi, *Capital and Language: From the New Economy to the War Economy* (Cambridge, MA: MIT Press, 2008), 54.

47. Marazzi, *Capital and Language*, 51.

48. David Harvey, *The Limits to Capital* (New York: Verso, 2007), xxi.

49. Cédric Durand, *Fictitious Capital: How Finance Is Appropriating Our Future* (New York: Verso, 2017), 1.

50. Robert Hassan, *The Chronoscopic Society: Globalization, Time and Knowledge in the Network Economy* (New York: Peter Lang, 2003).

51. Massimiliano Tomba, *Marx's Temporalities* (Leiden: Brill, 2013), viii.

52. Christina Lupton and R. John Williams, "Essays from the English Institute 2016: Time," *ELH* 85, no. 2 (2018): 285.

53. Lupton and Williams, "Essays from the English Institute," 285.

54. Boxall, *The Value of the Novel*, 97.

55. See Bill Gates, *Business @ the Speed of Thought: Succeeding in the Digital Economy* (New York: Grand Central, 1999).

56. Jameson, "The End of Temporality," 710.

57. Jean Baudrillard, *The Illusion of the End* (Palo Alto, CA: Stanford University Press, 1994), 1.

58. Franco Berardi, *The Soul at Work: From Alienation to Autonomy* (Los Angeles: Semiotext(e), 2009), 11, emphasis in the original.

59. Paul Virilio, *The Futurism of the Instant—Stop-Eject* (London: Polity, 2010), 70–71.

60. Baudrillard, *The Illusion of the End*, 2.

61. Franco Berardi, *After the Future* (Baltimore: AK Press, 2011), 17–23.

62. Franco Berardi, *The Uprising: On Poetry and Finance* (Los Angeles: Semiotext(e), 2012), 10.

63. Maurizio Lazzarato, *The Making of the Indebted Man: An Essay on the Neoliberal Condition* (Los Angeles: Semiotext(e), 2012), 8.

64. Mark McGurl, "Real/Quality," in *Time: A Vocabulary of the Present*, ed. Joel Burges and Amy J. Elias (New York: New York University Press, 2016), Kindle location 4554.

65. Elissa Marder, *Dead Time: Temporal Disorders in the Wake of Modernity (Baudelaire and Flaubert)* (Palo Alto, CA: Stanford University Press, 2001), 2–3.

66. McGurl, "Real/Quality," Kindle location 4503.

67. Don DeLillo, *Point Omega* (New York: Scribner's, 2010), 5–6.

68. Karen Newman, Jay Clayton, and Marianne Hirsch, eds., *Time and the Literary* (New York: Routledge, 2002), 1.

69. Will Self, "The Novel Is Dead (This Time It's for Real)," *Guardian*, May 2, 2014, https://www.theguardian.com/books/2014/may/02/will-self-novel-dead-literary-fiction.

70. Newman, Clayton, and Hirsch, eds., *Time and the Literary*, 1.

71. Jean-Paul Sartre, "On John Dos Passos and *1919*," in *Situations 1* (Paris: Gallimard, 1968), 16.

72. Theodor W. Adorno, "On Lyric Poetry and Society," in *Notes to Literature*, vol. 1 (New York: Columbia University Press, 1991), 40.

73. Georg Lukács, *Ästhetik II* (Neuwied: Luchterhand, 1976), 35.

74. Boxall, *The Value of the Novel*, 108.

75. Peter Osborne, *Anywhere or Not at All: Philosophy of Contemporary Art* (New York: Verso, 2013), 2–3.

76. Giorgio Agamben, "What Is the Contemporary?," in *Time*, ed. Amelia Groom, Documents of Contemporary Art (London: Whitechapel Gallery; Cambridge, MA: MIT Press, 2013), 84.

77. Agamben, "What Is the Contemporary?," 85.

78. Ernst Bloch, *The Utopian Function of Art and Literature: Selected Essays* (Cambridge, MA: MIT Press, 1987), 207.

79. Bloch, *The Utopian Function of Art and Literature*, 207.

80. Ernst Bloch, *The Principle of Hope*, vol. 1 (Cambridge, MA: MIT Press, 1995), 180.

81. Bloch, *The Utopian Function*, 207.

82. Henri Lefebvre, *Rhythmanalysis: Space, Time and Everyday Life* (New York: Continuum, 2004), 88.

83. Don DeLillo, *Zero K* (New York: Scribner, 2016), 157.

84. Giorgio Agamben, "Time and History: Critique of the Instant and Continuum," in *Infancy and History: On the Destruction of Experience* (New York: Verso, 2007), 99.

85. Bloch, *The Utopian Function*, 208.

86. Levine, *Forms*, 51.

87. Lupton and Williams, "Essays from the English Institute," 283.

88. Timothy Bewes, "The Novel Problematic," *Novel: A Forum on Fiction* 44, no. 1 (2011): 17, 19.

89. Guido Mazzoni, *Theory of the Novel* (Cambridge, MA: Harvard University Press, 2017), 2.

90. Jean-Paul Sartre, "Time in Faulkner: *The Sound and the Fury*," in *William Faulkner: Three Decades of Criticism*, ed. Frederick J. Hoffman and Olga W. Vickery (New York: Harcourt Brace, 1960), 225–27.

91. Sartre, "Time in Faulkner," 227, emphasis in the original.

92. Marc Augé, *The Future* (New York: Verso, 2015), 5.

93. Mark McGurl, "Ordinary Doom: Literary Studies in the Waste Land of the Present," *New Literary History* 41, no. 2 (2010): 344.

94. Sartre, "Time in Faulkner," 232.

95. Cristina Diniz Mendonça Crema, "Théorie du roman et théorie de la revolution dans la penseé de Sartre," *Trans/Form/Ação* 15 (1992): n.p., translation mine, http://www.scielo.br/scielo.php?script=sci_arttext&pid=S0101-31731992000100001

96. Jean-Paul Sartre, *Situations I* (New York: George Braziller, 1965), 346.

97. Jean-Paul Sartre, "For Whom Does One Write?" in *What Is Literature?* (New York: Philosophical Library, 1948), 109.

98. Bloch, *The Utopian Function*, 217.

99. Sartre, "On John Dos Passos and *1919*": 16.

100. A. A. Mendilow, *Time and the Novel* (London: Peter Nevill, 1952), 55.

101. DeLillo, *Cosmopolis*, 36.

102. Hans Robert Jauß, *Zeit und Erinnerung in Marcel Prousts "A la recherche du temps perdu": Ein Beitrag zur Theorie des Romans* (Frankfurt: Suhrkamp, 1986), 40, translation mine.

103. Katrin Stepath, *Gegenwartskonzepte: Eine philosophisch-literaturwissenschaftliche Analyse temporaler Strukturen* (Würzburg: Königshausen und Neumann, 2006): 177, translation mine.

104. Jauß, *Zeit und Erinnerung*, 40–41.

105. Giorgio Agamben, "Infancy and History," 99.

106. Boxall, *The Value of the Novel*, 114.

107. Lupton and Williams, "Essays from the English Institute," 283.

108. Lupton and Williams, "Essays from the English Institute," 284.

109. We find such accounts of the novel in Michael Clune's *Writing against Time* (Palo Alto, CA: Stanford University Press, 2013); and Laura Miller's "Dark Futures: What Happens When Literary Novelists Experiment with Science Fiction," *Slate*, May 25, 2017, http://www.slate.com/articles/arts/books/2017/05/literary_fiction_is_borrowing_the_tools_of_the_science_fiction_genre.html.

CHAPTER 2

1. Gary Shteyngart, *Super Sad True Love Story* (New York: Random House, 2010), 275.

2. Adam Kelly, "David Foster Wallace and the Novel of Ideas," in *David Foster Wallace and "The Long Thing": New Essays on the Novels*, ed. Marshall Boswell (New York: Bloomsbury, 2014), 18.

3. Philip Rahv, "The Cult of Experience in American Writing," in *American Literature, American Culture*, ed. Gordon Hutner (Oxford: Oxford University Press, 1999), 283–85.

4. Sorin Radu Cucu's *The Underside of Politics: Global Fictions in the Fog of the Cold War* (New York: Fordham University Press, 2013) is a particularly noteworthy example of scholarly work that unearths the complex relation between American and European fiction.

5. Kelly, "David Foster Wallace," 19n1.

6. Mark McGurl, "The Zombie Renaissance" *n+1* 9 (2010): n.p. Referenced without citation in Kelly, "David Foster Wallace," 19n1.

7. Kundera, *The Art of the Novel*, 16.

8. David Couzens Hoy, *The Time of Our Lives: A Critical History of Temporality* (Cambridge, MA: MIT Press, 2012), 90.

9. For examples of these debates, see David Steiner, "Reading," in *Profession* (2009): 50–55; in the same issue, Mark Edmundson, "Against Readings," 56–65; volumes 37 and 38 (2007) of *New Literary History*, which are dedicated to the problem of "literature now"; Amanda Anderson's 2006 book *The Way We Argue Now: Studies in the Cultures of Theory* (Princeton University Press); the lively debates that were triggered by Stephen Best and Sharon Marcus's "Surface Reading: An Introduction" *Representations* 108.1 (2009); the special volume "Reading Remains" of *differences* 21, no. 3 (2010); and the special issue "Literary Criticism for the Twenty-First Century," *PMLA* 125, no. 4 (2010).

10. For a sustained discussion of the problem of reading, time, and immediacy in the recent "method wars" in literary studies in general and the topic of postcritique in particular, see Mathias Nilges and Tim Lanzendörfer, "Literary Studies After Postcritique: An Introduction," in "Literary Studies After Postcritique," ed. Mathias Nilges and Tim Lanzendörfer, special issue, *Amerikastudien / American Studies* 64, no. 4 (2019): 491–514.

11. Hans Ulrich Gumbrecht, *After 1945: Latency as Origin of the Present* (Palo Alto, CA: Stanford University Press, 2013); and *Unsere Breite Gegenwart* (Frankfurt: Suhrkamp, 2010).

12. Hans Ulrich Gumbrecht, *Production of Presence: What Meaning Cannot Convey* (Palo Alto, CA: Stanford University Press, 2004), xiii.

13. Hans Ulrich Gumbrecht, "Reading for the *Stimmung*? About the Ontology of Literature Today," *boundary 2* 35, no. 3 (2008): 221.

14. Gumbrecht, "Reading for the *Stimmung*?," 221.

15. Hans Ulrich Gumbrecht, *Atmosphere, Mood, Stimmung: On a Hidden Potential of Literature* (Palo Alto, CA: Stanford University Press, 2012).

16. Gumbrecht, "Reading for the *Stimmung*?," 214.

17. Charles Altieri, "The Sensuous Dimension of Literary Experience: An Alternative to Materialist Theory," *New Literary History* 38, no. 1 (2007): 89.

18. Altieri, "The Sensuous Dimension," 72.

19. Carolyn Lesjak, "Reading Dialectically," *Criticism* 55, no. 2 (2013): 234.

20. Altieri, "The Sensuous Dimension," 72.

21. *Löschpapier*, literally "extinguishing paper," is the German word for blotting paper, sheets of lightly woven paper used when writing with fountain pens to soak up excess ink in order to avoid smudging. The joke: a school is on fire. A young student approaches the burning building and begins to throw paper into the fire. "What do you think you're doing!?" an outraged firefighter asks the boy, who replies: "Don't worry, it's *Löschpapier*."

22. Rahv, "The Cult of Experience in American Writing," 285.

23. Lesjak, "Reading Dialectically," 238–39.

24. Yu, *How to Live Safely*, 4.

25. See, for instance, the exchange between Walter Benn Michaels and Jonathan Flatley: Walter Benn Michaels, "Grimstad on Experience, Flatley on Affect: A Response" *nonsite* 22 (2018); and Jonathan Flatley, "Reading for Mood," *Representations* 140, no. 1 (2017).

26. Rachel Greenwald Smith, *Affect and American Literature in the Age of Neoliberalism* (Cambridge: Cambridge University Press, 2015).

27. Sean Austin Grattan, *Hope Isn't Stupid: Utopian Affects in Contemporary American Literature* (Iowa City: University of Iowa Press, 2017).

28. Jauß's 1986 book *Zeit und Erinnerung in Marcel Prousts "A la recherche du temps perdu"*, which began as Jauß's doctoral dissertation in 1952 and was subsequently revised several times before being published in its current form in 1986, must also be considered before the backdrop of Jauß's own dark history. This is particularly important because the temporal contradictions of our era produce their own moments of darkness and regressive desires that are directly connected to the rise of a new extreme Right. The memory of the atrocities of previous moments must serve as a reminder that crises of futurity have led to some of the most horrific excesses of humankind, and we must never fail to make legible the darkest versions of non-contemporaneity that mark the time of our present. I attempt to do this in my book *Right-Wing Culture in Contemporary Capitalism*. We find one of the most insightful examinations of the relation between Jauß's work and his past in the commentary of one of his former students: Gumbrecht. Gumbrecht locates the significance of Jauß's work precisely in the relation between his past and the significance of matters of time, memory, and the tension between experience and interpretation in his work. See Gumbrecht: "Mein Lehrer, der Mann von der SS. Die Universitätskarriere von Hans Robert Jauß zeigt, wie man mit NS-Vorgeschichte eine bundesrepublikanische Größe werden konnte." *Die Zeit*. April 7, 2011. In other words, we should engage with Jauß's thought on time, memory, and art because of his dark past, not in spite of it. For we find in Jauß's work ideas that help us ensure that fascism's murderous history and the ideas that made it possible will be remembered but never repeated.

29. Jauß, *Zeit und Erinnerung*, 93. The translations that follow from this work are mine.

30. Jauß, *Zeit und Erinnerung*, 166, 94.

31. Jauß, *Zeit und Erinnerung*, 42.

32. Jauß, *Zeit und Erinnerung*, 43.

33. Jauß, *Zeit und Erinnerung*, 45–46.

34. Jauß, *Zeit und Erinnerung*, 49.

35. Ben Lerner, *10:04* (New York: McClelland and Stewart, 2014), 4.

36. Judy Wajcman, *Pressed for Time: The Acceleration of Time in Digital Capitalism* (Chicago: University of Chicago Press, 2016), 27.

37. Boethius, *The Consolation of Philosophy* (New York: Penguin, 1981), 165.

38. See Jorge Luis Borges, *The Aleph and Other Stories* (New York: Penguin, 2004), 120–32.

39. Jacques Rancière, *Aesthetics and Its Discontents* (Cambridge: Polity, 2009), 1.

40. Rancière, *Aesthetics and Its Discontents*, 39.

41. Rancière, *Aesthetics and Its Discontents*, 45.

42. See Darko Suvin's formative essay "Estrangement and Cognition," *Strange Horizons*, November 24, 2014, http://strangehorizons.com/non-fiction/articles/estrangement-and-cognition/.

43. Boxall, *The Value of the Novel*, 103.

44. I examine the relation between realism and speculative fiction in detail in other essays, including "The Realism of Speculation: Contemporary Speculative Fiction as Immanent Critique of Finance Capitalism," *CR: The New Centennial Review* 19, no. 1 (2019): 37–60.

45. Mitchum Huehls, "Knowing What We Are Doing: Time, Form, and the Reading of Postmodernity" *Cultural Critique* 61 (2005): 55.

46. Huehls, "Knowing What We Are Doing," 56, emphasis in the original.

47. Pierre Bourdieu, *The Rules of Art: Genesis and Structure of the Literary Field* (Palo Alto, CA: Stanford University Press, 1996), 328.

48. Theodor W. Adorno, *Minima Moralia: Reflections on a Damaged Life* (New York: Verso, 2003), 16.

49. Walter Benjamin, *Illuminations* (New York: Schocken, 1968), 262.

50. Benjamin, *Illuminations*, 261.

51. Benjamin, *Illuminations*, 263.

52. Jennifer Egan, *A Visit from the Goon Squad* (New York: Anchor, 2010), 23, emphasis in the original.

53. The interview can now be found as the original recording (not the transcript): https://www.cbc.ca/player/play/2446544636.

54. Byung-Chul Han, *Duft der Zeit: Ein philosophischer Essay zur Kunst des Verweilens* (Bielefeld: Transcript Verlag, 2009), Kindle locations 51–53. The translations of Han's work that follow are mine.

55. Han, *Duft der* Zeit, 54–56.

56. Han, *Duft der* Zeit, 1560–62.

57. Han, *Duft der* Zeit, 1563–64.

58. Han, *Duft der* Zeit, 331.

59. See Rachel Kushner's *The Flamethrowers* (2013), Ruth Ozeki's *A Tale for the Time Being* (2013), and Paul Harding's *Tinkers* (2008).

60. Han, *Duft der Zeit*, 1568–72.

61. Boris Groys, "Comrades of Time," *e-flux* 11 (2009): n.p.

62. See Mathias Nilges, *Right-Wing Culture in Contemporary Capitalism: Regression and Hope in a Time without Future* (New York: Bloomsbury, 2019), esp. ch. 3, "The New Paternalism," and ch. 4, "Mystifications or, Lumberjacks without Forests."

63. Rachel Kushner, *The Flamethrowers* (New York: Scribner, 2013), 30.

64. Alexander Nagel and Christopher Wood, "The Plural Temporality of the Work of Art," in *Time, ed. Amelia Wood* (Cambridge, MA: MIT Press, 2013), 41.

65. Agamben, "What Is the Contemporary?," 88.

66. David Carr, *Time, Narrative, and History* (Bloomington: Indiana University Press, 1991), 146–47.

67. Carr, *Time, Narrative, and History*, 167.

68. Peter Dimock, *George Anderson: Notes for a Love Song in Imperial Time* (New York: Columbia University Press, 2013), 40, 9.

CHAPTER 3

1. Marcial González, "The Future as Form: Undoing the Categorical Separation of Class and Gender in Ana Castillo's *Sapogonia*," in *Class and the Making of American Literature: Created Unequal*, ed. Andrew Lawson (New York: Routledge, 2014), 215.

2. Samuel Delany, *Stars in My Pocket Like Grains of Sand* (Middletown, CT: Wesleyan University Press, 2004), 66.

3. José Esteban Muñoz, *Cruising Utopia: The Then and There of Queer Futurity* (New York: New York University Press, 2009), 12.

4. Lloyd Pratt, *Archives of American Time: Literature and Modernity in the Nineteenth Century* (Oxford: Oxford University Press, 2010), 3.

5. Pratt, *Archives of American Time*, 4.

6. Pratt, *Archives of American Time*, 3.

7. Pratt, *Archives of American Time*, 6.

8. See, for instance, Richard Russo's novels *Empire Falls* (2001), *Bridge of Sighs* (2007), and *Everybody's Fool* (2016).

9. Colson Whitehead, *Apex Hides the Hurt* (New York: Anchor, 2006), 90.

10. Colson Whitehead, *John Henry Days* (New York: Anchor, 2002), 127.

11. Kiese Laymon, *Long Division* (Chicago: Bolden, 2013), 38.

12. Pratt, *Archives of American Time*, 4–5.

13. See Nilges, *Right-Wing Culture*, esp. ch. 4, "Mystifications."

14. Cindy Weinstein, *Time, Tense, and American Literature* (Cambridge: Cambridge University Press, 2015), 2.

15. Mat Johnson, *Pym* (New York: Spiegel and Grau, 2011), 7–8.

16. Berlant, *Cruel Optimism*, 68.

17. Rebentisch, "The Contemporaneity of Contemporary Art," 226.

18. Theodore Martin, "The Currency of the Contemporary," in *Postmodern/Postwar and After: Rethinking American Literature*, ed. Jason Gladstone, Andrew Hoberek, and Daniel Worden (Iowa City: University of Iowa Press, 2016), 237.

19. Osborne, *Anywhere or Not at All*, 26.

20. Osborne, *Anywhere or Not at All*, 15, emphasis in the original.

21. Ernst Bloch, "Nonsynchronism and the Obligation to Its Dialectics," *New German Critique* 11 (1977): 22.

22. Bloch, "Nonsynchronism and the Obligation to Its Dialectics," 23–27.

23. Martin, "The Currency of the Contemporary," 229.

24. Brendan Dooley, *The Dissemination of News and the Emergence of Contemporaneity in Early Modern Modern Europe* (Burlington, VT: Ashgate, 2010), xiii–xiv.

25. Joel Burges and Amy J. Elias, eds., *Time: A Vocabulary of the Present* (New York: New York University Press, 2016), 8.

26. Benedict Anderson, *Imagined Communities: Reflections on the Origin and Spread of Nationalism* (New York: Verso, 1991), 43.

27. Anderson, *Imagined Communities*, 45.
28. Burges and Elias, *Time*, 8.
29. Dooley, *The Dissemination of News*, 11.
30. Wajcman, *Pressed for Time*, 34.
31. Rancière, "In What Time Do We Live?," n.p.
32. Burges and Elias, *Time*, 3.
33. Burges and Elias, *Time*, 4.
34. See, for instance, Ziauddin Sardar, *Rescuing All Our Futures: The Future of Futures Studies* (Santa Barbara: Praeger, 1999); *Future: All That Matters* (New York: McGraw-Hill, 2014).
35. Osborne, *Anywhere or Not at All*, 27.
36. Lim, *Translating Time*, 76.
37. Terry Smith, "Contemporary, Contemporaneity," Keywords Project, University of Pittsburgh, http://keywords.pitt.edu/pdfs/contemporary_and_contemporaneity.pdf. Smith borrows the account of contemporaneity's multiplicitous character from Giorgio Agamben, who introduces this term in his essay "What Does It Mean to Be Contemporary?"
38. Smith, "Introduction," 1.
39. Smith, "Introduction," 9.
40. Terry Smith, "Contemporary Art and Contemporaneity," *Critical Inquiry* 32 no. 4 (2006): 702.
41. Osborne, *Anywhere or Not at All*, 27.
42. Smith, "Contemporary, Contemporaneity," n.p.
43. Smith, "Contemporary, Contemporaneity," n.p.
44. Daylanne K. English, *Each Hour Redeem: Time and Justice in African American Literature* (Minneapolis: University of Minnesota Press, 2013), Kindle locations 3180–84, 3171.
45. English, *Each Hour Redeem*, 3183.
46. Honoré de Balzac, *Un prince de la bohème* (Paris: Michel Lévy, 1865), 189.
47. Ernst Bloch, *Heritage of Our Times*, trans. Neville Plaice and Stephen Plaice (Cambridge: Polity, 2009), 33.
48. West-Pavlov, *Temporalities*, 154.
49. Rancière, "In What Time Do We Live?," n.p.
50. Madhu Dubey, *Signs and Cities: Black Literary Postmodernism* (Chicago: University of Chicago Press, 2003), 22–23.
51. Rancière, "In What Time Do We Live?," n.p.
52. Other examples of such early novels include Ishmael Reed's *The Terrible Twos* (1982) and *The Terrible Threes* (1989), and Octavia E. Butler's *Xenogenesis/Lilith's Brood* (1987–89).
53. Toni Morrison, *Beloved* (New York: Vintage, 2004), 4.
54. Kimberly Chabot Davis, "'Postmodern Blackness': Toni Morrison's *Beloved* and the End of History," *Twentieth Century Literature* 44, no. 2 (1998): 242.
55. Boxall, *The Value of the Novel*, 100.
56. Samuel Delany, *Starboard Wine: More Notes on the Language of Science Fiction* (Pleasantville, NY: Dragon Press, 1984), 35.
57. *Delany, Starboard Wine*, 31.

58. Osborne, *Anywhere or Not at All*, 23.

59. Colson Whitehead, *The Intuitionist* (New York: Anchor Books, 1999), 12.

60. Colson Whitehead, *Zone One* (New York: Doubleday, 2011), 31.

61. S. D. Chrostowska, "Thought Woken by Memory: Adorno's Circuitous Path to Utopia," *New German Critique* 40, no. 1 (2013): 94.

62. Peter Thompson, "Ernst Bloch, *Ungleichzeitigkeit* and the Philosophy of Being and Time," *New German Critique* 42, no. 2 (2015): 56.

63. Thompson, "Ernst Bloch," 56.

64. Vincent Geoghegan, "Remembering the Future," in *Not Yet: Reconsidering Ernst Bloch*, ed. Jamie Owen Daniel and Tom Moylan (New York: Verso, 1997), 29.

65. Geoghegan, "Remembering the Future," 22.

66. David Kaufmann, "Thanks for the Memory: Bloch, Benjamin, and the Philosophy of History," in *Not Yet: Reconsidering Ernst Bloch*, ed. Jamie Owen Daniel and Tom Moylan (New York: Verso, 1997), 51.

67. Rancière, "In What Time Do We Live?," n.p.

68. Rancière, "In What Time Do We Live?," n.p.

69. Rancière, "In What Time Do We Live?," n.p.

CHAPTER 4

1. Fredric Jameson, *Archaeologies of the Future: The Desire Called Utopia and Other Science Fictions* (New York: Verso, 2005), 384.

2. William Gibson, "Will We Have Computer Chips in Our Heads?," in *Distrust That Particular Flavor* (New York: Putnam, 2012), 214.

3. Phillip E. Wegner, "Recognizing the Patterns," *New Literary History* 38 (2007): 186. It is also important to foreground Wegner's suggestion that cyberpunk science fiction can itself be regarded as "a kind of literary realism" (187).

4. William Gibson, *Burning Chrome* (New York: Harper Voyager, 2003), 28.

5. Kim Stanley Robinson, *The Gold Coast: Three Californias (Wild Shore Triptych)* (New York: Orb, 1995), 67.

6. Amy Hungerford, "On the Period Formerly Known as Contemporary," *American Literary History* 20, nos. 1–2 (2008): 418.

7. Gumbrecht, "Shall We Continue," 522.

8. Smith, "Contemporary Art and Contemporaneity," 703–4.

9. Tomba, *Marx's Temporalities*, ix.

10. Gumbrecht, "Shall We Continue," 528.

11. See Gordon Hutner, "Historicizing the Contemporary: A Response to Amy Hungerford," *American Literary History* 20, nos. 1–2 (2008): 410–19.

12. Ursula K. Heise, "Martian Ecologies and the Future of Nature," *Twentieth-Century Literature* 57, nos. 4–5 (2011): 447.

13. Andrew Hoberek, "Introduction: After Postmodernism," *Twentieth-Century Literature* 53, no. 3 (2007): 233.

14. John Frow, "What Was Postmodernism?," in *Past the Last Post: Theorizing Post-colonialism and Post-modernism*, ed. Ian Adam and Helen Tiffin (Calgary: University of Calgary Press, 1990), 139–59; Raymond Federman,

Critifiction: Postmodern Essays (Albany: State University of New York Press, 1993), 105. The death of Samuel Beckett on December 22, 1989, marks for Federman the death of postmodernism, and Beckett's *Stirrings Still* the "last gasp of postmodern fiction" (105), an argument that also directly finds its way into Federman's 2001 novel *Aunt Rachel's Fur*.

15. Smith, "Introduction," 13.

16. Timothy Melley, *The Covert Sphere: Secrecy, Fiction, and the National Security State* (Ithaca, NY: Cornell University Press, 2012), 6.

17. Melley, *The Covert Sphere*, 7.

18. Jeffrey T. Nealon, *Post-Postmodernism, or The Cultural Logic of Just-in-Time Capitalism* (Palo Alto, CA: Stanford University Press, 2012), 23.

19. Nealon, *Post-Postmodernism*, 10.

20. Nealon, *Post-Postmodernism*, 26.

21. Irving Howe, *Decline of the New* (New York: Harcourt, Brace, 1963), 30, emphasis in the original.

22. Howe, *Decline of the New*, 33.

23. Fredric Jameson, *Postmodernism, or, The Cultural Logic of Late Capitalism* (Durham, NC: Duke University Press, 1991), 307–11.

24. Jameson, *Postmodernism*, 310.

25. Donald Barthelme, *The Dead Father* (New York: Farrar, Straus and Giroux, 2004), 5, emphasis in the original.

26. Federman, *Critifiction*, 114.

27. The Smiths, "How Soon Is Now?," *Hatful of Hollow* (Rough Trade, 1984), LP.

28. William Gibson, *Neuromancer* (New York: Ace, 2000), 6.

29. Philip E. Wegner is developing a project that historicizes the year 1984 as a rich, significant moment in history. Since I am a big fan of Wegner's work and cannot think of any other scholar of contemporary American literature and culture better suited for this project, I would like to encourage all those who come across this note to keep an eye out for what will no doubt be a wonderful book.

30. Thomas Pynchon, *Vineland* (New York: Penguin, 1997), 32.

31. Don DeLillo, *White Noise* (New York: Penguin, 1998), 191.

32. Rachel Adams, "The Ends of America, the Ends of Postmodernism," *Twentieth Century Literature* 53, no. 3 (2007): 249.

33. Nealon, *Post-Postmodernism*, 23.

34. Gérard Duménil and Dominique Lévy, *The Crisis of Neoliberalism* (Cambridge, MA: Harvard University Press, 2013).

35. Pierre Bourdieu, "The Essence of Neoliberalism," *Le Monde diplomatique*, December 1998, http://mondediplo.com/1998/12/08bourdieu.

36. Federman, *Critifiction*, 107–8.

37. Federman, *Critifiction*, 129.

38. Amir Eshel, *Futurity: Contemporary Literature and the Quest for the Past* (Chicago: University of Chicago Press, 2013), 2.

39. Eshel, *Futurity*, 2.

40. Eshel, *Futurity*, 176.

41. Eshel, *Futurity*, 3.

42. John Henry Raleigh, "The English Novel and the Three Kinds of Time," in *The Novel: Modern Essays in Criticism*, ed. Robert Murray Davis (Englewood Cliffs, NJ: Prentice Hall, 1969), 248.

43. Raleigh, "The English Novel," 249.

44. Kurt Vonnegut, *Slaughterhouse Five* (New York: Dell, 1991), 221.

45. Kurt Vonnegut, *Breakfast of Champions* (New York: Dial, 2011), 302.

46. Bret Easton Ellis, *American Psycho* (New York: Vintage, 1991), 23, emphasis in the original.

47. Eshel, *Futurity*, 11.

48. Eshel, *Futurity*, 5.

49. McGurl, "Ordinary Doom," 331.

50. James I. Porter, *Selected Essays of Erich Auerbach: Time, History, and Literature* (Princeton, NJ: Princeton University Press, 2014), 158.

51. Porter, *Selected Essays of Erich Auerbach*, 161.

52. See Alan Kirby, *Digimodernism: How New Technologies Dismantle the Postmodern and Reconfigure Our Culture* (New York: Bloomsbury, 2009). The term *altermodern* was coined by Nicolas Bourriaud for the Tate Triennial 2009, https://www.tate.org.uk/whats-on/tate-britain/exhibition/altermodern.

53. Kojin Karatani, *History and Repetition* (New York: Columbia University Press, 2011), 50.

54. Peter Osborne, *The Politics of Time: Modernity and Avant-Garde* (New York: Verso, 2011), 14.

55. See Mathias Nilges and Michael D'Arcy, "Introduction: The Contemporaneity of Modernism," in *The Contemporaneity of Modernism: Literature, Media, Culture*, ed. Mathias Nilges and Michael D'Arcy (New York: Routledge, 2015), 1–16.

56. David James and Urmila Seshagiri, "Metamodernism: Narratives of Continuity and Revolution," *PMLA* 129, no. 1 (2014): 90–91.

57. Hayot quoted in James and Seshagiri, "Metamodernism," 91.

58. James and Seshagiri, "Metamodernism," 92.

59. Boxall, *The Value of the Novel*, 98.

60. Tomba, *Marx's Temporalities*, viii.

61. Brown, "Literature in Time," 5.

62. Fredric Jameson, *The Political Unconscious: Narrative as Socially Symbolic Act* (Ithaca, NY: Cornell University Press, 1982), 28.

63. Brown, "Literature in Time," 4.

Bibliography

Adam, Barbara. *Time*. New York: Wiley, 2004.

Adams, Rachel. "The Ends of America, the Ends of Postmodernism." *Twentieth Century Literature* 53, no. 3 (2007): 248–72.

Adorno, Theodor W. *Aesthetic Theory*. Translated by Robert Hullot-Kentor. Minneapolis: University of Minnesota Press, 1998.

———. *Minima Moralia: Reflections on a Damaged Life*. Translated by E. F. N. Jephcott. New York: Verso, 2003.

———. *Negative Dialectics*. Translated by E. B. Ashton. New York: Bloomsbury, 1981.

———. *Notes to Literature*. Vol. 1. Translated by Shierry Weber Nicholsen. New York: Columbia University Press, 1991.

Agamben, Giorgio. *Infancy and History: On the Destruction of Experience*. Translated by Liz Heron. New York: Verso, 2007.

———. "What Is the Contemporary?" In *Time*, edited by Amelia Groom, 82–88. Documents of Contemporary Art. London: Whitechapel Gallery; Cambridge, MA: MIT Press, 2013.

Altieri, Charles. "The Sensuous Dimension of Literary Experience: An Alternative to Materialist Theory." *New Literary History* 38, no. 1 (2007): 71–98.

Anderson, Amanda. *The Way We Argue Now: Studies in the Cultures of Theory*. Princeton, NJ: Princton University Press, 2006.

Anderson, Benedict. *Imagined Communities: Reflections on the Origin and Spread of Nationalism*. New York: Verso, 1991.

Arac, Jonathan. "What Kind of History Does a Theory of the Novel Require?" *Novel: A Forum on Fiction* 42, no. 2 (2009): 190–95.

Armitage, David, and Jo Guldi. "Bonfire of the Humanities." *Aeon*, October 2, 2014. https://aeon.co/essays/the-role-of-history-in-a-society-afflicted-by-short-termism.

Augé, Marc. *The Future*. Translated by John Howe. New York: Verso, 2015.

AYR. "Famili: Proxy Paranoia or Technological Camaraderie." *Harvard Design Magazine* 41 (2015). http://www.harvarddesignmagazine.org/issues/41/famili-proxy-paranoia-or-technological-camaraderie.

Balzac, Honoré de. *Un prince de la bohème*. Paris: Michel Lévy, 1865.

Barthelme, Donald. *The Dead Father*. New York: Farrar, Straus and Giroux, 2004.

Baudrillard, Jean. *The Illusion of the End*. Translated by Chris Turner. Palo Alto, CA: Stanford University Press, 1994.

Benjamin, Walter. *Illuminations*. Translated by Harry Zohn. New York: Schocken, 1968.

———. *Selected Writings*, vol. 4, *1939–1940*. Cambridge, MA: Belknap, 2003.

Benn Michaels, Walter. "Grimstad on Experience, Flatley on Affect: A Response." *nonsite* 22 (2018).

Berardi, Franco. *After the Future*. Translated by Arianna Bove et al. Baltimore: AK Press, 2011.

———. *The Soul at Work: From Alienation to Autonomy*. Translated by Francesca Cadel and Giuseppina Mecchia. Los Angeles: Semiotext(e), 2009.

———. *The Uprising: On Poetry and Finance*. Los Angeles: Semiotext(e), 2012.

Berlant, Lauren. *Cruel Optimism*. Durham, NC: Duke University Press, 2011.

Berlatsky, Noah. "When Science Fiction Stopped Caring about the Future." *The Atlantic*, December 5, 2014. https://www.theatlantic.com/entertainment/archive/2014/12/the-new-star-wars-isnt-really-new/383426/.

Bernstein, J. M. *The Philosophy of the Novel: Lukács, Marxism, and the Dialectics of Form*. Minneapolis: University of Minnesota Press, 1984.

Best, Steven, and Sharon Marcus. "Surface Reading: An Introduction." *Representations* 108, no. 1 (2009): 1–21.

Bewes, Timothy. "Introduction: Temporalizing the Present." *Novel: A Forum on Fiction* 45, no. 2 (2012): 159–64.

———. "The Novel as Absence: Lukacs and the Event of Postmodern Fiction." *Novel: A Forum on Fiction* 38, no. 1 (2004): 5–20.

———. "The Novel Problematic." *Novel: A Forum on Fiction* 44, no. 1 (2011): 17–19.

Bloch, Ernst. *Heritage of Our Times*. Translated by Neville Plaice and Stephen Plaice. Cambridge: Polity, 2009.

———. "Nonsynchronism and the Obligation to Its Dialectics." Translated by Mark Ritter. *New German Critique* 11 (1977).

———. *The Principle of Hope*. Volume 1. Translated by Neville Plaice, Stephen Plaice, and Paul Knight. Cambridge, MA: MIT Press, 1995.

———. *The Utopian Function of Art and Literature: Selected Essays*. Translated by Jack Zipes and Frank Mecklenburg. Cambridge, MA: MIT Press, 1987.

Boes, Tobias. *Formative Fictions: Nationalism, Cosmopolitanism, and the* Bildungsroman. Ithaca, NY: Cornell University Press, 2012.

Boethius. *The Consolation of Philosophy*. Translated by Victor Watts. New York: Penguin, 1981.

Borges, Jorge Luis. *The Aleph and Other Stories*. Translated by Andrew Hurley. New York: Penguin, 2004.

Bourdieu, Pierre. "The Essence of Neoliberalism," *Le Monde diplomatique*, December 1998, http://mondediplo.com/1998/12/08bourdieu.

———. *The Rules of Art: Genesis and Structure of the Literary Field.* Translated by Susan Emanuel. Palo Alto, CA: Stanford University Press, 1996.

Boxall, Peter. *The Value of the Novel.* Cambridge: Cambridge University Press, 2015.

Bridle, James. *New Dark Age: Technology and the End of the Future.* New York: Verso, 2018.

Brown, Marshall. "Literature in Time." *MLQ* 65, no. 1 (2004): 1–5.

Burges, Joel, and Amy J. Elias, eds. *Time: A Vocabulary of the Present.* New York: New York University Press, 2016.

Canales, Jimena. "Clock/Lived." In *Time: A Vocabulary of the Present*, edited by Joel Burges and Amy J. Elias, 113–28. New York: New York University Press, 2016.

Carr, David. *Time, Narrative, and History.* Bloomington: Indiana University Press, 1991.

Caruth, Cathy. "Afterword: Turning Back to Literature." *PMLA* 125, no. 4 (2010): 1087–95.

Cazdyn, Eric, and Imre Szeman. *After Globalization.* Hoboken, NJ: Wiley-Blackwell, 2012.

Chabot Davis, Kimberly. "'Postmodern Blackness': Toni Morrison's *Beloved* and the End of History." *Twentieth Century Literature* 44, no. 2 (1998): 242–60.

Chrostowska, S. D. "Thought Woken by Memory: Adorno's Circuitous Path to Utopia." *New German Critique* 40, no. 1 (2013): 93–117.

Clune, Michael. *Writing against Time.* Palo Alto, CA: Stanford University Press, 2013.

CO.EXIST staff. "The End of the Future and the Rise of the Present." *Fast Company*, May 16, 2013. https://www.fastcompany.com/2682076/the-end-of-the-future-and-the-rise-of-the-present.

Couzens Hoy, David. *The Time of Our Lives: A Critical History of Temporality.* Cambridge, MA: MIT Press, 2012.

Cucu, Sorin Radu. *The Underside of Politics: Global Fictions in the Fog of the Cold War.* New York: Fordham University Press, 2013.

Delany, Samuel. *Starboard and Wine: More Notes on the Language of Science Fiction.* Pleasantville, NY: Dragon Press, 1984.

———. *Stars in My Pocket Like Grains of Sand.* Middletown, CT: Wesleyan University Press, 2004.

DeLillo, Don. *The Body Artist.* New York: Simon and Schuster, 2001.

———. *Cosmopolis.* New York: Scribner, 2003.

———. "In the Ruins of the Future." *Guardian*, September 22, 2001. http://www.theguardian.com/books/2001/dec/22/fiction.dondelillo.

———. *Point Omega.* New York: Scribner, 2010.

———. *White Noise.* New York: Penguin, 1998.

———. *Zero K.* New York: Scribner, 2016.

Dimock, Peter. *George Anderson: Notes for a Love Song in Imperial Time.* New York: Columbia University Press, 2013.

Doherty, Mike. "William Gibson on the End of the Future." *National Post*, November 27, 2014. https://nationalpost.com/entertainment/books/william-gibson-on-the-end-of-the-future.

Dooley, Brendan. *The Dissemination of News and the Emergence of Contemporaneity in Early Modern Modern Europe*. Burlington, VT: Ashgate, 2010.

Dubey, Madhu. *Signs and Cities: Black Literary Postmodernism*. Chicago: University of Chicago Press, 2003.

Duménil, Gérard, and Dominique Lévy. *The Crisis of Neoliberalism*. Cambridge, MA: Harvard University Press, 2013.

Durand, Cédric. *Fictitious Capital: How Finance Is Appropriating Our Future*. Translated by David Broder. New York: Verso, 2017.

Edmundson, Mark. "Against Readings." *Profession* (2009): 56–65.

Egan, Jennifer. *A Visit from the Goon Squad*. New York: Anchor, 2010.

Ellis, Bret Easton. *American Psycho*. New York: Vintage, 1991.

English, Daylanne K. *Each Hour Redeem: Time and Justice in African American Literature*. Minneapolis: University of Minnesota Press, 2013.

Eshel, Amir. *Futurity: Contemporary Literature and the Quest for the Past*. Chicago: University of Chicago Press, 2013.

Federman, Raymond. *Critifiction: Postmodern Essays*. Albany: State University of NewYork Press, 1993.

Felski, Rita. *Doing Time: Feminist Theory and Postmodern Culture*. New York: New York University Press, 2000.

Ferrell, Will. "Where's the Future? Will Ferrell's Tour of Tech That Never Took." *Wired*, August 3, 2010. https://www.wired.com/2010/08/ff_future_ferrell/.

Finn, Ed. "The Inspiration Drought." *Future Tense*, September 16, 2014. https://slate.com/technology/2014/09/project-hieroglyph-why-our-science-fiction-needs-new-dreams.html.

Flatley, Jonathan. "Reading for Mood." *Representations* 140, no. 1 (2017): 137–58.

Foster, Hal, et al. "Questionnaire on 'The Contemporary.'" *OCTOBER* 130 (2009): 3–124.

Frow, John. "What Was Postmodernism?" In *Past the Last Post: Theorizing Post-colonialism and Post-modernism*, edited by Ian Adam and Helen Tiffin, 139–59. Calgary: University of Calgary Press, 1990.

Fukuyama, Francis. *The End of History and the Last Man*. New York: Free Press, 2006.

Gallagher, Catherine. "Formalism and Time." *MLQ* 61, no. 1 (2000): 229–51.

Gates, Bill. *Business @ the Speed of Thought: Succeeding in the Digital Economy*. New York: Grand Central, 1999.

Geoghegan, Vincent. "Remembering the Future." In *Not Yet: Reconsidering Ernst Bloch*, edited by Jamie Owen Daniel and Tom Moylan, 15–32. New York: Verso, 1997.

Gibson, William. *Burning Chrome*. New York: Harper Voyager, 2003.

———. *Neuromancer*. New York: Ace, 2000.

———. *Pattern Recognition*. New York: Berkley, 2003.

———. "Will We Have Computer Chips in Our Heads?" In *Distrust That Particular Flavor*, 211–18. New York: Putnam, 2012.

González, Marcial. "The Future as Form: Undoing the Categorical Separation of Class and Gender in Ana Castillo's *Sapogonia*." In *Class and the Making of American Literature: Created Unequal*, edited by Andrew Lawson, 215–28. New York: Routledge, 2014.

Grattan, Sean Austin. *Hope Isn't Stupid: Utopian Affects in Contemporary American Literature*. Iowa City: University of Iowa Press, 2017.

Greenwald Smith, Rachel. *Affect and American Literature in the Age of Neoliberalism*. Cambridge: Cambridge University Press, 2015.

González, Marcial. "The Future as Form: Undoing the Categorical Separation of Class and Gender in Ana Castillo's *Sapogonia*." In *Class and the Making of American Literature: Created Unequal*, edited by Andrew Lawson, 215–28. New York: Routledge, 2014.

Groys, Boris. "Comrades of Time." *e-flux* 11 (2009).

Gumbrecht, Hans Ulrich. *After 1945: Latency as Origin of the Present*. Palo Alto, CA: Stanford University Press, 2013.

———. *Atmosphere, Mood, Stimmung: On a Hidden Potential of Literature*. Translated by Erik Butler. Palo Alto, CA: Stanford University Press, 2012.

———. "Mein Lehrer, der Mann von der SS. Die Universitätskarriere von Hans Robert Jauß zeigt, wie man mit NS-Vorgeschichte eine bundesrepublikanische Größe werden konnte." *Die Zeit*, April 7, 2011.

———. *Production of Presence: What Meaning Cannot Convey*. Palo Alto, CA: Stanford University Press, 2004.

———. "Reading for the *Stimmung*? About the Ontology of Literature Today." *boundary 2* 35, no. 3 (2008): 213–21.

———. "Shall We Continue to Write Histories of Literature?" *New Literary History* 39 (2008): 519-32.

———. *Unsere Breite Gegenwart*. Frankfurt: Suhrkamp, 2010.

Han, Byung-Chul. *Duft der Zeit: Ein philosophischer Essay zur Kunst des Verweilens*. Bielefeld: Transcript Verlag, 2009.

Harding, Paul. *Tinkers*. New York: HarperCollins, 2008.

Harvey, David. *The Limits to Capital*. New York: Verso, 2007.

Hassan, Robert. *The Chronoscopic Society: Globalization, Time and Knowledge in the Network Economy*. New York: Peter Lang, 2003.

Heise, Ursula K. "Martian Ecologies and the Future of Nature." *Twentieth-Century Literature* 57, nos. 4–5 (2011): 447–71.

Hillman, Roger. *Zeitroman: The Novel and Society in Germany, 1830–1900*. New York: Peter Lang, 1983.

Hoberek, Andrew. "Cormac McCarthy and the Aesthetics of Exhaustion." *American Literary History* 23, no. 3 (2011): 483–99.

———. "Introduction: After Postmodernism." *Twentieth-Century Literature* 53, no. 3 (2007): 233–47.

Howe, Irving. *Decline of the New*. New York: Harcourt, Brace, 1963.

Huehls, Mitchum. "Knowing What We Are Doing: Time, Form, and the Reading of Postmodernity." *Cultural Critique* 61 (2005): 55–86.

Hungerford, Amy. "On the Period Formerly Known as Contemporary." *American Literary History* 20, nos. 1–2 (2008): 410–19.

Hutner, Gordon. "Historicizing the Contemporary: A Response to Amy Hungerford." *American Literary History* 20, nos. 1–2 (2008): 420–24.

Insko, Jeffrey. "Prospects for the Present." *American Literary History* 26, no. 4 (2014): 836–48.

James, David, and Urmila Seshagiri. "Metamodernism: Narratives of Continuity and Revolution." *PMLA* 129, no. 1 (2014): 87–100.

Jameson, Fredric. *Archaeologies of the Future: The Desire Called Utopia and Other Science Fictions*. New York: Verso, 2005.

———. "The End of Temporality." *Critical Inquiry* 29 (2003): 695–718.

———. "The Experiments of Time: Providence and Realism." In *The Novel*, vol. 2, *Forms and Themes*, edited by Franco Moretti, 95–130. Princeton, NJ: Princeton University Press, 2006.

———. "On the Power of the Negative." *Mediations* 28, no. 1 (2014): 71–74.

———. *The Political Unconscious: Narrative as Socially Symbolic Act*. Ithaca, NY: Cornell University Press, 1982.

———. *Postmodernism, or, The Cultural Logic of Late Capitalism*. Durham, NC: Duke University Press, 1991.

———. *The Seeds of Time*. New York: Columbia University Press, 1994.

———. *A Singular Modernity*. New York: Verso, 2013.

Jauß, Hans Robert. *Zeit und Erinnerung in Marcel Prousts "A la recherche du temps perdu": Ein Beitrag zur Theorie des Romans*. Frankfurt: Suhrkamp, 1986.

Johnson, Mat. *Pym*. New York: Spiegel and Grau, 2011.

Karatani, Kojin. *History and Repetition*. New York: Columbia University Press, 2011.

Kaufmann, David. "Thanks for the Memory: Bloch, Benjamin, and the Philosophy of History." In *Not Yet: Reconsidering Ernst Bloch*, edited by Jamie Owen Daniel and Tom Moylan, 33–52. New York: Verso, 1997.

Kelly, Adam. "David Foster Wallace and the Novel of Ideas." In *David Foster Wallace and "The Long Thing": New Essays on the Novels*, edited by Marshall Boswell, 3–22. New York: Bloomsbury, 2014.

Kirby, Alan. *Digimodernism: How New Technologies Dismantle the Postmodern and Reconfigure Our Culture*. New York: Bloomsbury, 2009.

Kubler, George. *The Shape of Time*. New Haven, CT: Yale University Press, 1970.

Kundera, Milan. *The Art of the Novel*. Translated by Linda Asher. New York: Harper Perennial, 1993.

Kunkel, Ben. *Indecision*. New York: Random House, 2006.

Kushner, Rachel. *The Flamethrowers*. New York: Scribner, 2013.

Laymon, Kiese. *Long Division*. Chicago: Bolden, 2013.

Lazzarato, Maurizio. *The Making of the Indebted Man: An Essay on the Neoliberal Condition*. Translated by Joshua David Jordan. Los Angeles: Semiotext(e), 2012.

Lefebvre, Henri. *Rhythmanalysis: Space, Time and Everyday Life*. Translated by Stuart Elden and Gerald Moore. New York: Continuum, 2004.

Lerner, Ben. *10:04*. New York: McClelland and Stewart, 2014.

Lesjak, Carolyn. "Reading Dialectically." *Criticism* 55, no. 2 (2013): 233–77.

Levine, Caroline. *Forms: Whole, Rhythm, Hierarchy, Network*. Princeton, NJ: Princeton University Press, 2015.

Lim, Bliss Cua. *Translating Time: Cinema, the Fantastic, and Temporal Critique*. Durham, NC: Duke University Press, 2009.

Lukács, Georg. *Ästhetik II*. Neuwied: Luchterhand, 1976.

———. *Theory of the Novel: A Historico-Philosophical Essay on the Forms of Great Epic Literature*. Translated by Anna Bostock. Cambridge, MA: MIT Press, 1972.

Lupton, Christina, and R. John Williams. "Essays from the English Institute 2016: Time." *ELH* 85, no. 2 (2018): 283–87.

Mann, Thomas. "Einführung in den *Zeuberberg*." In *Gesammelte Werke in Zwölf Bänden*, vol. 11. Oldenburg: Fischer, 1960.

Marazzi, Christian. *Capital and Language: From the New Economy to the War Economy*. Translated by Gregory Conti. Cambridge, MA: MIT Press, 2008.

Marder, Elissa. *Dead Time: Temporal Disorders in the Wake of Modernity (Baudelaire and Flaubert)*. Palo Alto, CA: Stanford University Press, 2001.

Martin, Theodore. "The Currency of the Contemporary." In *Postmodern/Postwar and After: Rethinking American Literature*, edited by Jason Gladstone, Andrew Hoberek, and Daniel Worden, 227–40. Iowa City: University of Iowa Press, 2016.

Marx, Karl. *The Poverty of Philosophy*. Moscow: Foreign Languages Publishing House, n.d.

Mazzoni, Guido. *Theory of the Novel*. Translated by Zakiya Hanafi. Cambridge, MA: Harvard University Press, 2017.

McCarthy, Cormac. *No Country for Old Men*. New York: Vintage, 2005.

———. *The Road*. New York: Vintage, 2007.

McGurl, Mark. "Ordinary Doom: Literary Studies in the Waste Land of the Present." *New Literary History* 41, no. 2 (2010): 329–49.

———. "Real/Quality." In *Time: A Vocabulary of the Present*, edited by Joel Burges and Amy J. Elias, 209–24. New York: New York University Press, 2016.

———. "The Zombie Renaissance." *n+1* 9 (2010).

Medina, Cuauhtémoc. "Contem(p)torary: Eleven Theses." *e-flux* 12 (2010). http://www.e-flux.com/journal/12/61335/contemp-t-orary-eleven-theses/.

Melley, Timothy. *The Covert Sphere: Secrecy, Fiction, and the National Security State*. Ithaca, NY: Cornell University Press, 2012.

Meltzer, Brad. *Identity Crisis*. New York: DC Comics, 2005.

Mendilow, A. A. *Time and the Novel*. London: Peter Nevill, 1952.

Mendonça Crema, Cristina Diniz. "Théorie du roman et théorie de la revolution dans la penseé de Sartre." *Trans/Form/Ação* 15 (1992). http://www.scielo.br/scielo.php?script=sci_arttext&pid=S0101-31731992000100001.

Miller, Laura. "Dark Futures: What Happens When Literary Novelists Experiment with Science Fiction." *Slate*, May 25, 2017. http://www.slate.com/articles/arts/books/2017/05/literary_fiction_is_borrowing_the_tools_of_the_science_fiction_genre.html.

Morrison, Toni. *Beloved.* New York: Vintage, 2004.

Müller, Silke, and Susanne Weiss. *Studienbuch neuere deutsche Literaturwissenschaft, 1720–1848.* Würzburg: Königshausen und Neumann, 1999.

Muñoz, José Esteban. *Cruising Utopia: The Then and There of Queer Futurity.* New York: New York University Press, 2009.

Nagel, Alexander, and Christopher Wood. "The Plural Temporality of the Work of Art." In *Time*, edited by Amelia Groom, 38–42. Cambridge, MA: MIT Press, 2013.

Nealon, Jeffrey T. *Post-Postmodernism, or The Cultural Logic of Just-in-Time Capitalism.* Palo Alto, CA: Stanford University Press, 2012.

Neubauer, John. "Bakhtin versus Lukács: Inscriptions of Homelessness in Theories of the Novel." *Poetics Today* 17, no. 4 (1996): 531–46.

Newman, Karen, Jay Clayton, and Marianne Hirsch, eds. *Time and the Literary.* New York: Routledge, 2002.

Nilges, Mathias. "The Realism of Speculation: Contemporary Speculative Fiction as Immanent Critique of Finance Capitalism." *CR: The New Centennial Review* 19, no. 1 (2019): 37–60.

———. *Right-Wing Culture in Contemporary Capitalism: Regression and Hope in a Time without Future.* New York: Bloomsbury, 2019.

Nilges, Mathias, and Michael D'Arcy. "Introduction: The Contemporaneity of Modernism." In *The Contemporaneity of Modernism: Literature, Media, Culture*, edited by Mathias Nilges and Michael D'Arcy. New York: Routledge, 2015.

Nilges, Mathias, and Tim Lanzendörfer. "Literary Studies After Postcritique: An Introduction." In "Literary Studies After Postcritique," edited by Mathias Nilges and Tim Lanzendörfer. Special issue, *Amerikastudien/American Studies* 64, no. 4 (2019): 491–514.

Osborne, Peter. *Anywhere or Not at All: Philosophy of Contemporary Art.* New York: Verso, 2013.

———. *The Politics of Time: Modernity and Avant-Garde.* New York: Verso, 2011.

Ozeki, Ruth. *A Tale for the Time Being.* New York: Penguin, 2013.

Porter, James I. *Selected Essays of Erich Auerbach: Time, History, and Literature.* Translated by Jane O. Newman. Princeton, NJ: Princeton University Press, 2014.

Pratt, Lloyd. *Archives of American Time: Literature and Modernity in the Nineteenth Century.* Oxford: Oxford University Press, 2010.

Pynchon, Thomas. *Vineland.* New York: Penguin, 1997.

Rahv, Philip. "The Cult of Experience in American Writing." In *American Literature, American Culture*, edited by Gordon Hutner, 283–91. Oxford: Oxford University Press, 1999.

Raleigh, John Henry. "The English Novel and the Three Kinds of Time." In *The Novel: Modern Essays in Criticism*, edited by Robert Murray Davis, 242–53. Englewood Cliffs: Prentice Hall, 1969.

Rancière, Jacques. *Aesthetics and Its Discontents.* Translated by Steven Corcoran. Cambridge: Polity, 2009.

———. "In What Time Do We Live?." *Politica Comun* 4 (2013). https://quod.lib.umich.edu/p/pc/12322227.0004.001?view=text;rgn=main.

Rebentisch, Juliane. "The Contemporaneity of Contemporary Art." *New German Critique* 42, no. 1 (2015): 223–37.

Rich, Nathaniel. *Odds against Tomorrow*. New York: Farrar, Straus, and Giroux, 2013.

Ricoeur, Paul. *Time and Narrative*. Vol. 2. Chicago: University of Chicago Press, 1985.

Robinson, Kim Stanley. *The Gold Coast: Three Californias (Wild Shore Triptych)*. New York: Orb, 1995.

Rushkoff, Douglas. *Present Shock: When Everything Happens Now*. London: Current, 2013.

Russo, Richard. *Bridge of Sighs*. New York: Vintage, 2007.

———. *Empire Falls*. New York: Vintage, 2001.

———. *Everybody's Fool*. New York: Vintage, 2016.

Sardar, Ziauddin. *Future: All That Matters*. New York: McGraw-Hill, 2014.

———. *Rescuing All Our Futures: The Future of Futures Studies*. Santa Barbara: Praeger, 1999.

Sartre, Jean-Paul. "On John Dos Passos and *1919*." *Situations 1*. Translated by Chris Turner. 13–30. New York: George Braziller, 1965.

———. "Time in Faulkner: *The Sound and the Fury*." In *William Faulkner: Three Decades of Criticism*, edited by Frederick J. Hoffman and Olga W. Vickery, 225–32. New York: Harcourt Brace, 1960.

———. *What Is Literature?* Translated by Bernard Frechtman. New York: Philosophical Library, 1948.

Self, Will. "The Novel Is Dead (This Time It's for Real)." *Guardian*, May 2, 2014. https://www.theguardian.com/books/2014/may/02/will-self-novel-dead-literary-fiction.

Shteyngart, Gary. *Super Sad True Love Story*. New York: Random House, 2010.

Silverman, Nathan. "Future Fail." *The Baffler* 36 (September 2017). https://thebaffler.com/outbursts/future-fail-silverman.

Smith, Terry. "Contemporary Art and Contemporaneity." *Critical Inquiry* 32, no. 4 (2006): 681–707.

———. "Introduction: The Contemporaneity Question." In *Antinomies of Art and Culture: Modernity, Postmodernity, Contemporaneity*, edited by Terry Smith, Okwui Enwezor, and Nancy Condee, 1–22. Durham, NC: Duke University Press, 2008.

Steiner, Peter. "Reading." *Profession* (2009): 50–55.

Stepath, Katrin. *Gegenwartskonzepte: Eine philosophisch-literaturwissenschaftliche Analyse temporaler Strukturen*. Würzburg: Königshausen und Neumann, 2006.

Suvin, Darko. "Estrangement and Cognition." *Strange Horizons*, November 24, 2014. http://strangehorizons.com/non-fiction/articles/estrangement-and-cognition/.

Taylor, Mark C. *Speed Limits: Where Time Went and Why We Have So Little Left*. New Haven, CT: Yale University Press, 2014.

Thiel, Peter. "The End of the Future." *National Review*, October 3, 2011. https://www.nationalreview.com/2011/10/end-future-peter-thiel/.

Thompson, Peter. "Ernst Bloch, *Ungleichzeitigkeit* and the Philosophy of Being and Time." *New German Critique* 42, no. 2 (2015): 49–64.

Tomba, Massimiliano. *Marx's Temporalities*. Leiden: Brill, 2013.

Trenkle, Norbert. "Value and Crisis: Basic Questions." In *Marxism and the Critique of Value*, edited by Josh Robinson et al., 1–16. Chicago: MCM Prime, 2014.

Van, Annette. "Novel Futures." *Novel: A Forum on Fiction* 41, no. 1 (2010): 157–62.

Virilio, Paul. *The Futurism of the Instant—Stop-Eject*. London: Polity, 2010.

Vonnegut, Kurt. *Breakfast of Champions*. New York: Dial, 2011.

———. *Slaughterhouse Five*. New York: Dell, 1991.

Wajcman, Judy. *Pressed for Time: The Acceleration of Time in Digital Capitalism*. Chicago: University of Chicago Press, 2016.

Wegner, Phillip E. "Recognizing the Patterns." *New Literary History* 38 (2007): 183–200.

Weinstein, Cindy. *Time, Tense, and American Literature*. Cambridge: Cambridge University Press, 2015.

West-Pavlov, Russell. *Temporalities*. New York: Routledge, 2012.

Whitehead, Colson. *Apex Hides the Hurt*. New York: Anchor, 2006.

———. *The Intuitionist*. New York: Anchor Books, 1999.

———. *John Henry Days*. New York: Anchor, 2002.

———. *Zone One*. New York: Doubleday, 2011.

Yu, Charles. *How to Live Safely in a Science Fictional Universe*. New York: Vintage. 2010.

Žižek, Slavoj. *Living in the End Times*. New York: Verso, 2010.

Index

FLASHPOINTS

1. *On Pain of Speech: Fantasies of the First Order and the Literary Rant*, Dina Al-Kassim
2. *Moses and Multiculturalism*, Barbara Johnson, with a foreword by Barbara Rietveld
3. *The Cosmic Time of Empire: Modern Britain and World Literature*, Adam Barrows
4. *Poetry in Pieces: César Vallejo and Lyric Modernity*, Michelle Clayton
5. *Disarming Words: Empire and the Seductions of Translation in Egypt*, Shaden M. Tageldin
6. *Wings for Our Courage: Gender, Erudition, and Republican Thought*, Stephanie H. Jed
7. *The Cultural Return*, Susan Hegeman
8. *English Heart, Hindi Heartland: The Political Life of Literature in India*, Rashmi Sadana
9. *The Cylinder: Kinematics of the Nineteenth Century*, Helmut Müller-Sievers
10. *Polymorphous Domesticities: Pets, Bodies, and Desire in Four Modern Writers*, Juliana Schiesari
11. *Flesh and Fish Blood: Postcolonialism, Translation, and the Vernacular*, S. Shankar
12. *The Fear of French Negroes: Transcolonial Collaboration in the Revolutionary Americas*, Sara E. Johnson
13. *Figurative Inquisitions: Conversion, Torture, and Truth in the Luso-Hispanic Atlantic*, Erin Graff Zivin
14. *Cosmopolitan Desires: Global Modernity and World Literature in Latin America*, Mariano Siskind
15. *Fiction beyond Secularism*, Justin Neuman
16. *Periodizing Jameson: Dialectics, the University, and the Desire for Narrative*, Phillip E. Wegner
17. *The Practical Past*, Hayden White
18. *The Powers of the False: Reading, Writing, Thinking beyond Truth and Fiction*, Doro Wiese
19. *The Object of the Atlantic: Concrete Aesthetics in Cuba, Brazil, and Spain, 1868–1968*, Rachel Price
20. *Epic and Exile: Novels of the German Popular Front, 1933–1945*, Hunter Bivens
21. *An Innocent Abroad: Lectures in China*, J. Hillis Miller
22. *Form and Instability: East Europe, Literature, Postimperial Difference*, Anita Starosta
23. *Bombay Modern: Arun Kolatkar and Bilingual Literary Culture*, Anjali Nerlekar
24. *Intimate Relations: Social Reform and the Late Nineteenth-Century South Asian Novel*, Krupa Shandilya
25. *Media Laboratories: Late Modernist Authorship in South America*, Sarah Ann Wells
26. *Acoustic Properties: Radio, Narrative, and the New Neighborhood of the Americas*, Tom McEnaney

27. *The New Woman: Literary Modernism, Queer Theory, and the Trans Feminine Allegory*, Emma Heaney
28. *Civilizing War: Imperial Politics and the Poetics of National Rupture*, Nasser Mufti
29. *Late Colonial Sublime: Neo-epics and the End of Romanticism*, G. S. Sahota
30. *Globalizing Race: Anti-Semitism, Empire, and the Politics of Scale in Modern French and European Culture*, Dorian Bell
31. *Domestications: American Empire, Literary Culture, and the Postcolonial Lens*, Hosam Mohamed Aboul-Ela
32. *Behold an Animal: Four Exorbitant Readings*, Thangam Ravindranathan
33. *Capital Letters: Hugo, Baudelaire, Camus, and the Death Penalty*, Ève Morisi
34. *Immaterial Archives: An African Diaspora Poetics of Loss*, Jenny Sharpe
35. *Figures of the World: The Naturalist Novel and Transnational Form*, Christopher Laing Hill
36. *Imperfect Solidarities: Tagore, Gandhi, Du Bois, and the Global Anglophone*, Madhumita Lahiri
37. *Fictional Environments: Mimesis, Deforestation, and Development in Latin America*, Victoria Saramago